THE RULES OF INFLUENCE

THE RULES

OF INFLUENCE

Winning When You're in the Minority

WILLIAM D. CRANO

ST. MARTIN'S PRESS ❧ NEW YORK

www.stmartins.com

Design by Level C

ISBN 978-0-312-55229-9

First Edition: April 2012

10 9 8 7 6 5 4 3 2 1

To Suellen, the light of my life

Contents

The Majority Rules . . . or Does It?

> The minority is sometimes right; the majority always wrong.
>
> —*George Bernard Shaw*

Anyone can be influential if they carry a big enough stick. Al Capone was right when he said, "You can go a long way with a smile. You can go a lot farther with a smile and a gun." Al's observation points to a problem with what we know about persuasion and social influence, which is that much of our understanding is based on studies in which the influencer controls both the smile *and* the gun. This focus is somewhat reasonable, because in many contexts, the influencer does hold all the cards. When implementing changes in an organization, for example, the boss might try to persuade the rank and file to go along with the new arrangements. You may or may not agree, but you know that you'd better listen to what is being proposed, because when persuasion fails, the boss still has the stick. We know how to persuade when the audience is obliged to listen. In many circumstances, however, the influencer is not in the driver's seat, and so the established research tells only half the story, and not the more interesting half, at that. More exciting are those clashes in which the individual or group without any obvious clout tries and succeeds in changing the beliefs of a more powerful opponent. Understanding how and why such attempts sometimes succeed (and why they often fail) tells us much about the process of social influence, and it is what this book is all about.

Understanding how the weak influence the strong, how the minority changes the majority, is the least understood, most puzzling, and perhaps most important aspect of social influence. Think about the last time you held an unpopular position on an important issue, when you knew you were right but few people agreed with you. And you didn't have a big stick. No matter your social status, education, wealth, race, or religion, your view placed you firmly in the (opinion) minority. Even in this position, however, you might have carried your argument, moving most or all of your former challengers to your side of the ledger. Do you understand how you did it?

On other occasions, you did not prevail. Your best arguments had little apparent impact, and the opposition maintained its resistance to your views. Do you understand why you succeeded in the first instance and failed in the second? This book is meant to answer that question. Its analysis is based on new understandings drawn from recent social psychological research. Unlike other analyses of social influence, we assume a starting position of vulnerability rather than invincibility. It's easy to persuade people if you have a gun to go along with your smile. But influencing the smiling guy who's holding the gun is a much bigger challenge. Winning under those circumstances is considerably more difficult, but it can be done, and this book will show you how.

Influence

Influencing others is an art—with a lot of science behind it. This book is intended to reveal the rules of influence that must be followed to achieve persuasive success when your views place you firmly in the minority, when you do not have capacity to force people to listen to you, much less agree with you. It is meant to help you win when you don't control the game, when you are outnumbered and surrounded. Understanding the how and why of successful influence is neither easy nor obvious, and the job is even tougher when you do not have the power to insist on your position, but social scientists have amassed a body of evidence that allows us to do just that.

The Good Old/New Days

Older, more established research on social influence offers some insights, but the classic approaches are limited because they implicitly assume that persuaders have greater resources than their targets of influence, or at a minimum can compel them to listen to their pitch. Under these circumstances, a few formulas seemed sufficient to do the trick: establish credibility, mount a strong argument, create conditions in which resistance is difficult, offer psychic rewards for being on the right side, and so on. Do all of this and you're in. There are many really good books that detail how this can be done, and they are quite useful if you assume that the persuader has enough clout to oblige the audience to listen, but they don't help much if you do not enjoy that advantage.

The new rules of influence begin with the assumption that you are operating from a position of weakness rather than strength, and that you cannot insist that others listen, much less conform. The new rules of influence identify tactics by which weakness can be turned to strength. The basis of these new understandings is found in research on minority influence, a relatively new field of scientific investigation that is concerned with the ways in which groups with little or no power to coerce overcome the resistance and inertia of the larger group (the majority) to achieve their goals. The relevance of this research for the new rules of influence is obvious, because the minority almost by definition is incapable of forcing its will on the majority. You should understand that in this research, the minority most often is identified not on the basis of demographic features (race, social class, ethnicity), but rather by its attitudes, values, or positions, which are at odds with those of the larger group. If I am a delegate to the Republican National Convention and admit on TV that I like the Democratic nominee better than I like any of the Republican hopefuls, I have put myself in a minority group—it does not matter that I am, like most of my fellow delegates, a well-off white male.

As this new approach to understanding and using influence starts with the premise that the influencer is in a weak position, understanding how minorities affect the dominant group (sometimes called the *power majority* or, in this book's language, simply the *majority*) is indispensable. If you're in a powerful position, persuasive subtlety is largely unnecessary. Brute force works well for those who possess it, at least for a while, and its use is commonplace. It is evident any time a majority party in Congress votes along straight party lines. On Christmas Eve 2009, for example, after months of haggling with their Republican counterparts over a universal health care bill, the Democratic majority in the U.S. Senate quit trying to use influence and simply overran the recalcitrant minority. Every Democrat voted yea on the universal health care bill, and every Republican voted nay. Holding an insurmountable electoral edge, the Senate Democrats could not be stopped, and so the bill became law. Their less numerous opponents could not stop them. In stark terms, there was no need for the majority to have spent months trying to persuade the minority that it should comply—the numbers were sufficient to force the issue from the start. However, to their credit, the Democrats understood that such applications of force often end badly, and they were correct in this case. Republican reaction to the new law was unyielding and fierce, and remains so. Although it is true that the majority rules, the use of brute majority force often backfires in the long run.

In this book, we are not concerned with the majority rules, the ways the majority can make the most of its power, but rather with the more interesting question of the minority rules, influencing others when the odds are stacked against us. Can the minority ever prevail? History suggests that this is an absurd question. Think of the minority spokespersons or groups that have made their mark, including Jesus and the early Christians, Gandhi, Pasteur, Hitler, Freud, Darwin, Einstein, Betty Friedan, the women's suffrage movement, Martin Luther King Jr. and the battle for civil rights. The list is not endless, but it is long. Whether we agree or not with the spokespersons or their movements, there is little doubt that originally unpopular views can have enormous impact on the world in which we live.

The rules that governed how these movements prevailed, how they moved resistant majorities, are the focus of the story that unfolds as this book progresses. As we will see, there are plenty of examples in which minorities won despite apparently insurmountable obstacles. We will consider how they did it, how influence agents in exceptionally weak positions carried their arguments and won their fights.

Minority status can come about in many ways. A group may be a minority because it is outnumbered by others who have different ideas or different demographic features. On the other hand, some groups are in the numeric majority but still are considered minorities because they occupy weak "outsider" positions in the society. Think of the black population in South Africa before apartheid was lifted. Despite their numbers, black people effectively were the minority in their country. A group might be considered a minority because it holds a set of beliefs, or perhaps a single belief that is considered odd or dangerous or salacious by the group that runs the show. No matter the source of minority status, the rules all minorities must follow to exert influence are the same. This is the central premise: All minorities must follow the same rules if they are to influence the majority. Following these rules of influence makes it possible for those with little or no power to survive and even prosper in the influence game. The rules have been deduced from experimental results and historical analysis, and are the basis of many surprising and originally unexpected research outcomes.

Principal support for the recommendations that will be made is found in scientific research on minority influence. We focus on this body of research because the rules of influence are most clearly revealed in the study of individuals and groups that *must* use persuasion to navigate their world. They cannot use brute force to get their way, and when they try to do so, they usually are destroyed without a second thought. The history of most militant minority movements is a history of destruction and defeat. The Black Panthers, the Tamil Tigers, the Italian Brigate Rosse, and the Students for a Democratic Society all had one thing in common: They were minority factions that attempted to forgo persuasion and instead to take on the majority in frontal assaults. Whether or not you agree with their positions, it is obvious that they chose unwisely. They no longer exist as credible forces for change.

Outcomes such as these should leave no one in doubt about the power of the majority, and maybe this is not all bad. Most democratic systems are premised on the principle that the majority rules, and most of us, most of the time, are mostly content to go along with the arrangement. The majority makes the rules and enforces them. It rewards the conventional and punishes the un-usual. The minority, on the other hand, defines the unusual, the outsider. It is the mirror image of the majority. The minority is not powerful. It does not make the rules. It is not rewarded by convention. Yet, the minority sometimes gets its way, and how it gets its way is a fascinating story.

Why should you care? Because sooner or later and more often than once, you will hold a weak, outsider position on an impor-tant issue, with little power to coerce, but with a strong convic-tion that the larger group is on the wrong path. You might prevail if you apply the right strategies. You surely will fail if you do not.

Gift of God to My Brothers and Me . . . [1]

On July 20, 2010, the city council of Oakland, California, ap-proved a measure that would grant industrial cultivation licenses to large-scale marijuana growers. The asking price was a cool $211,000 per year. There were more than two hundred applicants for the four licenses. Like most communities, Oakland is in dire need of hard cash, and the city council's price tag was not a pipe dream—these farms can be enormous, up to 100,000 square feet, and they can generate colossal profits. This is not your "grow light in the back closet" marijuana enterprise. In addition to license fees, the city hoped to realize $38 million in taxes from the sale of medicinal marijuana, which has been legal in California since 1996. Considering that activist and social critic John Sinclair was sentenced in 1969 to ten years' imprisonment for holding two joints, you may begin to appreciate the persuasive power of the minority, of how a weak and disdained group of (mostly) young people moved public opinion, the majority view, from strongly

---

[1] Line from an old Phish tune, "Marijuana."

anti-pot to a city council hearing in which industrial cultivation of marijuana was seriously entertained. It took some time, but time is part of the influence process. As we'll see, minority positions are almost never adopted instantaneously.[i]

Is there a way to understand how and why some minorities enjoy spectacular success while others fail miserably? Are there general rules of procedure that improve the minority's possibilities? What are common traps the minority must avoid if it is to succeed? This book is designed to answer these questions, which as I have argued, are relevant to all of us. No matter your sex, age, race, wealth, or social standing, we all have done time in the minority barrel. This book is designed to show how to make the most of it while there.

The Majority's Not-So-Secret Weapons

The majority exerts control through its capacity to harm or ostracize anyone who fails to get with the program. Ostracism might seem like the lesser of the two outcomes, but we have learned that the threat of banishment or expulsion from the group is exceptionally intimidating, sometimes even more intimidating than physical injury. We have evolved over thousands of years as social animals, deeply dependent on our group for physical sustenance and social support. Our survival depends on our relations with the groups that claim us, and so ostracism carries with it a sense of dire peril.

Ostracism has a long history as a method of social control. It was formally developed in the Athenian democracy around 500 B.C. The ostracism procedure allowed citizens to banish anyone for a period of ten years for whatever reason they chose. Once a year, all citizens voted to decide whether the ostracism process should take place. Sometimes the citizenry decided against it, but if enough voted in favor, the process went forward. The procedure was straightforward. Citizens gathered in the agora, Athens's central square, scratched the name of a man[2] they wished to ostracize on a shard (an ostracon—a broken piece of pottery, the Athenians' equivalent of scrap paper) and dropped it into an urn. If a sufficient number of votes were cast, the person who received the most was kicked out of the city for ten years. No trial was held, no witnesses were called, and the ostracized person had no means of defense or appeal—if your name came up more often than anyone else's, you were out. The ten years' banishment was viewed as an extreme punishment, even though the ostracized person's home and wealth were not confiscated, nor was his family harmed. Although most of those banished were wealthy and influential, and thus could carry on life outside Athens, many considered ostracism a fate almost worse than death.

In a similar vein, over its long history, the Roman Catholic Church systematized and elaborated the banishment process in its ritual of excommunication. The Church holds some articles of faith to be sacrosanct, untouchable, and Catholics who disagree with these established dogmas and are bothersome enough are drummed out. In earlier days, these individuals (sometimes called heretics) lost not only their church membership cards but their heads as well. The combination of physical threat and ostracism worked pretty well, and even though today's Church has given up the more extreme forms of the practice, now settling for separation from the Church without separating head from shoulders, excommunication is still seen by most Catholics as a grave punishment. The Church's kinder form of official ostracism is not the case everywhere. In Pakistan, for example, being a Christian or even belonging to the wrong Muslim minority sect appears to

---

2 Women were never ostracized.

make one fair game for execution by those who belong to the state's official religious majority.

Can the threat of exclusion from our social group really prove so intimidating today? Considerable research in social psychology has shown that people find it extremely unpleasant to be ignored or excluded even from trivial, ad hoc groups having no past and no future. In one such study, three research subjects were stationed in different rooms and interacted via computer. This setup was necessary because each subject actually was interacting with a computer that simulated the responses of the other two people. The subjects, of course, did not know this. While waiting for the real experiment to begin, they were told that they could pass the time by tossing a virtual ball from one to another on their computer monitors. This Pong-like game was an amusing diversion for the subjects, who did not know that the other two "players" were avatars that had been programmed to ostracize them after a short period of peaceful coexistence.

After a brief interval in which the three threw the virtual ball among themselves, the avatars systematically excluded the live subject from the game, hogging the ball and throwing it exclusively to each other. The whole interaction only lasted three to four minutes, but the subjects reported that it seemed like an eternity. Psychological measures taken afterwards indicated that as a result of the experience, the ostracized players' self-esteem had fallen through the floor, along with their positive mood. The striking impact of the game was clearly observable in the faces of the research participants, who were not aware that they were being filmed. Almost invariably, exclusion from the game perplexed, then angered, then saddened them. Some blamed themselves, reporting they thought they had done something wrong to be put on the sidelines by the other two players. Others scorned their ostracizers. Without exception, all found the experience distasteful. Imagine their feelings if they had been banished from a group they really valued and depended on for physical or emotional support. For us social animals, "the social kiss of death," may be one of the worst punishments of all, and the majority uses this threat as a means of maintaining control.[ii]

Ostracism is only one of the many weapons the minority uses to maintain itself in the catbird seat. The majority typically controls resources, physical, social, and emotional, and uses this control to keep its members in line. It's not by accident that the majority usually finds itself on the winning side, while the minority gets to wear the jacket with the big target painted on the back, so it's not surprising that people maneuver to be included in the ruling majority of *any* group to which they belong. Even though the majority shifts from time to time, from place to place, and from issue to issue, we strive to keep ourselves in it because the majority controls the game, the rewards and punishments, and it can change the rules whenever it likes.

Being in the Majority of the Minority

Striving to attain majority status in the group we belong to is evident even when the group is itself in the minority. Think about a complex business organization, with many factions vying for influence. Top management holds the power and by definition runs the show. Subordinate groups within the organization may have considerable control within their respective divisions, but they may be well removed from the power brokers, the executives who hold overall control. Even so, those who belong to an "outside" division work hard to attain membership in their division's leadership, to belong to the "majority within the minority." It's a safe bet that every middle manager has thought about what it would be like to be the boss and enjoy the power and prestige that go with the job—and probably more than once. Members of peripheral divisions strive to attain status in their group so that they can maneuver themselves into the division's leadership and ultimately control the group's directions. From there, the move to the top becomes feasible, or at least imaginable.

There's more to striving to be in the majority of one's group than merely acquiring power. We work to be in the majority of our groups not just because the majority controls material and psychological resources, but also because who we are is largely defined by those who claim us as their own. Drawing distinctions between who's in and who's out, between who's right and who's wrong, between privileged or disadvantaged—in short, between *us* and *them*—motivates us to be counted among those who do the counting. We seek to belong to the majority of our group, even if our group is in the minority, not just because the majority holds the power, but because the privilege attached to being in the majority position is commonly viewed by others and by ourselves as deserved. We had it coming. This perception contributes to our sense of worth, of who we are, and to others' assessments of our value as well.

Sometimes the feeling of advantage or privilege that accompanies membership in the majority of one's group can have terrible repercussions. The expression "Rank has its privileges" was not invented just for royalty. When the CEOs of America's three major carmakers were called to Washington, D.C., to explain why the government should bail out their ailing companies, all used their private corporate jets for the flight from Detroit to the Capitol. Their mode of conveyance did not go unnoticed. It was estimated that the flight cost GM about twenty thousand dollars to fly their CEO to the hearing. The cost of a normal airline coach seat at that time was $238. You can guess what their congressional critics made of these numbers. Obviously, someone in the automakers' shops should have told these men that their arrival with all the perks of office would not go over well under the circumstances at the time, but apparently no one did. And, of course, the CEOs probably never gave a second thought to the uproar their implicit show of privilege might cause. It's as if the privileges of rank blinded them and their advisers. They had climbed the ladder, were afforded great benefits as captains of one of America's major industries, and appeared to believe that they deserved their place at the table's head with all the rights and privileges attached thereto. They were quickly disabused of those beliefs. On their next visit to D.C., all three drove. There is no report of how their cars fared on the trip.

The need to belong, to help us identify ourselves and to present ourselves, to show the world who we are, motivates us to seek membership in our group's majority, because the majority garners the lion's share of respect. The downside of this largely positive process is that our attempts to define who we are require us to define who we aren't. We categorize, classify, and ultimately discriminate not only to incorporate ourselves more securely in the groups that claim our allegiance, and through which we form our own identities, our sense of who we are, but also to distance ourselves from outsiders.

Yet another reason people strive to belong to their group's majority is that most assume the majority view is correct and, obviously, the majority is supported by most of those who matter. If two heads are better than one, then dozens or hundreds or thousands of heads certainly must be even better. We like to be right, and the majority usually is—or at least is perceived as being right. After most elections, for example, more people say they voted for the winning candidate than possibly could have done so. Why? Not just because we like winners, but because by identifying with winners, we can bask in the reflected glory of the champ. If we're associated with the winner, we're winners, too.

An intriguing study conducted on seven large U.S. college campuses—including USC, Ohio State, Michigan, and Louisiana State, schools known for their students' passionate feelings about their football teams as well as for their fine academic programs— makes this point well. At each school, researchers calculated the proportion of students who wore clothing that identified them as belonging to their schools—team jackets, sweatshirts, hats, T-shirts, and so on. The data were collected in the same classrooms on every Monday in the fall. Why Mondays? Because generally, college football games are played on Saturdays, and Monday is the first class day following each school's games. On some Saturdays, the school's team won; on others, it didn't.

Analysis of the data of this study revealed that the proportion of students wearing school regalia on Mondays was much greater when their team had won the previous Saturday. At Ohio State, for example, on average, nearly 70 percent of the students wore Buckeye regalia on the Mondays after a win, but only 30 percent after a tie or a (rare) loss. The proportions were even more skewed at LSU, where 80 percent of the students, on average, were decked out in school apparel after a victory, but only 33 percent after a loss.

The researchers followed this study with interviews, and found that when their school had won, students used *we* (versus *non-we*) responses when answering a survey item that posed the following question: "In the third game of the season, your team played . . . Can you tell me the outcome of that game?" When describing a victory, students used *we* nearly one third of the time—"We won," "We killed 'em," and so on; when their team lost, the proportion dropped to 18 percent: "They lost," "The score was . . . ," and similar answers were more common responses. Intuitively, these results ring true. Think about the usually inebriated celebrants who jump in front of TV cameras after their team's victory—they don't scream "THEY'RE NUMBER ONE!" They identify themselves with the victors by screaming "WE'RE NUMBER ONE!" even though they had nothing whatsoever to do with the game's outcome.[iii]

Being (in the) Right

There's yet another reason for people's preference for membership in more powerful groups. If the majority is on one side of an issue, the position it supports is generally accorded the moral high ground—because the majority defines what's good and what's not. At the Nuremberg Trials conducted at the end of World War II, the victorious allies prosecuted the defeated Nazis for war crimes. In the first of the trials, twenty-four high-ranking members of the Nazi war machine were brought to the bar of justice. The crimes of which they were accused were horrific, and most of those charged were found guilty. There's no doubt that these men (they were all men) deserved the worst, and most got it. Who could argue for Martin Bormann or Hermann Göring? But there were critics of this tribunal, and they argued that the crimes the defendants had committed were defined as crimes only *after* the war was over, the definition having been fashioned by the winning side. Critics saw the trial as a sham, as "victors' justice," in which the winners had the power to do whatever they wished, and did so. The pretense of legality was just that—a pretense.

Were the critics a bunch of Nazi sympathizers, sore losers who wanted better treatment than the defendants deserved? Obviously not. The Chief Justice of the U.S. Supreme Court, Harlan Stone, called the proceedings a "high-grade lynching party." He expanded his remarks by saying, "I don't mind what he [the Chief U.S. Prosecutor Robert Jackson] does to the Nazis, but I hate to see the pretense that he is running a court and proceeding according to common law. This is a little too sanctimonious a fraud to meet my old-fashioned ideas." In a note to President Harry Truman, Robert Jackson himself wrote that the Nuremberg tribunal was prosecuting Nazis for some of the very behaviors the Allies had practiced (and were practicing), including forced labor, internment camps, plunder, aggressive war, attacks on civilians, and other unsavory undertakings. Supreme Court Justice William O. Douglas, a champion of civil liberties and an avowed hater of all the Nazis stood for, found the tribunals guilty of substituting "power for principle," and that is precisely my point. The winners, the power majority, decide what's good and what's evil, and adapt the rules of the game accordingly. Who is to stop them? Certainly not the losers.

The opposite side of the righteousness coin is palmed off onto the minority, whose positions often are judged as misguided, self-serving, and vaguely reprehensible if not downright immoral. The Nuremberg critics were not honored for their principled stand— they were castigated as being "soft" on Nazis and suspected of ulterior motives despite their reputations as among the best and most honorable people the country had produced.

Obviously, the majority has power. It reflects the social consensus, and with consensus come safety and stability. It provides a shorthand version of right and wrong. There's nothing *necessarily* wrong with any of this, and in the main, "majority rules" work pretty well, most of the time.

So why bother with minority influence? Because when we must apply social influence, we usually are in the minority on issues that may matter greatly to us, and while it's obvious that the majority holds most of the cards, it doesn't hold *all* the cards. It's right most of the time, but not all the time. The minority offers a corrective to the majority, an alternate point of view that often points to the better route. As agents of influence, dissidents are almost always in weak, but not impossible positions. These influence agents can prevail. Sometimes the influencer wins by taking over, becoming the majority, the new power player. But even when the weaker group cannot take over, its members often can influence the more powerful to see things its way and ultimately to accede to its wishes. To do so, influencers must adhere strictly to a number of rules that govern success or failure. We'll consider these *rules of influence* over the course of this book.

All Dummies Think Alike

There is a danger in striving for majority or leadership status in our groups. The need to be a part of the majority of the groups we care about can lead to ruinously bad outcomes, because it may squelch our motivation to voice divergent viewpoints that could have resulted in more optimal outcomes for us and our identity groups. The inclination to go along with the prevailing wisdom without expressing even strongly held reservations has been studied for many years. The tendency has been labeled *groupthink,* a common failing brought about by the desire to fit in, to maintain group unanimity, and to create for oneself a more secure place in the group. The potentially disastrous outcome of groupthink was starkly evident in the events leading to the Bay of Pigs fiasco, John F. Kennedy's failed attempt to "liberate" the Cuban people from the oppressive regime of Fidel Castro.

In deciding how the United States should deal with Castro, the newly elected president and his advisers inherited a CIA plan that pressed strongly for an invasion of Cuba's Bay of Pigs. The plan's authors practically guaranteed Kennedy that an invasion would incite a popular revolution against Castro and his regime, resulting in a change of government that was friendlier to the United

States. Arthur Schlesinger, a Harvard professor on the edges of Kennedy's inner circle, warned the president in a memorandum that the invasion would be a disaster, but over the course of extended high-level deliberations among the president's closest advisers, groupthink took over. The "need" to invade became increasingly evident, at least to those intimately engaged in the discussion, advisers who were largely isolated from outsiders' dissenting opinions. Isolation was necessary because the Bay of Pigs plans were top secret, but it had severely negative consequences for the quality of the decisions being made.

It was obvious to everyone in Kennedy's circle, including Schlesinger, that the decision to invade was moving relentlessly toward unanimity. Schlesinger had grave reservations about this apparently unstoppable course of action, and although he had expressed them in a private memorandum to the president, he never went public with his doubts. How did he respond when at the meetings of Kennedy's brain trust, how did he react to the pressure brought about by the majority's need for unanimity? In his own words, he "shrank into a chair at the far end of the table and listened in silence."

Schlesinger could have persisted in his opposition to the advice developed in Kennedy's war council, bringing his doubts to the table, and his action might have encouraged others to voice their disquiet and thus help to avert the debacle that was to come. Even if he had failed to move JFK and his inner circle, he would not have had to carry the burden of guilt over his silence, as he himself admitted:

In the months after the Bay of Pigs, I bitterly reproached myself for having kept so silent during those crucial discussions in the cabinet room. . . . I can only explain my failure to do more than raise a few timid questions by reporting that one's impulse

to blow the whistle on this nonsense was simply undone by the circumstances of the discussion.[iv]

The "circumstances of the discussion" is an exceptionally uninformative explanation of inaction, especially for a person as perceptive as Arthur Schlesinger. The groupthink process evident in Kennedy's White House during those critical days happened because Schlesinger wanted in. It happened because members of the decision-making group were extremely cohesive and largely isolated from information and interpretations other than their own, which they had developed themselves under highly stressful circumstances. Ultimately, it happened because members of the inner circle valued group unanimity more than they valued being right. Not a flattering picture, but not so uncommon either. Groupthink is a widespread and universal phenomenon that affects group decision making whenever the "circumstances of the discussion" are right. The lack of a minority voice doomed the discussion from the start, and John Kennedy's charismatic personality didn't help matters. A somewhat less forceful character by mere disposition might have naturally, encouraged more doubts to surface.

What has groupthink to do with the dynamics of social influence and our membership in, and identification with, strong and weak groups? Everything. On its own, the majority has little incentive to change the standard operating procedures. Creativity is stifled and the same old bad decisions are repeated, with identically bad outcomes. One of the smartest men the world has known, Albert Einstein, saw this clearly when he is said to have defined insanity as "doing the same thing over and over and expecting different results." Without a vocal minority suggesting an alternative view, the entropy in the system is never diverted. Course changes never occur. Nothing progresses. Those caught in the jaws of groupthink are practically guaranteed that their creative ideas will not be adopted, and their actions ensure that the group they wish to impress with their silence will neither prosper nor value them highly.

After the Bay of Pigs disaster, Kennedy set up arrangements to ensure that all voices, especially dissenting ones, would be heard whenever important decisions were on the table. His reaction was entirely correct. Groupthink, which springs from the strong need to maintain our place in the ruling clique, constricts alternative views, undermines problem solving, fosters self-censorship, and *almost always* results in poorer decisions. Kennedy was forced to face up to the disastrous outcomes of groupthink, and developed mechanisms to alleviate its dangers.[v]

Stifling Groupthink

Coming from a Catholic background, it is surprising that JFK needed the Bay of Pigs to alert him to the terrible consequences of groupthink. He had centuries of Church history to draw upon. From 1587 until recently, the Roman Catholic Church, arguably one of world's most successful organizations, appointed a special skeptic when deciding whether or not to elevate a person to sainthood. Officially, this professional skeptic was known as the *Promotor Fidei,* the "Promoter of the Faith." Unofficially, he was known as the *Advocatus Diaboli,* the "devil's advocate." It was the advocate's job to punch holes in cases that argued for canonization, to question all evidence that attested to the holiness of the nominee for sainthood. Whenever possible, the devil's advocate cross-examined available witnesses, scrutinized testimony of the contender's saintliness, and advanced all *reasonable* arguments against canonization. The Church instituted this role as insurance against groupthink—though they did not call it that in

1587. The devil's advocate's job was to force consideration of all points of view, thereby enhancing the quality of these important decisions. Not everyone, after all, should be sainted.

In 1983, Pope John Paul II discontinued the devil's advocate role, and in his remaining years, he canonized five times more men and women than had been sainted *in the previous eighty years.* In fact, over the course of his twenty-seven-year papacy, John Paul II sainted more people than the combined number of saints canonized over the previous five hundred years! Interestingly, John Paul II was himself beatified less than five years after his death. This first step to sainthood was the fastest in modern Church history. It occurred in the absence of a devil's advocate.

You can draw your own conclusions, but it's arguable that over the centuries, devil's advocates fulfilled their roles by applying brakes to irrationally exuberant evaluations of saintliness, brakes that were no longer available after John Paul II eliminated the office. Although most businesses are concerned with more worldly issues than the Catholic Church is, they might do well to consider this example. Clearly, a devil's advocate in the ranks might pay great dividends for a company. Of course, reckless devil's advocacy can put a stop to good ideas as well, but this is not what I am promoting. Devil's advocates should shoot holes in arguments or propositions only if they also can come up with better ideas. It is incumbent on the devil's advocate to use the role responsibly. When it is done right, devil's advocacy mitigates the dangers of groupthink, resulting in materially better decisions. Rather than harass and fire the whistle-blower or skeptic, corporate advocates of this type might prove an important benefit to the corporation. This is not to argue that the critics will be well liked, but they could be well worth the aggravation they might cause.[vi]

Obviously, the majority sometimes gets it terribly wrong. Yet, the opposing position often is weak and ineffective. It's difficult to count the number of times many of us have been asked to vote for futile political incumbents or their opponents, who we fear will be equally inadequate. How can the weak, the dissidents, the outsiders, in short, the minority, succeed? How can it generate support for its position? And, more important, when we find ourselves in a similar position—when all our colleagues or friends want to go in a direction we believe will prove disastrous—how do we resist the temptation to shrink into the chair at the far end of the table and instead rise up, make ourselves heard, and insist the larger group get it right? How do we succeed when the odds are stacked against us? Can it be done?

Obviously.

Some Minorities That Beat the Odds

Although no one questions the power of the majority, it's a mistake to assume that it always wins. Minorities often fail to carry the day, but they succeed far more frequently than most of us realize. The conflict minorities create often rouses the majority to resistance, but it also can provoke new ways of thinking that can boost creativity and innovation, and sometimes it promotes real advances. Positive minority-based changes are not all that rare, so it is important to recognize the productive features of minorities and to understand why some succeed where most fail. They can and do stir the pot, and when they do, good things sometimes happen. Some social scientists insist that minority groups are responsible for *all* major social innovations.

This is not to suggest that majority resistance to minority innovations is not to be expected at all turns. Why would it be otherwise? Why would the majority stand still while the minority changes the status quo? Why would the white U.S. majority in the 1950s, for example, willingly afford equal rights to African

Americans, women, or gay people? To do so does not appear to be in their immediate self-interest. They're in the driver's seat. They run the show, and change could end this cozy state of affairs. Majorities almost always can be expected to resist minority appeals, and their resistance succeeds most of the time. Make no mistake, the minority's job is far from easy. Entrenched interests oppose the minority influence agent from the start and can be expected to persist until one or the other faction prevails. Those who swim against the current incite conflict, and they usually lose.

But when they win, they can win big.

Polio

Consider the early career of Dr. Jonas Salk, the father of the first widely used polio vaccine, and acknowledged by many as a genuine hero of medical science. Most of us can't remember the bad old days when polio haunted the country, but the threat this dreaded disease posed was terrifying. In 1946, for example, there were twenty-five thousand new polio cases in the United States alone. By 1953, new cases numbered fifty-eight thousand, and the country was in a state of mild panic.[vii] In 1948, Salk began working on a vaccine that he hoped would put an end to this scourge. Consistent with his earlier research on other viruses, Salk attempted to develop a so-called killed-virus vaccine, which he believed held the promise of putting an end to the epidemic.

Most people today consider Salk a genius, but what you might not know is that many established scientists of his time viewed him as an outsider, a lightweight technician who did not fit in the more rarefied world of orthodox virus researchers, most of whom believed that only a "live virus" vaccine would work. This was not a trivial academic quibble—thousands of lives hung in the balance. The establishment scientists largely controlled the agencies that provided the lion's share of research funding, and though Salk found it difficult to secure the necessary money to advance his research, he steadfastly refused to quit and continued to plug away at his cure. The battle in the scientific community was intense, but the smart money was not being bet on Jonas Salk.

Scientific arguments aside, the numbers kept getting worse. Fostered by extreme necessity and prodded by Salk's persistence, the dam broke in 1954. In desperation, the March of Dimes and the National Foundation for Infantile Paralysis, a private philanthropic group founded by President Franklin Roosevelt in 1938, paid the costs of vaccinating nearly 2 million U.S. school-children with Salk's vaccine. The action was taken despite the bitter and resolute opposition of the powerful American Medical Association (AMA), which argued that proper scientific safeguards had been ignored in the rush to bring the vaccine to the field.

The AMA was correct. One batch of the vaccine produced by a sloppy laboratory killed eleven children, and the vaccine was not effective 100 percent of the time. But on the other side of the ledger, the program had to be judged an enormous success. The results were quick and startling and beyond everyone's expectations except, perhaps, Salk's. By 1961, polio cases in the United States had dropped below one thousand for the first time in years. Except for the one horribly unfortunate batch, none of the millions of children inoculated died from the vaccine. Seemingly overnight, Salk became a national hero, receiving the kudos of a grateful and relieved nation.

It is critical that we not gloss over the backstory of this hero's tale. Like all successful minorities, Salk exhibited dogged tenacity. His overnight hero status was twenty years in the making. That he did not falter is certainly a tribute to his character, but it also is an invaluable lesson to any influencer who hopes to succeed.

The general plot of Salk's story, of how an outsider changed the face of the world as we know it, is rare but not singular. From the very first days of his work on the polio vaccine, Salk was an outsider, clearly not a member of the medical establishment. His ideas were considered insubstantial, and he was judged as lacking the intellectual depth necessary to address the incredibly difficult medical problem he sought to solve. But as history has shown, outsiders who persist *can* influence the majority, they *can* prevail against incredible odds. Outsiders like Salk not only can provoke uncomfortable moments in the life the majority, but if they are to succeed, they *must* do so.

You can imagine mainstream live-virus researchers' reactions when they learned that Salk had acquired the means of inoculating millions of schoolchildren. In addition to believing that he was dead wrong, and that his vaccine might kill many children, or that it simply would not work, in small recesses in the corners of their minds they also had to wonder whether his success, unlikely as it appeared, would have negative repercussions for their own professional careers. For all these reasons, worthy and unworthy, the majority of virology researchers fought Salk tooth and nail. In this case, the majority did not derail the train, and the rest is history. Polio is now relegated to the fringes of Western society. The last indigenous case of "wild" polio in the United States was diagnosed in 1979. Like most successful minorities, Salk showed that persistence paid. Without it, he never would have had the opportunity to test and validate his ideas.

In research on minority influence in the psychology laboratory, this same result consistently recurs. Unless the minority is persistent and unwilling to take a backward step, it will not prevail. Without dogged devotion to the cause, without a willingness to suffer the onslaughts of the majority without ever taking a backward step, the minority's cause is lost. Salk intuitively recognized this fact from the start. Many others in a similar underdog position have not. By compromising or moderating their positions even slightly in hopes of dampening resistance, they fall into a fatal trap, succeeding only in adding fuel to the majority's fire, energizing rather than defusing further resistance.

To most people, minority groups appear relatively powerless. The gay rights movement, which has suffered a series of legal and electoral defeats; the Christian minority in Pakistan, whose members are slowly but systematically being killed; the proponents of equal pay for equal work, whose goal is far from realized despite federal law—all are minority groups that apparently lack the power to win the hearts and minds of the majority. While it is clear that they cannot compel the majority to accept their ideas about how things are or ought to be, the question remains, can a minority group ever persuade the majority to understand and acknowledge the legitimacy of its point of view? I believe it can. And although, as we will see, the outcomes of the influence process might not achieve all they had hoped, it may improve minorities' situations considerably. That such groups have failed to realize their goals does not necessarily indicate that they cannot. Rather, it is evidence that they have not stumbled on how to do so.

When underdogs succeed, it is easy to attribute their victory to luck or incredible coincidence, but this interpretation betrays laziness, ignorance, or a profound misreading of the historical record. Over the years, some minorities have been surprisingly effective. They not only have moved the power structure, but they sometimes have even taken it over. Were all these successes attributable to luck or incredible circumstance? Consider some minority groups and individuals who revolutionized society. The leaders of the early Christian Church; Martin Luther and the Protestant Reformation; Charles Darwin and his theory of evolution; Thomas Jefferson and the Second Continental Congress; Joseph Smith, Brigham Young, and the Mormon Church; Steve Jobs and Apple Computer—all these individuals and their groups prevailed, even though they started out with no apparent power, no influence, few obvious possibilities of success, and almost no advocates. What's more, they often were targets of an unfriendly majority, but in one way or another, their ideas were adopted, their visions realized. How did they do it?

Social and Minority Influence

Social psychologists have studied the general question of social influence for more than sixty years, and for the last thirty have specifically examined how minorities wield influence. We focus on minority influence because in most cases, the influencers with whom we are concerned are in weak positions, underdogs unable to force acceptance of their views or appeals. The principles discovered in the scientific research on minority influence are complex, exceptionally relevant for our purposes, and remarkably consistent. We know how minorities succeed. The rules of influence have been unearthed and verified, allowing us to understand how some individuals and groups have overcome incredible odds to prevail, while others with apparently better odds of success have fallen by the wayside. The rules are complicated and poorly organized, and so the complete picture is only dimly perceived even by scholars who have devoted their research lives to the issue, but they can be distilled from the large and largely disorganized research literature. The rules are exposed and developed throughout this book, but one central truth stands out: *The processes that govern the success (but not the failure) of a minority are the same in every case, no matter who the majority or minority is, irrespective of the issues involved or the moral righteousness of the minority's position.*

This is particularly important, as it suggests that the rules work irrespective of the identity of the minority. The rectitude of the group does not matter. The rules of influence hold whether the minority group is the early Christian Church or al-Qaeda, Mother Teresa's Missionaries of Charity or Adolf Hitler's Nazi Party, Barack Obama's Presidential Exploratory Committee or the Baader-Meinhof Red Army Faction. Applying the identical set of rules allows us to understand the factors that determine persuasive success or failure, and will illuminate the fundamental processes of minority influence.

In light of some of these minority successes, it is important to understand that the minority's story does not always have a happy ending. It is easy to point to successful minority movements precisely because they're rare, and so the successes stand out. Examples of minority groups' failures to move their respective majorities are considerably more numerous, and these failures will come in for attention as well, as they are as instructive as the successes are.

By seeing both sides of the coin, we can appreciate how apparently trivial changes in strategies or conditions spell the difference between success and failure, sometimes even between life and death.

People Who Need People

Strange as it may seem, the majority needs the minority, and the minority needs to prevail at least some of the time if it, *and the majority*, are to survive. Minority influence is the engine of progress, the driving force for change. If we are to learn how to influence others, it is imperative to understand how minorities work, how they persevere, and how they prevail. After years of research, we have succeeded in doing so. We have uncovered rules of influence that clearly point to the actions that maximize the persuasive effectiveness of those with little or no power to impose their will. As a convenient shorthand, we will identify these people and groups as the minority, even though by all outward appearances they may not be distinguishable from the majority. In this case, as we will see in the coming chapter, minority status has more to do with ideas than with physical or demographic features.

If followed precisely, these rules of influence can lead to success in moving a more powerful, if recalcitrant, group in your direction. This is not to say that every influence attempt will lead to certain success, or that influence agents always get precisely what they want. However, the changes induced will almost inevitably prove beneficial to its cause. The rules are unforgiving. One false step, one violation of the rules, and the likelihood of successful influence is significantly diminished. But let's not think about failure, at least not for now. The remainder of this book is devoted to detailing the rules of influence with compelling research and examples that all will recognize. It is presented not as a how-to-do-it manual, but rather as a set of strategies and broad-spectrum guidelines that smart people will be able to tailor to their specific needs.

Following the rules of influence should become second nature for you, and this book is my attempt to expose them and make them so. The rules of influence are research-based principles that enable and empower us to present ourselves and our arguments in as persuasive a manner as possible. They help us bring others to our way of seeing things. The rules obviously can be used for ill, but it is more likely that they will appeal to people of good conscience, as they reject brute force in favor of logic and wit. Demagogues will not find the advice presented here compatible with their way of doing things. The book is designed to change the way you think about social influence, to enable you to create better outcomes for yourself and the groups that claim your allegiance. Absorbing the lessons laid out in this book will enable readers to materially improve their persuasive success, even when they have no power to enforce their wishes.

Unsuccessful influence agents fail in many different ways, but successful ones all follow the same script. We will consider this script throughout the book, but before we do, it is important to remember that we are assuming that the influencer has little power to coerce. I am not concerned with persuading people who have no choice but to follow. Anyone can do that. Rather, I care about the ways in which a person in a weak position can move the powerful. If we can crack that nut, the rest is easy, but before we begin, let's consider the meaning of majority and minority, because our understanding of minority influence forms the basis of the new rules of influence.

ONE

Who and What Is a Minority?

> Everything great and intelligent resides in the minority.
>
> —*Goethe*

Although race and ethnicity often spring to mind when the word *minority* is used, these features are, for our purposes, not particularly important determinants of minority status. Minority groups come in all shapes, sizes, and colors, and while it is true that minorities sometimes are identified by obvious physical features like skin color, sex, height, or weight, even definitions based on physical features can shift according to circumstance. Princeton University was established in 1746, and for more than 200 years, Old Nassau admitted only males as full-time students. In 1961, Sabra Meservey was accepted into the Oriental Studies graduate program.[3] She was the first and only woman officially enrolled in the school at the time, and to her credit gained a master's degree two years later. Then, as now, women outnumbered men in the state and the country. Women were the numeric majority, but Sabra Meservey, a woman, was decidedly

---

[3] In keeping with Princeton's long-standing male-oriented traditions, Meservey's letter of acceptance began, "Dear Sir:"

in the minority at Princeton University. Place and circumstance matter.

Along with demographics, majority or minority status also can be based on beliefs or behaviors. Suppose you are a member of the Republican National Committee. At a meeting of the state chairpersons, you realize that the vast majority of the committee's membership is male. If you are a male, you are by simple arithmetic in the group's demographic majority; if female, you are in the minority. These demographic differences might not affect your work on the committee or the reception you receive from your fellow delegates, but suppose that while talking with them, you mention that you heartily agreed with President Obama's decision to bail out the auto companies. This position is unquestionably contrary to the committee's and the party's stated position, and no matter your demographic features, you have just jumped squarely into the minority.[4] Your deviation from the company line has placed you there, irrespective of your sex, age, race, religion, height, weight, or accent. Even if all these other features conform perfectly to the picture of the average Republican National Committee state chairperson, you still are in the minority. Opinions matter, and most of the time, they matter more than demographics when determining your status in the groups in which you find yourself.

This example points to at least two different types of minorities, demographic minorities and opinion minorities. Demographic minorities consist of individuals with physical features that differ from those of the majorities of their membership groups. Opinion

---

[4] If you are a committeewoman who happens to favor President Obama's economic stimulus plan for the auto companies, you are a *double minority,* a person (or group) that differs from the majority demographically *and* attitudinally. Research indicates that you will have almost no chance whatsoever of persuading the majority to accept your point of view. As we will see, however, even double minorities can influence the majority if they follow the rules.

minorities, on the other hand, hold positions at odds with the majority's. Because we are concerned primarily with influence, opinion minorities will command most of our attention, but the rules of influence operate irrespective of the type of minority—remember, in our work, *minority* is shorthand for groups or individuals with limited (or no) power to force acceptance of their positions. At the individual level, we are concerned with your capacity to influence others when they, not you, hold the upper hand, and research on minority influence provides the basis for this understanding. I believe it is critical to understand how minority groups exercise influence to understand how we can influence others when we do not have the power to force compliance.

Number and Power and the Definition of Legitimacy

To understand minority influence, it is important to understand what is meant by minority. In social research, minorities usually are defined in terms of number or power, neither of which, individually, captures the full meaning of the word. In combination, however, they paint a useful picture.

Number

In experimental laboratory research, *number* is the most common feature used to define minority or majority group status. The group with the most members is the majority and groups with fewer members are minorities. This research typically creates or assembles real or virtual groups of strangers who hold (or are said to hold) perceptions or opinions that are divergent from those of the majority, to which you belong. Research subjects may be told that 82 percent of their group holds a particular attitude, which is consistent with theirs. The subjects themselves are in the majority in this situation. Or, they might learn that only 18 percent of their fellow research participants hold a position consistent with theirs. In this case, the subjects are in the minority. The research is concerned with people's reactions to this type of information. In some cases, the disagreement between majority and minority does not involve attitudes or opinions, but rather a simple perception—for example, you might be asked to judge the color of a large circle that is projected onto a movie screen or large flat-screen monitor. You and most of your group report seeing the circle as blue, but a small subset of the group might insist that the circle is green. How you come to grips with their disagreement on a fundamental perception, how the opposing groups interact with each other, and the conditions that lead to the minority's success or failure in influencing the majority are the kinds of questions asked in research of this type.[5]

Number is used frequently in laboratory research because it is a convenient and efficient way of creating majority and minority groups, but it is only one, and probably not the most important indicator of majority or minority status. Another factor, power, often overwhelms number in determining minority status. Among other features, power has the unique capacity to define virtue or propriety, which in turn affects persuasion.

Power (or Status)

Before the end of apartheid in South Africa, whites ran the show. The black population was probably ten times that of the white population, but was considered the minority despite its overwhelming

---

[5]   You might be surprised to learn that minorities apparently can affect participants' reports of even obvious and simple perceptual judgments!

numbers. White rulers had the power to enforce their will and applied it ruthlessly. For many years, the white power structure wielded sufficient force to maintain its dominance. Number did not define majority status—power did. When the civilized world ultimately responded to the injustice of the system of apartheid through boycotts and ostracism of all things South African, the balance of power shifted. The force the white rulers of the country wielded could not be supported, and the practice of apartheid disintegrated.

Power is a key factor in defining group status. As shown in this example, power and number are not synonymous. The majority is the group with the muscle, even if it lacks numbers. A group may be accorded majority status because it controls resources—power—even if it is numerically inferior.

Writings by and about Jack Welch, the former and wildly successful CEO of General Electric, provide many interesting and instructive examples of the creative use of power, and power's capacity to define majority and minority status. Welch was one of the most dynamic company CEOs in the history of American business. He was involved in the smallest details of his company. He seemed to know everything and everyone who worked at GE, no small feat for the boss of one of the largest and most powerful engines of the U.S. economy.

Welch often consulted with his division managers and their staffs on the many issues with which a company of GE's size had to contend. Sometimes in these meetings, the obvious solution to problems would emerge organically over the course of the discussion. Jack Welch was an intuitive leader with an uncanny ability to work through problems, and to bring his employees with him, so that the proper plan of action evolved progressively over the course of their interactions. When it did not, he would lay out the conflicting alternatives about the decisions that could be made. Although there might be twenty people in the room, and nineteen of them felt that GE should move in one direction, the remaining voice often prevailed—if it was Welch's.[viii] In this circumstance, as in many others we will consider, number did not rule, power did. Even when outnumbered, the person in charge is the majority. Number does not matter when it is confronted by superior force.

Power's Capacity to Define Morality (or Propriety)

Obviously, the more powerful group can compel others to do its bidding, but there's more to it than that. Beyond the obvious, power often defines what is good and what is not; it sets the guidelines of proper behavior. Those in power have the capacity to define the rules of goodness or propriety or morality—to decide or define *values,* good and evil. The powerful define what is right or wrong, proper or improper, and the majority almost always reserves the positive adjectives for itself. Who do you think is responsible for the quip, "To the victors belong the spoils"? Certainly not the losing team. It is extremely unusual, for example, for leaders of a victorious army to be prosecuted for war crimes, even if their armies committed atrocities as a matter of course. Conversely, leaders of losing armies are almost always defined as depraved criminals who violated the norms of good conduct, which of course are defined by the winners (who by virtue of power can define morality any way they want).

The Nuremberg War Crimes Trials, which we considered in the introduction, offer a good example of the majority's hold over the definition of morality. The trial of Saddam Hussein in 2005 and his subsequent execution a year later provides another illustrative example of the capacity of the group in power to define right and wrong. Almost nobody who objected to Hussein's trial argued that he was a nice guy who did not deserve his fate. However, lots of people argued that the tribunal was a sham, a show trial staged to lend legitimacy to his execution. The winners defined the law, good and evil, after the fact, just as the winners did at Nuremberg. The group in power decided that Hussein's response to a failed assassination attempt in 1982 constituted crimes against humanity. The charges seem reasonable. He literally wiped out every male, young or old, in Dujail, the town in which the attempt on his life occurred. Such actions provide legitimate grounds for prosecution, and many wondered why charges were not brought until more than twenty years had passed. The answer is that Hussein held power during the intervening years, and power defines legitimacy. Almost as soon as the "Coalition of the Willing" invaded Iraq, Hussein lost his place at the head of Iraq's power majority. His definitions of right and wrong no longer held, and he lost his life as a consequence. It's dangerous to play with fire—or power.

Number, Power, and Morality: Do Other Features Matter?

Although the distinctions we've considered so far—number, power, and power's capacity to define virtue or morality—have been used in theories designed to distinguish majorities from minorities, they might not be distinctions that people actually use when thinking about these kinds of groups. How can we tell? We asked them.

My colleagues and I conducted a study to determine the characteristics people actually considered when they thought about minorities and majorities.[ix] To do this, we assembled a large number of young adults (average age, twenty-six years) and asked them to describe majority and minority groups through a structured process, by filling in the blanks in a number of incomplete sentences. The sentences each read as follow:

A minority is _____ because _____, which is a positive/ negative thing.

You might want to try this yourself. We repeated the same sentence stem nine times so you can run through it more than once if you like.

Respondents were to fill in the blanks, completing as many of the sentences as they could. On average, the subjects completed five sentences. Then, they were given ten more identical sentences, but this time the word *majority* was substituted for *minority*. You might like to give this variation a try as well.

A majority is _____ because _____, which is a positive/ negative thing.

To keep things even, half the subjects got the majority questions first, while the others started with the minority sentences.

The instructions to the participants were minimal: They were to fill in the first blank on each stem, "A minority (or majority) is _____" with a word or phrase that characterized such groups.

The second part of the sentence, "because _____" was there to help us understand the characterization by providing a context for the answer. This was especially useful when the description was ambiguous.

In the third part of the sentence, subjects circled *positive* or *negative,* which indicated the favorability of the descriptors they had written in the second blank.

To give you an example, here is how an actual subject completed the first sentence stem:

A minority is *an exploited group* because *they are singled out for unequal treatment,* which is a *negative* thing.

On the next stem (remember, subjects were given ten stems of each sentence type to complete), he wrote,

"A minority is *usually misunderstood* because *people don't know the discrimination they have to deal with,* which is a *negative* thing.

The content of participants' responses was analyzed to detect the major themes that emerged in their sentence completions. The results of the analysis expanded the general three-part framework (number, power, and morality) somewhat, but were not inconsistent with it. Participants' descriptions revealed that when left to their own devices, their conceptions of majority and minority groups were somewhat more complicated than we originally thought. The most frequent and most salient descriptions used reflected power or status, and number (no surprise here). However, distinctiveness (similarity and difference between the strong and the weak) also entered in, as did personal or demographic features (ethnicity, education, sexual orientation, age, and so on), as expected. An interesting distinction related to power also emerged. It had to do with whether the group was a target of other people's actions or the initiator of actions. Majorities initiate action; minorities are on the receiving end. Obviously, power has much to do with the group's or individual's capacity to initiate, but what of the other features that emerged in the study? You will find that they, too, are connected to the features raised earlier. Distinctiveness connects with number. If a group is distinctive, its members stand out because they're rare. If they weren't, they would not be distinctive. Rare implies lack of number, but there's more to it. We also learned that some of our (majority group) subjects identified these "rare" groups, minorities, as different or strange or even dangerous. Dangerous groups need to be identified or distinguishable. Our subjects' responses suggested that minorities needed to be made distinctive so that their actions could be monitored.

The historical record is frighteningly consistent with this unexpected (at least, to us) response. When the Nazis forced Jewish people to wear the yellow Star of David on their clothing, they did so to make them readily identifiable (and so, more easily monitored and controlled). Jews could be watched more closely if it was clear who they were. The Nazis created a kind of demographic feature to facilitate their conscious and intended anti-Semitic discrimination. But the Nazis also implemented the Jewish badge to emphasize to its wearers and to all other German citizens the Jews' estrangement from the larger society. The Nazis believed it was in their best interests to demonstrate to everyone that the Jews were distinct from the larger majority, to facilitate casting them as illegitimate and not a part of the *Volk,* the German people. The badge served multiple purposes. It was meant to emphasize the Jews' separateness and outsider status to all who saw it, and the hopelessness of rising up against the state's might. With the Jewish badge law, the Nazis attempted to make the Jews distinctive, identifiable, outcast, and hopeless.

Capacity to Initiate Action

Distinguishing groups based on their capacity to initiate action was consistent with our earlier consideration of power. Many of our respondents saw the majority as the group that did things to others, and the minority as the group that had things done to it. For example, one respondent completed the minority item as follows:

A minority is *weak* because *they don't have the power to defend themselves,* which is a *negative* thing.

Another wrote,

"A majority *is able to do great things* because *it has the resources
to get things done,* which is a *positive* thing.

These categorizations indicate our respondents' recognition of
the power difference between the majority and minority groups,
a differentiation we've seen in our consideration of the Nuremberg and Saddam Hussein trials. When they were in the driver's
seat, the Nazis and members of Saddam's Ba'ath Party did as
they pleased, to almost anyone they could get their hands on.
When they lost power and themselves became minorities, neither
had the capacity to stop the new majorities from returning the
favor.

The misuse of power to define right and wrong is not confined
to those we hate. When the torture of prisoners at Abu Ghraib
was discovered, a great hue and cry was raised throughout the
civilized world, even in the United States, whose soldiers had
done the dirty work. Some of those involved were sentenced to
the brig. Can you name a single high-ranking officer who served
prison time as a result of his or her actions in that prison? If you
cannot, you are correct, because none did. Their status as members of the power majority insulated them from the consequences
that could have been meted out.[x]

Now let's consider the last part of the subjects' task. You will
recall that respondents evaluated the favorability of the descriptors they used in describing the majority's or minority's actions.
So, for example, one respondent wrote:

"A majority is *powerful* because *they have the law on their side,*
which is a *positive* thing.

The results of the analysis of favorability surprised us. Across all respondents, the sentences involving the majority were rated significantly more favorably than those involving the minority. This result held even for those who themselves were members of demographic minority groups. The subjects seemed to value the descriptions and products of the majority more than those of the minority. This result may point to the power of the majority to define what's good and bad, and also, perhaps, to people's desire to be on the right side of the equation. Even within minority groups, members vie to be in the clique that holds the power, and this preference was clearly reflected in our research participants' evaluations of the majority and minority group characterizations they themselves had made.

Our analysis of our subjects' answers corresponds nicely with research on the ways the mass media describe minorities and majorities. In a recent study, we analyzed the headlines that appeared in the five major newspapers in California from 2000 to 2003. These were large newspapers, which together accounted for more than 40 percent of the newspaper circulation in the state. We were interested in all headlines that used the words *minority* or *majority* in some form or another. Over the three years that we studied, these words appeared in 1,464 headlines. *Minority* appeared in significantly more headlines, but the real point of the study was to see how the newspapers characterized these two groups, and the context in which these references were used. We found that political and international issues were discussed most frequently in stories involving the majority ("Women make up the majority of workers in the factories of Shenzhen"), and social and economic issues were the most frequent focus of minority-headlined stories. Majority headlines often included the identity of the majority—"the House Majority Leader, Nancy Pelosi"— but minorities were typically described with broad, imprecise descriptions and references to ethnicity ("the Asian minority"). Finally, stories with majority headlines were longer than those involved with minority issues, suggesting perhaps that issues involving the majority's concerns deserved greater elaboration and analysis.[xi]

These findings reinforce what we already know, that no matter how we define the minority, the majority runs the show. Typically, the majority is defined in terms of number, power, the capacity to define morals—what's good and what isn't—and the ability to make things happen. The minority is found in the mirror image of these same features.

Putting all this together, we can define the *typical* minority group as a collective of people who are less numerous, less powerful, and who hold beliefs that those in power consider incorrect, subversive, dangerous, or in some way contrary to everyone's (that is, everyone who matters) best interests. A group can be in the minority even if doesn't satisfy all these criteria. Shiites in Saddam's Iraq were three times more numerous than the ruling Sunnis, but they lacked power, and so they were the minority group relative to the considerably less numerous Sunnis. Given their capacity to define morality or propriety, the Sunnis branded Shiite behaviors and beliefs as quaint, improper, or demonic, depending on the orthodoxy and needs of the perceiver, because they were contrary to standards defined by the majority as proper, appropriate, or godly. Minority status often carries with it the taint of foolishness, illegitimacy, or as we saw in our headline study, as lacking value, and this observation holds whether the minority is a Shiite in prewar Iraq, a Jehovah's Witness in Vatican City, or a Cleveland Indians fan almost anywhere.

Is there any hope for those stuck in the minority meat grinder? Can they possibly influence the powerful and suspicious majority? There is no question that they can, and understanding how to do it is crucial, because everyone at one time or another finds themselves in the minority. To stand a chance, we need to understand some fundamentals about the nature and function of the groups that claim our allegiance. And we also need to learn about the groups we hate, fear, or ignore, because they, too, help us define who we are.

Give It to Me Straight, Doc

The likelihood that the minority can resist the power of the majority, make, and win its claim is not great. Without understanding the new rules of influence, the odds are practically nonexistent. The group in control is inherently conservative, in the sense that it is intent on maintaining the power structure as it is, on maintaining the status quo, which helps its members maintain their privileged position. Outsiders, on the other hand, are inherently progressive, pushing for changes in the rules and regulations that govern and constrict their freedoms and opportunities. The minority pushes for change to increase both its power and its numbers.

Behind in numbers, outgunned, and without the moral authority to define values, it's a wonder minorities ever win. How the minority can influence the majority, credibly and effectively, has everything to do with the way in which it presents itself, and how this self-presentation affects the larger group's views of the outsiders. The next chapter examines the subtle and not-so-subtle ways we define ourselves through our group memberships and how our groups define us, sometimes even when we fight hard to avoid the classification. We will see that our identities can be influenced profoundly by the ways others see us, even if we, ourselves, reject their views. These identities, in turn, spell the difference between acceptance and rejection by the group in power, and acceptance has everything to do with our persuasive successes.

How Our Groups Define Who We Are

What characterizes a member of a minority
group is that he is forced to see himself as both
exceptional and insignificant, marvelous and
awful, good and evil.

—*Norman Mailer*

How we develop our self-identity, our sense of who we are, is
largely determined by the groups in which we claim membership, the groups that claim us as members, whether we like it
or not,[6] and the groups we aspire to join. Studies of radical Muslim extremists find that the newer and less established members
of the group, the wannabes, often are the most extreme in their
views and behaviors. It is as if they need to prove their mettle by
demonstrating greater commitment and conformity to the group's
orthodoxy than the more senior members.[xii]

These kinds of findings suggest that we need others to help us
define ourselves, to validate that identity. Greater uncertainty often
leads to more extreme behavior in the quest for self-identification.
The less certain we are about our place in a group relevant to our

---

[6] People can be "claimed" by some groups even if they would rather be left off their
rosters. For example, convicted child molesters are seen by the population at large
as members of a dangerous and repellent group, even though many molesters might
never have interacted with any other member of this group. They are identified by
the society at large as belonging to this group of undesirables, and *all* members of
the group receive largely the same response by the larger society.

identity, the more extreme we are willing to be. To help us define ourselves, we actively seek out other people's company, people with whom we wish to associate, and work to connect ourselves with them. If real people are not available or are not up to the job, we seek substitutes. We might, for example, become fanatic fans of a recording artist, an author, a movie star, or a sports figure. Although being a Facebook friend of Lady Gaga might not do much for some of us, it seems to have struck a responsive chord for more than 10 million people. Apparently, being a part of this group, as fluid and shapeless as it might be, helps individuals stake out their identities.

Personal and Social Identity

We use groups in many ways to build or bolster an identity we seek to capture. We wear the right clothes with the right logo, whether it's OshKosh or Armani, often to signal our preferences and to identify with others who do so as well. We affect the right accent, read the right books, go to the right clubs where the right people hang out on the chance we might hook up. In extreme cases, we buy dogs.

Why? Because in addition to those peculiar quirks and idiosyncrasies that distinguish us from everyone else (our personal identities), we use our group memberships to define ourselves, to round out ourselves, to tell the world who we are. There is good evidence that our group memberships are at least as important as our personal identity in creating our self-definitions. The importance groups assume as we develop our self-definitions or identities may surprise you, probably because groups are such common and inescapable features of social life. They saturate almost every aspect of our existence—they're everywhere, all the time, and so they fade from consciousness for the most part. You're an Eagle

Scout, a Tri Delt, the Executive Officer of a Navy destroyer, or a University of Michigan alumnus, and these identities, present or past, leave a mark on who you are. The groups that form our social identities become part of the background, the psychological scenery, but their importance in determining who we are is difficult to overestimate.

We belong to many groups by choice—we want to be counted among the group's membership. We're liberals or conservatives, Democrats or Republicans, Los Angeles Lakers or Boston Celtics fanatics, we fancy Botticelli or Modigliani, Klee or Kandinsky, Stravinsky or The Strokes, we say tomāto or tomăto. But there are some groups that you cannot avoid being a part of, simply because group membership is defined on the basis of features that you possess but did not necessarily choose. You're a man or a woman, black or white, Ethiopian or Irish, able bodied or disabled, speak the King's English or a variant of that language with a thick Scottish burr. These groups matter, too, and like your chosen memberships, they affect your characterization of yourself because, if nothing else, they affect the way others respond to you. If others consistently treat you as stupid, or dishonest, or sexy, or intellectual, chances are you will come to see yourself in this way, and your behavior will reflect these self-perceptions. The membership category others have assumed you belong to (ignoramuses, crooks, sexpots, intellectuals) will have a strong effect on your own view of yourself, and that self-image will certainly affect your consequent behavior.

In his early years, one of the world's wisest and most profound thinkers, Thomas Aquinas, was known to his pals as "the Dumb Ox." He thought of himself in this way for years and behaved accordingly. Only after he broke from this identity did he produce his incredibly interesting views on the nature of humanity and the meaning of life.[xiii] Our living up (or down) to others' expectations is a result of what has been called the self-fulfilling prophecy, and though we are not doomed inevitably to act out others' expectations of us, there's plenty of evidence indicating that the way others view and respond to us has much to do with the ways we think of ourselves and, ultimately, behave.

A colleague of mine and I addressed the question of the behavioral effects of the self-fulfilling prophecy with a study of data from a national survey of more than four thousand parents and their children (twelve to eighteen years of age). In the first year of the survey, which was readministered to respondents at yearly intervals for four years, parents and children were interviewed about a number of issues involving illicit drug use. One set of questions concerned the youngsters' use of marijuana. Parents and children answered privately. Most of the parents were accurate in their assessments of their children's marijuana use, but we were interested in those who misjudged their kids, and the effects of these misjudgments on the children's later behavior, which was assessed in the following year of the survey. Our research question was whether or not a parent's misjudgment was associated with their child's subsequent marijuana usage.

If you are a parent, the answer to this question might scare or delight you, depending on your tendency to see the best or the worst in your kids. Some parents *mistakenly* reported that their children had used marijuana in the first year of the survey (that is, the kids hadn't used marijuana, but the parents thought they had). We found that these children were significantly more likely to begin using marijuana by the second year's survey than were kids of parents who correctly reported that their children had not initiated marijuana use. On the positive side, some parents in the first year of the survey *mistakenly* reported that their children did not use marijuana (the kids themselves reported they did). In the second year of the survey, we found these kids were significantly more likely to have stopped using marijuana than children whose parents' were correct in their reports in the first year of the survey that their child had used marijuana.[xiv]

In a nutshell, these findings demonstrated that parents' incorrect views of their children's drug use seemed to push the children's behavior in the direction of their expectations. The self-fulfilling prophecy works, but apparently it works both ways, for good or ill. Would similar results be obtained on adult subjects? Based on mountains of evidence, there can be no doubt about this. The expectations others have of us play a role in our own identities, on who we think we are, and who we think we are affects the way we behave. There also should be no doubt that the groups we are associated with, by choice or owing to features we carry with us, have much to say about the expectations people form of us. The evidence is inescapable: The effects of others' expectations on our behaviors are real and they are powerful.

Groups and Identity

Groups must be viewed as more than mere associations of people we join to find like-minded associates. The groups to which we belong are the building blocks of *us,* of who we are, of how we perceive and relate to the world at large, and they help determine how the world at large perceives and relates to us. We join groups because, among other reasons, they are a source of rewards. Our memberships matter to us because of their potential to enhance our self-esteem. When our group does well, we take personal pride in the group's achievement, even if we had nothing to do with it. Remember the guys running through the introduction yelling "WE'RE NUMBER ONE!" They were hollering for lots of reasons, alcohol being among the likely causes, but they also were yelling because associating with a winner is highly satisfying.

Groups that choose us work in the same way—when these groups succeed, our self-esteem grows, and when they fail, we suffer. This is why antidefamation associations protest at what they consider to be caricatures of the groups they represent and seek to protect. They do so because the caricature affects group members and nonmembers alike. Many Italian-American antidefamation activists railed against *The Sopranos,* an award-winning television series that followed the lives of Mafia gangsters in New Jersey. They did not complain about the production values of the show, but rather that it portrayed Italians in an extremely bad light, almost relentlessly. There were too few positive images of good and successful law-abiding Italians in the show, which was so one-sided that the image of the Italian American was tarnished. They did not prevail in this case, but they did raise awareness among the general population that the portrayal was less than accurate. It bears repeating that even groups that we belong to through no fault of our own—you're a redhead, or Chinese, or short—groups that chose us, rather than groups we chose to join, can affect your sense of self-worth as a result of how redheads, or Chinese, or short people in general are treated and viewed by the larger society. If you belong to a group that has been devalued by the majority—garbage collectors, midgets, immigrants, Muslims post-9/11 in the United States and England—the mere fact that you belong to one or another of these groups may affect your self-esteem and sense of worth. Of course, people can rise above the judgments of the larger society, but there's a psychological and sometimes physical price to pay to do so.

The minority group must sustain its members in confrontations with the majority if it is to survive. The National Socialists (neo-Nazis) who every now and then on warm Saturday mornings parade down quiet college streets, asserting the First Amendment rights they would deny everyone if they only had the chance, are almost universally hated. However, they are sustained by fellow members, even though those individuals are equally hated by the larger society.

How Identities Form

For many years, social scientists have actively investigated the ways groups affect people's identities. Among the most creative of these researchers was Henri Tajfel, who as a young man journeyed from Warsaw to Paris to study chemistry at the Sorbonne, France's premier institution of higher learning. When World War II broke out after his arrival in the City of Light, he was drafted into the French Army, not an auspicious beginning to an academic career. Worse yet, after a year in the armed service of France, he was captured by the Nazis. He kept his Jewish heritage to himself, and spent the next two years in prisoner of war camps as a French soldier. Because the Nazis did not learn of his Jewish heritage, young Henri was not shipped off to the concentration camps that awaited so many other Jews caught in the Nazi vise. After the war, he switched his course of study from chemistry to psychology when he came to realize the incredible importance of the groups with which one was identified. In his case, being identified as French rather than Jewish spelled the difference between life and death.[xv]

He turned this realization into research that unmistakably illustrates the importance of even trivial group memberships on people's beliefs and actions. In an early study of the ways people use groups to form identities, Tajfel and his collaborators had their subjects estimate the number of black dots projected onto a white movie screen. The correct judgments were not obvious—

lots of dots were projected, and they were not visible for very long—but the job didn't take much effort and no one suggested to the subjects that the fate of the Western world depended on the quality of their perceptions. After a few judgments, the experimenter collected everyone's written estimates and appeared to tally their guesses. He told the participants that they differed in their tendency to over- or underestimate the dots. Some were told they were overestimators, others that they were underestimators. No particular value was placed on either designation. In fact, the overestimator and underestimator labels were assigned to subjects randomly. They had no connection to the actual judgments the research subjects had made.

Now, no reasonable person could possibly view this difference—the trivial distinction of over- or underestimating dots on a screen—as a defining attribute of good or evil. Yet, subjects used the information in precisely this manner, because in the next phase of the experiment, when given the opportunity to dispense rewards and to judge the relative morality and deservingness of their fellow participants, lo and behold, the subjects allocated significantly more of their limited pot to those who fell into their group at the expense of those who did not. Overestimators gave significantly more rewards to their fellow overestimators, and underestimators overrewarded their own kind at the expense of the overestimators. When judging social worth, deservingness, morality, intelligence, and other positive traits, people judged those from their own group as more moral, more righteous, smarter, and more deserving than people from the other group. These differences in evaluation and the behaviors that followed from them were based on a trivial distinction that would mean nothing to any thinking person.

Because these findings were so unexpected, literally hundreds of variations of the study were conducted in laboratories across Europe and the United States, with identical results. Clearly, Tajfel's findings were not anomalous. These studies consistently demonstrated the importance of group assignment on people's judgments and actions, even though the criteria used to define group membership were trivial to the point of meaninglessness. Participants always overrewarded their own group at the expense of the others.

We need not imagine how strongly people might discriminate when the factor that separates their group from other groups is truly important to them, like religion, ethnicity, race, clan, tribe, gang, political party, or national origin. We need not imagine because history is replete with examples of the terrible consequences that *can* come about as a result of social identification and the discrimination it can foster. Distinctions based on group memberships have encouraged torture, genocide, and mass murder. The genocide in Rwanda, which we will consider carefully in the next chapter, is but one of hundreds of gruesome examples of this fact. But group memberships also have encouraged prosocial behavior. Belonging to groups that are devoted to helping others obligates, or at least encourages people to be helpful, and this applies whether the group is the Boy Scouts, the clergy, or the healing professions, groups whose outward appearances signal their members' willingness to respond to the needs of others.

To make sense of the unexpected results he was finding in his research, Tajfel developed a theory to explain the ways we use groups to define our identity, and how this identity process, in turn, affects our relations with others. The basic idea of social identity theory, as it has come to be called, is simple —who you are, your identity, is largely the result of your group memberships or affiliations. We build our social identities from our group memberships. Our membership groups (the DAR, the Lubavitchers, the Geek Squad at Best Buy), and the groups we aspire to, the ones we'd like to join, reinforce and define our sense of who we are. They form our social identity, and our social identity regulates our social interactions. It is fashionable for the diet conscious to tell you that you are what you eat. Social identity theory suggests they're wrong, unless you eat your groups.

We belong to many groups, and they all contribute to our sense of who we are. Angie might be a Lutheran Yalie Los Angeleno Republican hockey mom, and that only begins to describe the many parts of her social identity. Her group memberships are crucial because they distinguish those who are part of her identity-forming and, therefore, valued groups from those who are not. At the Republican National Convention, for example, Angie may classify all Republicans as belonging to a group that defines a central part of her identity. Democrats fall outside the group, and Angie's distancing herself from them also helps her define herself. In-group and out-group distinctions of this type, based on group memberships and avoidances, affect our perceptions and evaluations, our willingness to associate with or avoid, and to reward or punish other people. These decisions are made on the basis of the similarity of others' group memberships with ours.

We discriminate between "us" and "them" because it is rewarding to do so. We use outsiders to give us a better fix on the insiders who form the groups that play a central role in our definition of ourselves. When we differentiate ourselves from other groups, we usually single out dimensions that tilt the evaluation in our favor. So, a high school football player might think, *Okay, our school's not as new as our rival's, our facilities are terrible, our teachers aren't as good, and our rival school always produces National Merit finalists. We never do . . . but we have a better football team.* We can outshine almost any group by picking the right comparison dimension, and this is not just sour grapes at work. It reflects a feature that in our eyes is important, precisely because it allows us to differentiate *us* from *them*. Our high schooler's comparison process may seem ludicrous to an unbiased outsider, but it allows him to maintain a sense of superiority over the rival group (students from the other high school) on a dimension that matters to him (football), while simultaneously boosting his own group (fellow schoolmates).

Winning these psychological contests is rewarding, and it strengthens our ties with our fellow group members. This is how groups retain their members and why people go to great lengths to preserve their membership status in their identity-defining groups. The essential message of social identity theory is that we do not define ourselves in terms of "I," but rather in terms of "we."

Who Am I (er, We)?

The "Who am I?" test is a measure that assesses the features that are important to people when they attempt to describe and define themselves. The test format is straightforward: Following the phrase "Who am I?" are twenty numbered blank lines on a page. Those taking the test are asked simply to fill in the blank lines with self-descriptive words or phrases—female, vegan, Democrat, Raiders fan, and so forth. Any descriptor is allowed. The format is illustrated on the next page. You might want to try it before reading on.

WHO AM I?

Please describe yourself. In the 20 lines that follow, write a word or phrase that describes who YOU are.

1. _____
2. _____
3. _____
4. _____
5. _____
6. _____
7. _____
8. _____
9. _____
10. _____
11. _____
12. _____
13. _____
14. _____
15. _____
16. _____
17. _____
18. _____
19. _____
20. _____

Typically, the responses people make on the test illustrate the importance of social groups in the construction of the self, their social identities. Usually, after people list the standard demographics (male, six feet tall, white, balding), they begin to list descriptors that refer to groups that they have joined of their own free will (Tea Party activist, Episcopalian, hunter, NRA member, and the like). These various memberships need not be formal groups to be important to a respondent.

How do we characterize the content of these descriptors? Sociologists have found it useful to break groups into two broad types—*achieved* groups and *ascribed* groups. To be a member of an achieved group takes some willful action on our part (Rotarian, Southern Baptist, member of Kobe Bryant's fan club, Eagle Scout, Stanford alumnus). You have to do something to achieve membership in achieved groups. On the other hand, we're part of ascribed groups because of who and what we are, the traits and features we carry with us through no action on our part. Skin color, height, national origin, age, and sex are all ascribed features. These features, too, can strongly affect our identities. Although we did not consciously do anything to attain them, other people use ascribed features to define us and make attributions about our motives and behaviors, and these reactions or expectations of others, in turn, affect our sense of who we are and often, our behavior as well.

The "Who am I?" test highlights the importance of our group memberships, ascribed and achieved, in the self-definition process. If you had tried the test yourself, go back and consider your answers. It's a good bet that almost all of what you entered on the test has to do with the groups to which you belong. This process of developing our identity through our group memberships is called social identification. Not only do we use our groups to define ourselves, other people join the action as well. In fact, people often use features we were born with to classify and judge us on traits and abilities that have nothing to do with the feature they are using. For example, a person might look at a tall, trim, young African American man and assume that he is a good basketball player, but not particularly good in school. While height might be grounds for a very risky bet on basketball ability—lots of tall people are terrible at the game—we know from years of research and hundreds of studies that neither height nor skin color predict an individual's IQ. Facile attributions based on ascribed features— let's call them stereotypes—are commonplace and often wildly off base. They are the building blocks of discrimination, and if you keep your eyes and ears open, you'll see that their potential for misdiagnosis does not retard their continual use.

Northeasterners often view a thick Southern accent as a possible indication of inbred mental retardation, while Southerners often think the Northeastern accent is an infallible indicator of snobbish condescension. Neither group is necessarily correct. Obviously, when we use ascribed features (sex, weight, skin color) to infer internal traits, the process can produce some seriously distorted misconceptions. And, as our research on the self-fulfilling prophecy has shown, it also can affect the actions of the person being (mis)judged.

The common stereotype of senior citizens holds that they are relatively inactive, slow-moving, cautious, slow to adopt progressive ideas, and, generally, politically conservative. But consider the marching orders of the Gray Panthers, which call for guaranteed health care and patients' rights, reproductive choice, legalization of medical marijuana, a comprehensive test ban treaty, a halt to the blockade of Cuba, and opposition to a military draft, among other progressive causes. Certainly these positions do not conform to expectations based on a stereotype of stodgy oldsters who oppose all change and every progressive idea.

Medical doctors who are members of the American Medical Association pay their dues at least in part so they can claim membership in the association, because this identity signals lots of positive information—their advanced educational background, relative wealth, social status, intelligence, training, perseverance, and talent. Whether the information is always correct is beside the point—the attributions people make because of this group membership are consistent, predictable, and positive.

We value our groups because in addition to their telling others who we are, they help *us* define who we are as well. Each of us has many group memberships, some more essential to us than others, and in total, they define our *social identity*. Although we belong to many groups, the varying contexts in which we find ourselves determine the relative importance of these memberships at any given moment. If we are sitting in the bleachers of Chicago's Wrigley Field in the middle of thousands of screaming Cubs fans, our "team" identity becomes salient, but our Cubs identity might not rise to the surface when we're sitting in the Caffé Greco on Rome's Via Condotti. Unless the context calls it to our attention, a particular group identity might not affect our actions. Except for our most central self-identities, which are "on" at almost all times, different identities come online depending on the circumstances in which we find ourselves. Our using a PC might not really mean too much to us, but when we are faced with an obnoxious Apple Computer booster, our identity as a PC person probably will suddenly become salient.

All the studies discussed in this chapter point inescapably to the conclusion that the impressions people form of themselves can have an immense effect on all aspects of their lives. Our self-conceptions can have a powerful effect on our capacity to influence other people as well. If we are unhappy about the identities that define us, whether they're ascribed (I hate being short) or achieved (and uneducated), we are unlikely to be persuasive when trying to influence people's opinions, because in addition to gauging the quality of our persuasive communications, targets of persuasion pay considerable attention to the social and physical characteristics of the people trying to influence them. Our evaluations of ourselves, then, have powerful effects on others' evaluations of us.

Positive self-evaluations affect others' responses to us, and these responses help spell the difference between the success or failure of our attempts to move people to our way of thinking. Even more important, as we will see in the coming chapter, is the correspondence of our social identity with that of the individual or group we are attempting to influence, because if these identities do not match, we have little chance of success.

THREE

You in or Out?

The most certain test by which we judge
whether a country is really free is the amount
of security enjoyed by minorities.

—*Lord Acton*

On the evening of April 6, 1994, the three-engine private jet of President Juvénal Habyarimana of Rwanda fell from the sky over Kinshasa after being hit by two surface-to-air missiles. All on board died, including Habyarimana and the acting president of Burundi, Cyprien Ntaryamira. The assassination sparked the Rwandan massacre of 1994, in which an estimated 2 million persons from the contending Hutu and Tutsi tribes were killed or displaced. In retrospect, this human catastrophe should have been anticipated, as influential Hutu voices calling for the elimination of the Tutsi had been strong and strident for many years. The slaughter of innocent civilians of all stripes began within hours of the assassination, and continued for the next hundred days. When the smoke cleared, nearly one quarter of the Rwandan population, 800,000 to 1 million men, women, and children had been exterminated.[xvi]

The massacre pitted Hutu against Tutsi, the two major Rwandan ethnic groups. Although a numeric minority, the Tutsi had exercised power in the country for decades. The Hutu had wrested control of Rwanda from the Tutsi after a bloody revolution in 1959, and when Habyarimana, himself a Hutu seized power in a bloodless coup in 1973, Hutu supremacy was assured. But after twenty years of dictatorship, events indicated that all this might change. Severe internal economic problems and external pressure from a revitalized Tutsi expatriate army camped on Rwanda's border had seriously destabilized the country, and Habyarimana was forced to make concessions to the Tutsi in a formal treaty assuring them a legitimate place in the government, the army, the educational system, and the police forces, organizations that had been closed to Tutsi for years. To many Hutu, these conciliatory actions appeared to be nothing more than appeasement that ultimately would lead to the Tutsi's return to power. Habyarimana's assassination seemed to confirm Hutu fears, and they struck out.

Two large, well-prepared, and heavily armed militias of Hutu extremists, aided by many untrained machete-wielding Hutu vigilantes, systematically swept through the country, killing with grim efficiency massive numbers of Tutsi and moderate Hutu. They appeared to believe that even Hutu were fair game if they were not willing to be complicit in the killing of their Tutsi neighbors. We've heard it all before—"If you're not with us, you're against us."

No one acquainted with the Rwandan situation would have suggested the Hutu and Tutsi liked each other, although the two groups lived in relative harmony for many centuries before the country was taken over and "civilized" by the Western colonial powers near the beginning of the nineteenth century. In colonial times, the Germans placed Tutsi in positions of authority to the massive disadvantage of the Hutu. When the Belgians took over Rwanda from the Germans after World War I, the pattern continued. Certainly there was ill will between the contending Hutu and Tutsi camps, but the ferocity and speed of the Rwandan massacre shocked even seasoned cynics. How could this slaughter have occurred, and how could it have been avoided?

From the perspective we have developed, the bad blood that characterized Hutu-Tutsi relations ultimately can be analyzed in terms of the different social identities ascribed to the groups. Most Tutsi would rather be caught dead than be called a Hutu, and the Hutu felt the same way about the Tutsi. This was not a match made in heaven. However, for many Rwandans, telling one from the other was not easy. To allow for discrimination, we must be able to differentiate one group from another. "You got to identificate before you can discriminate," as Johnnie Cochran might have phrased it. How did the marauding Hutu identify their victims? Physical features in the Rwandan context are an unreliable gauge. Generally, the Tutsi are thought to be taller than the Hutu, to have a thinner body build and more chiseled facial features. This might have been true a few centuries ago, but these differences have faded over the years. The groups have lived together and intermarried for centuries. In fact, genetic studies cannot distinguish the groups. The last colonial power in Rwanda, the Belgians, identified as Tutsi anyone who owned more than ten cows or had a long nose. Owning fewer cows was a Hutu feature, as Hutu traditionally engaged in farming rather than herding and animal husbandry. How the proboscis criterion was developed is anyone's guess.

In the end, the identity cards instituted by the Belgians to help them keep track of their wards provided the acid test. When gangs of marauding Hutu swept through villages, it was important to have Hutu on your ID card, because you would be killed if you did not—and your age or sex or occupation did not matter. The Hutu and Tutsi tended to live in relative isolation of one another, so some settlements were known to be Tutsi, others Hutu, and this facilitated the slaughter of the "right" people and the salvation of others. In mixed communities, the job was a bit more difficult, but neighbors would know the ethnic identity of those who lived nearby and had no choice but to provide the information to the marauding bands of killers.

One might argue that it should have been clear to the Tutsi that trouble was afoot, and the better part of valor—discretion—should have prevailed. It did not, and thousands upon thousands perished. Their reluctance to hide their important (ethnic) group identity is understandable even under extreme duress. We have found in our laboratory that people will rush to the defense of their identity group if it comes under attack from a rival group, even if they originally did not much care for the identity group. However, in our laboratory, "under attack" does not involve machetes.

The Tutsi were under heavy pressure for years before the crash that took Habyarimana's life. The state-supported propaganda machine had heaped vile slurs on them, and even went so far as to publish the "Hutu Ten Commandments," designed to regulate relations between the groups. These "commandments," which were authorized by the government, drew a stark distinction between the groups, and were meant to encourage the separation of Hutu from Tutsi. They laid the psychological foundation for the slaughter that has come to be called the Rwandan massacre.

THE HUTU TEN COMMANDMENTS

1. Every Hutu should know that a Tutsi woman, whoever she is, works for the interest of her Tutsi ethnic group. As a result, we shall consider a traitor any Hutu who

   - marries a Tutsi woman
   - befriends a Tutsi woman
   - employs a Tutsi woman as a secretary or a concubine.

2. Every Hutu should know that our Hutu daughters are more

suitable and conscientious in their role as woman, wife and mother of the family. Are they not beautiful, good secretaries and more honest?

3. Hutu women, be vigilant and try to bring your husbands, brothers and sons back to reason.

4. Every Hutu should know that every Tutsi is dishonest in business. His only aim is the supremacy of his ethnic group. As a result, any Hutu who does the following is a traitor:

- makes a partnership with Tutsi in business
- invests his money or the government's money in a Tutsi enterprise
- lends or borrows money from a Tutsi
- gives favors to Tutsi in business (obtaining import licenses, bank loans, construction sites, public markets, etc.).

5. All strategic positions, political, administrative, economic, military, and security should be entrusted only to Hutu.

6. The education sector (school pupils, students, teachers) must be majority Hutu.

7. The Rwandan Armed Forces should be exclusively Hutu. The experience of the October 1990 war has taught us a lesson. No member of the military shall marry a Tutsi.

8. The Hutu should stop having mercy on the Tutsi.

9. The Hutu, wherever they are, must have unity and solidarity and be concerned with the fate of their Hutu brothers.

- The Hutu inside and outside Rwanda must constantly look for friends and allies for the Hutu cause, starting with their Hutu brothers.
- They must constantly counteract Tutsi propaganda.
- The Hutu must be firm and vigilant against their common Tutsi enemy.

10. The Social Revolution of 1959, the Referendum of 1961, and the Hutu Ideology, must be taught to every Hutu at every level. Every

Hutu must spread this ideology widely. Any Hutu who persecutes his brother Hutu for having read, spread, and taught this ideology is a traitor. (from Berry & Berry, 1999—see Note xvi)

The Critical (Sometimes Life and Death) Distinction between In-group and Out-group Minority Status

To understand how the Hutu rulers distanced the Tutsi from the larger Rwandan society requires that we consider the factors that determine majority or minority status. For many years, the majority in pregenocidal Rwanda was Hutu. They were far more numerous than Tutsi, and they controlled the government, the educational system, the military, and the mass media, and used this control to stunning effect. There were considerably fewer Tutsi, they had little power, and as shown in the "Hutu Ten Commandments," were defined by the leaders of the country, the power majority, as scheming, self-interested, clan-centric, untrustworthy, traitorous villains. Not a pretty set of personal qualities.

Although the majority and minority status of the two groups was clearly established, the government still pushed hard to distance the Tutsi from the mainstream, much as Hitler did with the Jews in Germany. It was not sufficient that the Tutsi be a minority group; they had to be pushed out of the community of "legitimate" Rwandans. The government did this because identifying a group as being outsiders, which the Tutsi clearly were, is not sufficient to ensure that it will be ignored or persecuted, and this is precisely what the government wanted to happen. To prepare the fertile grounds of the killing fields, the minority had to be identified as outside the larger group of "true" Rwandans, the Hutu majority. The Tutsi had to be made not just a minority, but outsiders, an out-group that did not possess the qualities required to be considered a legitimate member of the larger group, and thus, unable to lay claim even to reasonable, much less equal treatment.

By way of contrast, the "true" Rwandans, members of the Hutu in-group, were viewed as sharing a common identity with all other majority group members (Rwandan Hutu). We are all Republicans, or Teamsters, or members of the Aryan Brotherhood, and we share the features of other Republicans, Teamsters, or Aryan Brothers, even if we sometimes disagree with some of the positions our fellow in-groupers express.[xvii]

When encountering the out-group, we typically assume its members hold beliefs and values that are antagonistic to ours, requiring great caution and a certain uneasy defensiveness when dealing with them. If we decide that the out-group is set on our group's destruction, we will do everything possible to protect our group, and consequently ourselves. The more important the group to our social identity, the faster we are willing to leap to the group's defense. If this means that the out-group must be attacked preemptively, so be it.

In-group and Out-group Minorities: A Critical Distinction

Members of the out-group are not seen as worthy of the same treatment the in-group deserves. They are fair game because they lack some fundamental quality that entitles them to the protections the in-group enjoys. In extreme cases, out-groupers are considered subhuman, and when this happens their extermination is not impeded by the usual prohibitions against mistreating a fellow human being.

For our analysis it is essential to distinguish in-group and out-group minorities. The Tutsi-Hutu disaster presents a vivid picture of in- and out-groups. In the minds of the contending parties, the out-group did not deserve to exist. It was believed to hold beliefs and values and intentions that threatened the very existence of the in-group, and so was subject to preemptive elimination. In most circumstances, the gulf between in- and out-group minorities is not so wide, but the distinction between these factions remains crucial. The in-group minority is judged by the majority as a legitimate part of the larger group. It is distinguishable from the majority because of a feature or belief that is inconsistent with the general norm, but this difference is not seen as sufficient to expel or disqualify them from membership in the larger group. For example, almost all members of the Beverly Hills Tea Party take a hard line on illegal immigration. They find it unacceptable under all conditions and situations, and believe the remedy requires speedy deportation of all those in the country illegally. However, it is conceivable that a few group members in good standing might see the issue as more nuanced, as requiring a close consideration of circumstances before deciding whether or not to deport the immigrant to his or her home country. This contrary opinion places the small faction of dissidents in the minority of the group's membership, but it does not necessarily result in their expulsion from the group. People holding this nuanced view still may be considered part of the party, but they are a minority within the group, in our terms, an in-group minority, and even though they are a minority, being in-group they retain the rights and privileges of members and are afforded the perks of group membership. People outside the group, the out-group (for example, Democrats), who may hold the identical nuanced view are judged more harshly and evaluated more negatively.

As we will see, the difference between in-group and out-group minority status is crucial, because members of out-groups are not viewed as being entitled to the same rights and privileges as in-group members, even when those in-group members are in the minority of the larger group. In the Rwandan case, the distinction between in-group and out-group minority disappeared. The Hutu who refused to cooperate in the killing spree were considered out-group, traitors, and their fate was at least as bad as that of the Tutsi. The difference between in-group and out-group spelled the difference between life and death for thousands.

What could the Tutsi have done to avoid the fate that awaited so many of them? Probably not much—the intensity of the Hutu propaganda was so profound that the majority was not likely to have listened to anything the Tutsi said in their defense. This is a fundamental problem for all out-group minorities—the majority often will simply not "hear" what it has to say. If they had threatened the Hutu, thus gaining their rapt attention, the Tutsi would only have succeeded in pouring fuel onto an already roaring fire of hatred. If the Tutsi had gained the majority's ear through conciliatory means, their best (and probably only) hope was to appeal to their common in-group status as fellow Rwandans. Appealing to a larger, more comprehensive status that both Hutu and Tutsi shared might have shifted the basis for comparison from differences to similarities, from Hutu versus Tutsi to the more inclusive category of Rwandan. At the time of the massacre, there was little hope that this tactic would have succeeded, the relations between the groups having been poisoned beyond recall, but if any hope remained, it was in establishing a common, overarching identity that superseded that of tribe membership.

Leaving Rwanda, let's consider how this would play out in more common and less deadly contexts. To be effective, the weaker group must establish a link with the group in power. This is critical because the majority must accept the outsiders as part of itself, as a part of the in-group, before it will give them a fair hearing. A minority that fails to be accepted as in-group is unlikely to have much chance of moving the larger group.[xviii] For the minority to influence the majority, it must persuade the majority that "we're all in this together, we are part of the larger group." This is the first and most critical rule of minority influence.

Rule 1. The "Us" Factor: The Minority Must Be Accepted as In-group, as a Legitimate Part of the Larger (Majority) Group, as "Us" Rather Than "Them."

To be accepted does not mean that the minority must deny differences between itself and the majority. Rather, it must show that the similarities between the contending groups matter more than the differences. A short, fat, balding guy wearing Converse All-Stars and too-short basketball shorts might have trouble persuading the hotshots at the local pickup game to choose him for their team—after all, there may be lots of money riding on the game's outcome. But if he can show that he is a deadly shooter from anywhere on the court, his physical dissimilarities from the ideal basketball player may be minimized, and his similarities to the ideal (he's a dead shot and a tenacious defender as well) may overcome the conflict between the ideal and the apparent reality. To be considered for membership on the team, Shorty would do well to display his shooting ability (of which he is proud) rather than his beefiness (of which he is not) or his 1980s-style Celtics basketball short shorts (of which he is oblivious). If the minority devalues the very characteristics it presents to the majority, which in most cases are largely responsible for its minority status in the first place, it will find it impossible to persuade the majority that "we are part of you." Who wants to be part of a group that detests itself?

When minorities attempt to become in-group with the majority, which they must do if they are to move the larger group to their position, they have to establish and emphasize the overarching identity features that inevitably are more inclusive than the features used as the basis for discrimination. Consider the rhetorical approach of Martin Luther King Jr. in his attempts at overcoming racism in the United States in the 1960s. Reading or listening to his speeches, you can see that his analysis of the problem of racial discrimination was that the (white) American majority used easily identifiable differences in physical characteristics (skin color) as bases for assuming differences on important attitudes and values. His most powerful speeches argued that this assumption was specious, that skin color was a very unreliable indicator of beliefs or values or basic humanity and goodness. African American parents, he argued, wanted the same opportunities for their children as white parents did. But if race was a faulty indicator of belief and value similarity, what then could be used to decide in-group or out-group status? In answer to this logically implied question, he attempted to shift the basis for deciding who was in- or out-group. His position was that we should not use race as the determining feature of group status, as race had nothing to do with the features that should decide group membership, but that the basis of comparison should involve membership or nonmembership in a higher-level group. Rather than base in-group status on the faulty indicator of skin color, he argued, in-group membership should be based on our common identity as Americans, and as human beings. These membership groups encompass black and white, rich and poor, liberal and conservative. We will see how King made use of this two-pronged attack to argue that African Americans were as much a part of the American in-group as any other citizens, and therefore entitled to all the rights of members of that group. He could not and did not argue that racial differences did not exist; they're there for all to see. But he could and did argue that they did not matter.

King's intuitive understanding of the necessity to establish a common identity with the majority is precisely the approach minority groups must adopt if they are to succeed. The minority must be accepted as part of the in-group, and to do this, it is necessary to shift the grounds for in-group and out-group comparison. The minority must move the focus of the conversation from the differences that separate us to the similarities that unite us. The groups' similarities must trump the differences that divide them.

In-groups and Out-groups: Who are these people? What's in it for them?

Over the years, researchers have learned that members of out-groups—groups not a part of our identity system, and sometimes in conflict with the ideals we value—rarely succeed. To understand why, my colleagues and I conducted a study using college students as our research subjects. They heard a persuasive message that was attributed either to a respected in-group or a group from a school that the students universally disrespected. The description of the groups was stripped down, but sufficient for the students to know if the source of the message was in- or out-group.

The message argued that too much had been spent on NASA and the space program, and that it was time to rein in the costs. A measure that we had administered earlier showed that the students initially did not agree with this position, but when the message was attributed to their in-group, it had a powerful effect on their later attitudes, which we measured at the end of the study. When the identical message was attributed to the out-group, however, *it had no effect whatsoever.* The students completely ignored what the out-group had to say—the extremity of the out-group's position was varied systematically, but degrees of disagreement simply did not register on their radar. A reason that out-groups find it so difficult to gain traction with the majority is that the majority often ignores the outsiders' appeals. It's easier to ignore someone you do not trust than to engage in a mental debate with their arguments.

This is not to suggest that the majority *always* ignores the out-group. In later research, we showed that if the message had been attributed to a rival school's students who had seriously demeaned the subjects' alma mater, they certainly would have reacted. However, in instances that do not involve a serious threat to the groups that contribute to our social identity, we often disregard the out-group's message. The reason for this refusal to engage is that the out-group's position generally is evaluated as self-interested, and at the expense of our own group's welfare. Because of this, members of out-groups are unlikely to get their way so long as they are perceived as outsiders—except in those rare cases when their out-group status is precisely relevant to the issue being considered, and no one from the in-group has similar qualifications. We might have nothing to do with the office geek—after all, he's a geek—until the copy machine breaks and he's the only one who knows how to fix it.

This should not be taken to mean that all groups strive to be counted in the majority, even though members of any group, even minority groups, usually strive to be in the ruling majority of their own groups. Some groups consciously distance themselves from the mainstream. At least in their early days, many religious organizations separated themselves from the larger community, partly to maintain theological purity—*we know the truth and don't want it diluted by all those heathens*—and partly because the group members feared persecution because of their beliefs. The history of the early Mormon Church is a good case in point. Mormons were concerned about maintaining the belief system laid down by their leader, Joseph Smith, and they also were concerned about persecution. They had experienced plenty of it first-hand.

To simultaneously stay alive and practice their beliefs, they became cautious about advertising their religious dogmas and practices in the communities they formed, which generally were closed to the outside world. When the Mormon Church had gained a large enough following and had modified some of its more controversial official positions, it was accepted as a legitimate part of the mainstream.[7] At that point members' concerns for physical safety became less pressing, and the Church initiated an active proselytizing campaign that carries forward today. This likely would not have occurred if the Church were under attack from the larger majority population and in self-defense had retreated into a defensive shell. To remain separate is to remain impotent. If it wishes to change the beliefs, policies, or actions of the majority, the minority has to come into contact with it and must endeavor to be acknowledged as part of the team. To succeed, the minority must work to be seen by the majority as being a part of the in-group, a different but legitimate part of the majority. To do this, they must establish criteria for inclusion that are accepted by the majority and that rise above the features that set them apart from the majority in the first place.

A textbook example of how becoming a part of the identity group changes the game was evident in the Barack Obama's 2008 presidential campaign. By any objective criterion, Barack had little chance of victory when he announced his intention to run for the presidency in February 2007. Among other things, he had

---

[7] For example, polygamy was outlawed by Brigham Young when in 1896 the Mormons' home base, Utah, sought entry into the Union. Most saw statehood as an impossibility if polygamy continued to be accepted as a legitimate feature of church doctrine.

very little experience at the national level, he was not well known, he was African American, his father was a Muslim, his middle name was Hussein, and he was opposed by a host of qualified, experienced, and well-heeled candidates. It turned out that his lack of exposure on the national scene helped him, because he wasn't tied to any particular policy and had not established a strong social identity. But he had to do so for voters to understand who he was, his person and his positions, so they could judge his qualifications. He had to become someone you knew and liked. So who did he become? He became *you*.

This is a common political maneuver. Many politicians labor to identify with the "common person." To their credit, the Republican Party has made an art form of this tactic. When George W. Bush ran against John Kerry in the 2004 presidential election, he enjoyed a clear advantage in his ability to connect with the electorate. Despite the fact that both men were born with silver spoons firmly in place, polls revealed that the majority of undecided voters found Bush more personally appealing than Kerry. As the undecided usually swing close elections, this discrepancy was a problem for Kerry's candidacy, a problem that he was unable to overcome.

In the Obama-McCain race, the Republicans had "Joe the Plumber," and Sarah Palin, but the Democrat's standard bearer was a master of integrating himself with the public, the majority, and this capacity to link with the majority decided the outcome of the race. In his campaign speeches, Mr. Obama almost never used the word *I* when discussing a goal, victory, or accomplishment. It always was *us* or *our* or *we*. "We won this campaign," "We can do it," "We shall overcome," and of course, "Yes, we can." In one of the most famous speeches of the campaign, perhaps of the generation, Obama proclaimed, "Yes, we can"—we can reclaim the American Dream. He did not say, "Yes, I can."

Obama's phrasing was not accidental. If he was to offset his negative ascribed and achieved features, of which there were many, he knew he had to become part of the great American "in-group," and he did.

FROM OBAMA'S "YES, WE CAN" SPEECH

This is **our** moment. This is **our** time to put **our** people back to work and open doors of opportunity for **our** kids . . . to reclaim the American Dream and reaffirm that fundamental truth that out of many **we** are one; that while **we** breathe, **we** hope, and when **we** are met with cynicism and doubt, and those who tell **us** that **we** can't, **we** will respond with that timeless creed that sums up the spirit of a people: Yes, **we** can.

In this sense, he was following in the footsteps of another master orator, the Rev. Martin Luther King Jr., whose "I Have a Dream" speech has been judged by many as the most powerful example of twentieth-century American oratory. Even more than Obama, King made a direct appeal for inclusion, for recognition that he and his cause were part of the larger in-group called America. Don't base your judgments of who we are on color, but on our common desires to achieve the American Dream, he argued, and those values and goals clearly supersede race if you believe in the very doctrines that created the country. He looked forward to the day when the "sons of former slaves and former slave owners will . . . sit down together," that "little black boys and black girls will be able to join hands with little white boys and white girls as sisters and brothers." King appealed to those whites who were at least willing to entertain the possibility that blacks and whites shared common hopes for their children, that their beliefs on fundamental issues were not all that different, and because of that they all shared the common identities of Americans and human beings.

FROM MARTIN LUTHER KING JR.'S "I HAVE A DREAM" SPEECH

I have a dream that one day this nation will rise up and live out the true meaning of its creed: "We hold these truths to be self-evident, that all men are created equal...." I have a dream that one day on the red hills of Georgia, the sons of former slaves and the sons of former slave owners will be able to sit down together at the table of brotherhood.... I have a dream that one day even the state of Mississippi, a state sweltering with the heat of injustice, sweltering with the heat of oppression, will be transformed into an oasis of freedom and justice.... I have a dream that my four little children will one day live in a nation where they will not be judged by the color of their skin but by the content of their character.... I have a dream that one day ... right there in Alabama little black boys and black girls will be able to join hands with little white boys and white girls as sisters and brothers.

Considerable research suggests that many prejudicial or racist reactions are based on people's underlying assumption that those "others," the minority out-group, hold beliefs, hopes, and values that differ from theirs in fundamental ways. If a minority out-group is to make any headway in influencing the majority, it must consider the basis of its status and the implications it holds for the majority's views—rightly or, equally often, wrongly.

In business contexts, the minority's job sometimes can be a bit easier. Although a small faction of the decision-making team might hold a position at odds with that of the majority, they usually don't have to persuade their peers that they're part of the team—after all, the same guy signs all their paychecks. If they're smart, members of the minority will make an attempt to link their identities with the overarching, common identity—we're all employees of this firm, we all have a big stake in its success—rather than that of their faction—"the IT group knows what's best for you technically challenged people."

Suppose the majority of the leadership of a small computer-oriented business is leaning toward a heavy investment in creating a specific piece of software. A small minority feels that this would be suicidal for the firm, as the industry seems to be moving to a different standard. As in-group members, the dissidents have a chance of persuading the others on the merits of their case, but first they must establish their link to a common identity by emphasizing their in-group status with the majority. They may move the company to their position at that point if they follow the rules of influence that are developed throughout this book.

In its early years, Microsoft's focus was fixed on building operating systems and other software applications. The firm largely ignored the Internet, although the Web showed signs of becoming an emergent giant in computing. Fresh out of college, Steven Sinofsky joined Microsoft in 1989 as a software engineer, and soon was promoted to Bill Gates's technical assistant. Obviously, his qualities had been noticed. He had a future in the company. After seven years at Microsoft, he paid a visit to his alma mater, Cornell University, where he was amazed at the extent to which the Web had altered the complexion of everyday intellectual life on the campus. It was clear to Sinofsky that the Web would change the face of communications and computing. He returned to Microsoft with the firm belief that the Web would become a major threat to Microsoft's profits if the company did not move seriously into the Internet game. Sinofsky teamed up with another up-and-comer, J Allard, and they argued persistently and persuasively against the established company culture, which was not particularly attuned to his vision or to people arguing with the boss, who had expressed strong reservations about Microsoft's getting into the Internet business. However, because of his relationship with Gates, Sinofsky was given a hearing. He was an accepted member of the Microsoft family; he was in-group in our terminology, even though his ideas about the Web were inconsistent with those of Microsoft's top brass. A few months later, he and Allard were allowed to present their position at a senior executive retreat. They argued with passion and persuasiveness. After some thought, Gates was sold on the idea, and as his vote counted the most, Sinofsky and Allard's vision was adopted. Microsoft radically changed its hugely successful business model, almost overnight, and threw in with the Web. The rest is history. In 2008 Microsoft was the forty-fourth largest company in the world with $60 billion in sales. Sinofsky is now president of Microsoft's Windows division, and Allard had risen to VP for design and development before his retirement from Microsoft.[xix]

The critical requirement to "get in-group" is reserved not only for minorities. Most politicians recognize the fact that they must identify with the mass of voters if they are to succeed. This is true even for those who clearly are not a part of the great middle. Think back to earlier elections, when Al Gore dropped his coat and tie, and took to wearing plaid shirts with rolled-up sleeves. Mitt Romney, perennial Republican candidate, did the same. Neither of these men were unaccustomed to formal business dress, they had worn suits all their working lives, but to get in-group, they left their suits at home.

Why do you think it was so important for George W. Bush's handlers in 2004 to parade him as the "kinda guy you'd like to have a beer with," whereas John Kerry was portrayed as an elitist who wouldn't know a Bud from a Miller Lite? The Bush crew needed to show that their candidate, who attended one of the country's elite prep schools, Phillips Academy, went on to Yale University and Harvard Business School, who not only was a multimillionaire, but whose father was the former director of the CIA, the U.S. Ambassador to the UN, an oil tycoon, and the forty-first President of the United States, was just like you and me. Some even believed that Bush's fractured English was really a ruse to ingratiate hisself with the masses, and this may be true, although relistening to his father's old speeches suggests a familial or possibly genetic contribution as well. The attempt to link this multimillionaire son of a multimillionaire with the common man (or woman) on the street worked brilliantly. During the Bush versus Kerry presidential campaign, a Zogby poll indicated that 57 percent of the undecided voters would rather have a beer with Bush (though he had sworn off alcohol years earlier) than with Kerry. This discrepancy in the "swill index" was to prove telling. A Pew Research Center poll run about the same time found that 56 percent of possible swing voters rated Bush as more of a "real person" than Kerry, who captured only 38 percent of these voters. Did these perceptions matter? We cannot know for certain, but there's no doubt about who ended up sitting in the White House.

If nothing else, these examples should show that finding oneself in a minority faction is not particularly unusual. In fact, in most groups, members often disagree on issues, sometimes heatedly. As long as the issue does not threaten to destroy the group and thus compromise an important element of members' self-identities, as the prime function of all our group memberships is to build identity, these battles are tolerated, even expected. This openness of the majority to in-group minorities is critically important, because it provides the opportunity for the minority to influence majority positions.

Does the Issue Matter?

Minorities and majorities can form around any issue, and the extent to which firm positions are developed on the issue determines the leeway the majority will afford the minority in pushing its case. From considerable research, we know that the majority characteristically is reluctant to change and to adopt the alternative possibilities advanced by a minority. This resistance enables the majority to maintain stability of its defining beliefs. A group that swings from one position to its opposite wreaks havoc on members' identities, and would soon destroy itself. This is one of the many, but perhaps the most important reason that groups are reluctant to change the fundamental beliefs around which they are formed. The Young Republicans of The Ohio State University, for example, are not likely to switch allegiance to a Democratic candidate, for to do so would require its members to radically alter their self-definitions as Republican. Swings of this type would destroy the group.

This does not necessarily suggest that all majorities hold negative views of weaker groups that hold positions different from theirs. Majority groups often view in-group minorities positively, even if they do not succumb easily to their demands. We have a long tradition of pulling for the underdog. People who "speak the truth" regardless of the consequences usually are admired, even if we do not agree with the positions they advocate. Those willing to put their lives on the line sometimes gain our grudging respect even if we think their positions are off base.

In some cases the minority enjoys a persuasive advantage, especially when the issue is one on which the majority has not formed a strong position. In these circumstances, minority status may actually *improve* the likelihood of success. This is especially so when the minority is defined by number, rather than power. In the numeric minority case, the minority is, by definition, rare or distinctive, and the majority is more likely to take notice of the minority precisely because of this. This advantage is enhanced if agreeing with the minority's position does not seem to disadvantage the majority.[xx]

The reasons for the minority's advantage in these situations are rooted in considerable research. The first requirement in persuasion is that the persuader be noticed. People orient themselves to the unusual or the exotic, and numeric minorities by definition are rare, so they get noticed. The minority may use their salience to good effect when dealing with issues on which the majority does not hold a strong position. They can advance their case without strong opposition—after all, the majority has no horse in the race—and under the proper conditions, the majority will be inclined to agree with the minority. The proper conditions involve the identity of the minority group. If the minority belongs to the same identity group as the majority (we're all Yankee fans, or Mormons, or Alabama alumni, or goths), the increased visibility and attention-grabbing nature of the minority will further its cause. All bets are off if the minority group is not viewed by the majority as in-group. In that case enhanced visibility is a hindrance—it simply allows for a more certain identification of whom to target or ignore.

Summing Up

Why are we so consumed with being in the right group and in the right faction in the groups that claim our allegiance? It is because a major determinant of who we are is defined to a great extent by those with whom we associate, *and* those we avoid. We need out-group people as well as in-group members to define ourselves, to help us know who "we" are. Drawing distinctions between who's in and who's out, between us and them, is a natural consequence of our need to form an identity, to distinguish people with whom we belong from people we should avoid. We discriminate not only to distance ourselves from the out-group, but also to integrate ourselves more securely in our in-group.

It is reinforcing to discriminate between "us" and "them" on dimensions that matter to us, because we usually tilt the evaluation so that *we* come out on top. Winning these psychological contests is satisfying. It strengthens our social ties by bolstering our in-groups and confirms our sense of self. This is how groups retain members and why people go to great lengths to preserve their status in their membership groups. We do not define ourselves in terms of "I," but rather in terms of "us" versus "them."

Distinguishing those who belong to the groups we use to define ourselves from those who do not is not *necessarily* unfair or inequitable, but it often works out that way. Years of research and hundreds of studies have shown that merely assigning people to different groups, sometimes on the flimsiest basis, affords all that's needed to devalue outsiders.

Engineering a minority victory is not easy. Many conditions must be met if the minority is to prevail, and the primary condition concerns the minority's relations with the majority. How the majority views the minority largely determines the minority's likelihood of success. If the minority is judged to be a viable part of the overall group, although perhaps a strange part, the (in-group) minority has a chance. If it is viewed as being outside the group it is attempting to influence, as not having a legitimate claim to group membership, then the (out-group) minority will find it nearly impossible to succeed. And so, the first rule of minority influence is that the minority must create the conditions to be accepted as part of the majority—a deviant part, perhaps, but nonetheless a member of the larger group. Unless this happens, the outsider has no voice.

In the next chapter, we will begin to consider what the minority must do, how it must present itself, and how it must tailor its message to stand a chance of success. The probability that the minority will influence the majority is not great, but the factors that enhance this probability, the rules of influence, have been identified, they are clearly established, and they will be revealed in the coming chapters.

Resizing Goliath

It is unnatural for a majority to rule, for a
majority can seldom be organized and united
for specific action, and a minority can.

—*Jean-Jacques Rousseau*

I t happens all the time. The group in power falls from grace—or
is pulled from the throne kicking and screaming—and all
those who had been a part of the old regime suddenly contract
amnesia or insist that they didn't do it and would never again do
what they said they hadn't done in the first place. A gaggle of tell-
all books follows in the wake of almost every failed or deposed
power broker. This is not a new phenomenon. John Quincy Adams kept a diary for nearly seventy years, in which he skewered
nearly every politician and public figure, foreign or domestic, he
had encountered in his long life.[xxi] Thomas Jefferson did the
same. Second-guessing the former high and mighty is an ancient
art, and with the advent of modern technology, anyone can do it,
and does, even if the former leadership did a good job. Criticism
of the fallen or former seems almost genetically wired into the
human psyche.

Sometimes the criticism is well deserved. Sometimes the critics
are right. Maybe the emperor really had no clothes. Maybe the
idol did have feet of clay. But sometimes the former minority,

now the majority, unleashes its attack on the former power hold-
ers even though the old keepers of the flame did well. The new
majority has the power to define good and evil, and to apply their
definitions retrospectively, so this rewriting of history is not unusual. Truth is not the issue; power is. When the president of Iran
can deny the Holocaust despite the indisputable evidence of history, it is clear that being in power sometimes absolves the speaker
from an overly strong dependence on reality.

Witnessing the actions of "new" majorities, two facts stand
out: First, when the majority loses its power, there are plenty of
rats ready to desert the sinking ship and to claim innocence, ignorance, or amnesia when explaining their own actions while on
or near the throne. This is done because the new majority is busy
rewriting history, and the former leaders are attempting to get
ahead of the steamroller. The second fact, which follows from the
initial premise, is that majorities *do* fall, they are replaced, and
the process often is not very pretty. How majorities succumb is
not our primary focus—after all, this is a book about how the
weak, rather than the strong, get their point across—but it is useful to think about the ways the group in power can fail, because
the weaker group often has a lot to do with it, and it is important
to know how they accomplished the overthrow of the old regime.

Minority Ascent

The processes outsiders use to supplant the group in power are the
same as those it uses to influence it, but they are taken to an
extreme. Examples of outsiders scrambling to gain influence, to
become the new ruling majority are common. A homey example
is seen in school board recall elections that appear to occur with
increasing regularity in the United States, where in most school
districts local citizens are elected to boards that serve as the re-

sponsible trustees of the schools. When dissatisfaction with one or another policy arises within these complex structures, board members are put on the spot to maintain or change the system to address the problem. A tireless and dissatisfied minority can wreak havoc in these cases, often calling for the recall of incumbents and replacing them with new members sympathetic to their views. Given a relatively high degree of apathy in the electorate, especially on issues that do not concern many of the eligible voters, this takeover approach can accomplish the intended outcome.

It would be a mistake to lay all majority group failures at the feet of a devious and successful minority that has worked tirelessly to unseat the governing body. In many circumstances, the ruling party does not really lose control, but rather its power and direction are diluted by the absorption of outsiders into the larger group. In this case, the minority will not have changed the majority directly, but its form is altered, sometimes beyond recognition.

Outsiders' successful ascent via majority dilution is evident in state primaries that are designed to designate a political party's nominee for high office (president or senator, for example). In many states, the most politically extreme members become actively involved in their party's nominating process, essentially hijacking the election. Naturally, they work to nominate people like themselves, candidates who share their views. This process often overturns the usual applecart, resulting in the nomination of extremist candidates who do not appeal to the wider electorate, whose members tend to be moderates, and whose numbers make for electoral victory or defeat.[8]

---

[8] This skewed process has become a regular theme of the American political system. In operational terms, it means that to gain the Republican nomination, candidates must run hard to the right, whereas to gain the Democratic nod, candidates must run hard to the left. After the nomination is secured, there's a wild run to the middle, where most of the voters live.

At the national and international level, those holding the reins of power appear to recognize and fear the minority's capacity to infiltrate and overtake a system. Politicians in Europe, for example, have begun to raise warnings about the Islamification of their world. They are responding implicitly to the threat of minority dilution. On July 13, 2010, for example, France's lower house voted 355 to 1 to ban women (and men, too, presumably) from wearing the burka, the full Islamic veil. The French Senate followed suit, voting 246 to 1 to support the ban. Violations call for a first-time fine of €150, and it escalates from there. The law change had overwhelming support across the French populace. Lawmakers in Belgium and Spain also have considered similar regulations.

The official reasons for the French ban are nebulous at best. An official French government paper stated that "The French Republic lives in a bareheaded fashion." In an equally baffling justification, Justice Minister Michèle Alliot-Marie observed, "This (law) is not about security or religion, but respecting our republican principles. . . . France, the land of secularism, guarantees respect for all religions (but) hiding the face under a face-covering veil is against public social order, whether it is forced or voluntary." Why wearing a veil is against the public order is anyone's guess, but there is no doubt that the French Parliament didn't take to the style.

Though there is considerable doubt that it will pass constitutional muster, the law change, passed with only a single dissenting vote in both houses, was a clear and decisive expression of the majority's views. The action has caused uproar throughout Europe and the Middle East. The overwhelming passage of this law would have you imagine that there were hordes of burka-clad Muslim women trooping down the Champs-Élysées eating every croissant in sight, decimating the escargot population, and wreaking general havoc, but this was not so. In fact, research indicated that only about two thousand Muslim women in France wear the full veil. As the population of France is about 65 million, and more than half of them are women, the obvious question must be raised: Why bother? Why stir up a hornet's nest to constrain the behavior of a minuscule portion of the population? The question, if not the answer, says more about the mind-set of the lawmakers and the population than it does of the actual threat that women wearing the burka pose for the state of France. It suggests that the majority of the French people, and their representatives, fear the implicit menace posed by the Islamic "invasion." It's not that they fear that burka-wearing Muslim women will storm the Bastille and violently overthrow the French government. Rather, the lawmakers and those who favor their actions (almost everyone in France, apparently) let slip the much deeper fear that Muslims will take over the country by dint of a high birth rate and a stubborn refusal (or inability) to integrate into France's social mainstream. They will overcome the power structure from the inside, joining the society and changing it, rather than by brute force from the outside. The result of this internal invasion will be, they fear, a country that none of them recognize as France.

Minority Ascent via Majority Overreach

These fears betray a hidden and sometimes almost unmentionable truth about the majority that many in the leadership hierarchy implicitly understand. They acknowledge that on the surface, the majority seems invincible. Holding power, it can do no wrong—you do its bidding or get out of town. But the majority's hold is tenuous, and those at the top—at least those who know a little history—recognize the fragility of their mandate. Because of its threat of punitive power (which sometimes is grossly exaggerated), the majority can demand behavioral compliance. However, it cannot force people to accept its position. The powers that be can force people to behave in a prescribed fashion, but they cannot make people believe in what they're being forced to do—they cannot control what and how people think. And even if the majority is sufficiently powerful to force compliance to its will, in the long run forced compliance cannot be sustained. It requires too many resources and too much motivation to keep people in line. Even true believers eventually get tired, and their messianic enthusiasm flags.

This does not prevent authoritarian groups and states from using force to ensure their members comply with the wishes of the majority's leadership. The ruling class can maintain a heavy-handed strategy with respect to demanding minority compliance as long as enough of its members believe they can exercise the power to make the strategy work, *and* members of the minority accept this proposition. When either of these requirements goes unmet, the majority's power to force its will weakens, and eventually dissipates in futile control attempts. The Arab Spring of 2011, in which the population of a number of Arab states (Egypt, Bahrain, Tunisia, Libya, Algeria, Jordan, Morocco, Syria, and Oman, among others) rose in revolt against their rulers is a striking and dramatic example of the minority's power to call for a reckoning. This does not imply that all these rebellions will succeed, but even those that fail will have left an indelible mark on the dominant group.

In reality, the power of the majority is almost always constrained, either by law or tradition, and those in the majority who recognize this either moderate their exercise of power or try to persuade the opposition that the constraints do not exist. Those in power who push their advantage can forestall losing their grip on the rudder, as in Libya, but not for long. In poker, pretending to have a stronger hand than you hold is called bluffing. Bluffs work, except when they're called.

The landslide electoral victory of Barack Obama in 2008, which swept a Democratic majority into the House and a supermajority into the U.S. Senate, supplies a perfect example of the limits of majority power. In this case, the overwhelming Democratic majority was shown to have few teeth, and those that it did have were not very sharp. With a strong majority in the Congress and sixty Democrats in the Senate, the majority had the capacity to do almost anything it wanted. Whether you accept the administration's position that the majority did all it could in the face of a terrible inheritance from the prior administration, or the opposition's view, that it failed miserably to lead the country to greener pastures owing to a lack of leadership and planning is not at issue here, but neither is the widespread perception in the electorate that the Democrats did not use their mandate effectively. Even most Democrats agree on this proposition. The general agreement on the answer, however, begs the question—Why did the Democratic majority not exercise the overwhelming power it apparently had?

The answer to the question lies in its adverb. Despite its size, the makeup of the majority (and the minority) severely limited the majority's power to do much more than it did. The supermajority did not realize all its goals rapidly and efficiently, because of a strong, consistent, and almost always unified minority opposition. This united opposition was coupled with the reality that the majority, like almost all majorities, contained factions or subgroups that were ready to pull out or revolt if the majority did not honor its claims, commitments, or demands. This is a fact of life with which the majority, often to its surprise, almost always must contend. The Democrats were not prepared for the disparity of views that existed within their own party. Together, these two factors, a united minority opposition and a less-than-united majority seriously retarded the Democrats' agenda. This process is not restricted to senatorial brawls. Whenever a united minority rises in opposition to a less-than-united majority, the outcome always is put in doubt.

Is disunity a hallmark of the majority? Not always—but usually. Except in the most extreme groups, the majority embraces a variety of sometimes inconsistent or conflicting positions. The latitude of beliefs the majority will accept as legitimate is wide, except on issues that are central to the very life and identity of the group. In these circumstances, departures from orthodoxy elicit very strong reactions from the group, often resulting in ostracism. However, in all but the most extreme groups, or under the most extreme circumstances, the majority is not monolithic or single-minded. As social animals whose lives revolve around the groups to which we belong, we have learned to live with this state of affairs. When we manage to land in the majority of our group, most of us are not particularly surprised if there is some degree of disagreement on issues, even ones we consider important, if not absolutely essential to the group's continuance.

Diversity of opinion is not severely sanctioned if it does not threaten to splinter the group—in fact, most of the time we expect it. So why did the majority Democrats in Congress not press their advantage? They did not do so, because their advantage was not sufficient for them to prevail. The majority was not internally consistent on almost any issue, *and* the Republican minority was almost always completely united and unequivocally opposed to the majority's wishes. This pattern is not unusual. The minority *must* maintain a united front if it is to prevail. The majority is under no pressure to do so, and so it is rare to find a large majority unequivocally united on almost anything—at least, not for long.

Two requirements must be met before the majority can push its agenda effectively and efficiently, and the Democrats could not satisfy either of them. To run roughshod over the Republican minority, the Democrats required unanimity of belief, which they did not have, and at least some cooperation from the minority, which they also did not have. Satisfying even one of these requirements would have greased the skids of the Obama Administration's legislative agenda, but neither was forthcoming, and so whatever progress was made was destined to be slow and torturous.

How could this story have had a different ending? The majority would have been able to move its agenda rapidly if all its members backed the agenda without defections, *or* if there were a discernible break in the minority ranks. The legislative successes the majority eventually enjoyed occurred precisely under these circumstances. When either one or the other of these requirements was not met, the majority did not advance, at least not very rapidly.

This is not to suggest that the majority is a pushover. The majority *is* powerful. It *does* define good and bad. It *does* hold the keys to the kingdom (and the treasury), but it is not invincible. A strong and consistent minority in many cases can stop the majority in its tracks, if it is unyielding and unswerving in its opposition, if its opposition can be presented as rational and reasoned, and if the majority is not united. To Lord Acton's mot, "Power tends to corrupt and absolute power corrupts absolutely," we would add, "but power that does not induce acceptance will not long endure."

What all this means is that despite having power, the majority only rarely enjoys an absolute stranglehold even on its own members, much less its opposition. The majority doesn't absolutely *need* to convince its rank and file to follow its wishes—it can meet ingroup recalcitrance with threats, force, minimalization, or ostracism. We have seen that these threats are powerful inducements to good behavior, at least in the short term. Most times the majority is reluctant to use its power on its own members because to do so can threaten the group's cohesion. Group leaders cannot simply expel group members they find obnoxious or bothersome, because when they do, the obnoxious or bothersome member often takes other group members out of the group, and this inevitably weakens the group.

In extreme cases, disaffected members will bolt, and even the most autocratic leader comes to realize that defections ultimately weaken the group's hold on power. As the first rule of all groups is to persevere, to continue to exist, forcing deviant members out of the group usually is done only as a last resort.

If the majority cannot effectively force its members to toe the line, then it's even more certain that it cannot force the minority to do so, at least not over the long term. What this means is that in many circumstances, the majority is not nearly so unstoppable as it appears. It rarely is in a position to compel its members' allegiance, no matter how insistent its demands, and is in an even weaker position to insist on compliance from the minority.

Unanimity: The Majority's Real Advantage

It would be a mistake to overestimate the power of the minority, and by extension, to underestimate the majority's clout. Although using brute force to obtain in-group compliance is rarely successful for long, it also is rarely needed. We learned long ago that a gun is not required to induce people to act in ways inconsistent with their true beliefs. All that's called for is a bit of social pressure applied at the right time by the right people—and more often than not, the right people belong to the majority. Group pressure works because it can be extremely uncomfortable to be moving in one direction when everyone else is going the other way.

A study the great Solomon Asch conducted more than sixty

years ago showed that the majority doesn't have to do much to affect people's judgments. Even though he made no *obvious* attempt to influence people in his study, Asch found that he could induce many of them to deny even the clear and seemingly incontrovertible evidence of their own senses—under the right circumstances. Let's replay his study, with you as a research subject.

You and three fellow students come to Dr. Asch's lab to participate in a study. You'll get extra credit for your introductory psych course for your service. The research apparently involves easy perceptual judgments. You realize immediately that all the subjects attend the same small college, so you share a common in-group identity as Swarthmore College students. You don't know any of the others personally, but you've seen them around campus. They dress like you, use the same slang, they even cut their hair the same way. They are part of your in-group identity, of who you are, as a student at Swarthmore.

At the front of the room, a researcher shows all four of you a card that contains a reference line. On another card are three lines labeled *A* through *C,* and one of them exactly matches the reference line. The task, he explains, is for each of you to tell him in turn which of the three lines—*A, B,* or *C*—matches the reference line. You are to respond in order on each trial, and as luck would have it, you pick the short straw and get to respond last on each judgment trial, after the three others have done so.

You soon see that the judgments are extremely undemanding. The first set of stimulus lines are shown, the answer is clearly *A,* and the three subjects who respond before you all say "*A.*" The next set is shown, and *C* is the obviously correct answer, and all three subjects ahead of you respond "*C,*" as do you. The simplicity of these judgments was intentional. In fact, Asch purposely developed his stimulus cards so that almost no one ever made a mistake when they responded alone.

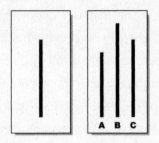

However, when the third (of twelve) judgment trial comes along, something goes haywire. What had started as a walk in the park begins to turn into something very different, because on this trial, all three of your fellow students make the same obvious mistake. (Remember, they respond before you do.) Judging the lines presented here, they all said *"B"* matched the reference line. You look again and it is clear to you that *C* is the right choice. Isn't it? A small dagger of doubt cuts into your early confidence—but it's a small dagger. The central question of the study is this: What will *you* say now that it's your turn?

You might wonder how the three students could have been so off base. What you didn't know is they were paid by Dr. Asch to give the wrong answer, unanimously, on cue, on specific judgment trials. All their judgments were scripted. The question that drove the research was whether or not their incorrect answers influenced anyone, even though the correct judgments were painfully obvious. The answer to this question might surprise you.

Fully *one third* of the time, the naïve respondents went along with the clearly incorrect majority, even though the threesome never tried to convince anyone that they were right. In fact, they never said anything except *A, B,* or *C*—but their influence was evident. You yourself might have resisted. A quarter of the subjects never went along with the majority; but that means that 75 percent of the participants did, at least once, so despite your anticipated protestations, the odds are that you, too, would have complied with the majority and reported a judgment that clearly was at odds with what you thought you saw.

Asch did not stop there. In an interesting extension of his basic study, he varied the number of confederates from one to fifteen. As usual, the game was rigged so that the real subject always responded last or next to last. Imagine if fifteen of your fellow college mates all reported seeing something that you clearly did not. Would you feel any pressure to comply and answer as they did? Contrary to what you might expect, it did not work out that way. The research showed that maximal influence was found with only three or four confederates. Piling on more and more false judgments didn't hurt, but it did not increase compliance either. Apparently, the *size* of the majority did not matter—what counted was the fact that the naïve subject was out of synch with it—*and that the majority was unanimous.*

You might find this research artificial, and it is, but that does not invalidate its implications, which are that you often will find yourself in circumstances in which you know you are right, and yet everyone else's judgments or behaviors indicate that you're not. You are in the minority, and how you respond in these circumstances will determine your success or failure in changing the group's actions. The stakes were not particularly high in Asch's experiment, yet filmed recordings of the real subjects' reactions showed that their conflict with their fellow participants was highly disturbing. Imagine if the conflict involved an issue about which they cared deeply. There is no doubt you will find yourself in just such a place, probably more often than you realize. How you decide to respond is your business, but if you decide to try to influence your group, the rules laid out here will help you succeed in doing so.

Asch extended his study to learn what would happen when the larger group was not unanimous, when a single confederate did not go along with the others. In this case, all bets were off. The research revealed that if *even one* confederate broke with the majority, if *just one* said *"B"* when the other fourteen said *"A,"* the majority's power to extract compliance evaporated, even if the deviant confederate's response also was incorrect. This result suggests that unanimity is all important when it comes to the majority pushing minorities around. Without it, the majority's capacity to influence the minority *and its own rank and file* is compromised. It is possible that unanimity was necessary because the judgments people were asked to make were really obvious. If they were a bit more difficult, perhaps something less than unanimity would have worked, but a high degree of majority consensus appears necessary if the majority is to control the situation. The lack of unanimity seems to motivate deviants to stand up for their positions. A majority that lacks unanimity is not in a strong position to force compliance.[xxii]

Reflecting on Asch in Real Group Contexts

Why should a single defection cause such problems for the majority's capacity to influence its dissident members? Probably because defection within the ranks compromises the credibility of the group's position. Consider some of the cues we use to determine if a persuader is speaking the truth, telling us something that we should believe. When communicators make statements that everyone expects them to make, statements that are in their self-interest, no one pays much attention. Obviously, if a person is running for office, it's reasonable that he or she would say, "I'm the best candidate for the job. Please vote for me." We *expect* people to speak in their own behalf, in favor of their beliefs and actions, and when they do, it doesn't surprise us. More important, it doesn't motivate us to listen carefully to what they are saying—or to accept what they have to say. But how would you react to a person who admitted that his or her well-established position was wrong, or was based on a lie. For example, suppose former Vice President Dick Cheney were to come onto the evening news and state, "You know, it's true. We really never believed that Iraq had weapons of mass destruction, but we were really mad at Saddam Hussein. He kept baiting us, thinking he could get away with it. He didn't seem to think we would do anything about it. We showed him and the rest of the world that we were serious. It's very dangerous to play chicken with the U.S."

What would your response be after having witnessed Cheney make this announcement on TV, before your very eyes? Would you believe that he did not think Iraq had weapons of mass destruction before arguing for the Iraq invasion? Under these circumstances, you would have almost no choice but to believe him. For years he had defended the U.S. entry into Iraq on the grounds that intelligence evidence indicated that the Iraqis had, or were developing, extremely dangerous weapons, and it was the administration's responsibility to ensure that they were never used. To hear him admit that this was a fabrication created simply to go after Saddam Hussein would be shocking, but it would be almost impossible to assume that he was lying. He had nothing to gain and much to lose by doing so. The message would take on truth value even if you originally believed that the invasion was completely justified because of the reasons the administration had given. Would your opinion of Cheney change? It might, but research evidence suggests that it would not. If you originally disliked the former VP, it's doubtful that you would like him for telling you that he had lied to you all these years. If you did like him originally, you might like him less for having lied, but this might be offset by your admiration for his willingness to take heat to come clean.

Experimental evidence bearing on these guesses regarding your likely response to Cheney's unlikely recanting can be found in a pair of experiments that a colleague and I performed to study people's beliefs when communicators presented messages that clearly were not consistent with what people expected them to say.[xxiii] The premise of the research was that unexpected (non-self-serving) messages would be more believable than self-serving ones, even though the "inconsistent" communications, when presented without attribution, were less believable than ones that were consistent with the speakers' positions.

To revisit this experiment, we need to journey back to the bad old days of the mid-1960s, when the United States was involved in a costly and to many, largely pointless war in Vietnam while enduring a fierce civil rights battle at home. The commanding officer of the American forces for much of the Vietnam War was General William Westmoreland. As CO, you would expect him to say that the tactics he had developed were working, but would the credibility of his statement suffer by being attached to the general, who had a vested interest in our accepting his analysis? We tested this possibility by asking some of our subjects to rate the credibility of the following statement:

U.S. bombing of North Vietnam has partially reduced the influx of men and military supplies to the South.

The bombing of North Vietnam had ignited a firestorm of protest in the United States. The military argued that it would choke off supplies to the south, and thus support the army's efforts in the field. Obviously, the general favored this tactic, even though critics claimed it had the possibility of massively widening the war.

When our subjects read this *unattributed* statement, they found it credible, despite the considerable controversy surrounding the bombing of North Vietnam at the time. However, when the exact sentence was attributed to General Westmoreland and presented to other subjects, they found it significantly less believable than the first group. The only difference was the attribution of authorship. In one case, the statement was presented without attribution, whereas in the other it was signed by General William Westmoreland.

We reversed the process with a different statement, which read

Generally speaking, the number of casualties in the Vietnamese conflict has far exceeded that reported in the U.S. press.

Subjects' ratings of the believability of this unattributed statement were quite low. However, when it was attributed to Westmoreland, the believability ratings went through the roof. Why? The statement clearly did not support Westmoreland's continued desire to bring more troops to the battlefield to prosecute the war more vigorously. He was telling us that the war was not going as well as we had been led to believe. This statement was more credible when attributed to the general because it seriously undercut his position. He would have had no reason to make the statement if it were untrue.

Was this result attributable to the issue, or the particular source, General Westmoreland, we chose to investigate? To answer this question, we repeated the study with a very different message source, Stokeley Carmichael, a hero of the Black Power movement at the time. Our assumption was that a student who liked Westy would not like Stokeley, and vice versa. This "inequality" helped us ensure that the results were not specific to a particular message source. In the Carmichael section of the study, students rated the believability of the following statement:

Often, Negroes have not taken the initiative required to benefit from civil rights legislation.

Most of our subjects did not find this statement credible. However, when the same statement was attributed to Stokeley Carmichael, participants rated it significantly more believable than the (same) unattributed statement. The opposite pattern was found when different subjects rated a statement that was consistent with Carmichael's known position. That statement read

There are many documented reports of police brutality in Negro neighborhoods.

When this statement was presented without any source attribution, our subjects found it highly credible. However, merely attributing the sentence to Carmichael significantly reduced its judged credibility.

Putting all this together helps us understand why a single in-group deviant can have such a devastating impact on the majority's power to affect the actions and beliefs of others in the group. Deviants from the in-group majority usually have nothing to gain and much to lose from defection, so communications delivered by people willing to behave in this manner assume an aura of credibility. Why take on the majority if you're not absolutely convinced you're right? It is for this reason that in-group majority defectors can have such a powerful impact. We believe what they have to say. On the other hand, the business-as-usual praises for one's positions and scorn for contrasting ones is common and expected. It doesn't raise any eyebrows and can be done without risk.

Preaching to the choir is "cheap talk" in the language of political science, and it doesn't buy much. It might help energize those who are already convinced, but it is not likely to persuade anyone. Speaking against one's obvious interest, however, carries the aura of truth, a sometimes rare and always valued commodity. It is for this reason that defectors from the majority carry such weight—people believe them. And it is for this reason that the majority does all it can to keep its sheep in the fold, even if the sheep are troublesome. In addition to weakening the majority's apparent mandate, defections within the ranks encourage the minority to challenge the majority's power, which we have seen is more tenuous than it appears at first glance. A single crack in the majority's unanimity emboldens the minority.

Coping with Internal Threats (Dissent)

Most successful majority group leaders recognize the danger of dissent within the ruling structure. They often resort to a direct approach to deal with it by imposing gag rules on their inner circles. In this way, even if dissent is rampant, no one outside the inner circle knows about it. Almost all U.S. presidents in recent memory have tried to make use of this tactic. George W. Bush's administration, and later, Barack Obama's, for example, were known for holding their cards close to the vest. This looks like a useful strategy, as it prevents policy disagreements from becoming public, which could encourage critics to propose ideas different from those favored by the leadership. Most administrations are not about to wash their dirty laundry in public. However, while the policy of maintaining a tight grip on all information is short-term smart, it is long-term stupid. Its unwitting side effect is to damp out the diversity of views whose adoption might help avoid egregiously wrong decisions to which all administrations sometimes are prone. No political party has a monopoly on good sense. By effectively blunting alternatives, good sense is lost and errors become more likely. Maintaining the appearance of a solid front by clamping down on all communication with the "outside," except those vetted by the boss, creates the impression of widespread internal consensus, but the process stifles internal debate, and we already know about the dangers of groupthink, an almost inevitable outcome of a false consensus created by a leader's overly tight grip.

More effective methods that have been used by groups in power to deal with internal disagreement employ persuasive techniques designed to win the allegiance of dissidents, the in-group minority. We'll consider in detail the communication tactics the majority uses to defuse recalcitrant in-group and out-group minorities in chapter 9, but for the moment let's consider some of the more obvious methods it uses to foster in-group acceptance of its positions. The tactics differ as a function of the target. When communicating with in-group dissidents, the successful majority typically avoids derogatory tactics (sarcasm, threats, and the like) because the in-group must be kept intact if the majority is to prevail. Dissent within the ranks is almost inevitable, but it is rarely so important to justify putting the group's integrity at risk to stifle it. That being the case, the smart majority uses logical arguments and soft persuasion to bring in-group dissidents into line. If possible, it avoids threats and strong pressure. Unsuccessful majorities are more prone to have threatened its dissident members, and although this tactic may produce the desired outcomes in the short run, there is a long-term price paid for it. That price is calculated in terms of the in-group minority's disaffection with, and distancing itself from the majority. This is a steep price to pay for compliance to majority wishes, even though it sometimes is required when the majority is desperate for unanimity.

When the persuasion target is an out-group minority, the majority often will begin with reasoned appeals to logic to persuade, as it does with in-group dissidents. If these appeals do not work, and they usually don't, the majority resorts to personal criticism (Any fool should be able to understand this . . .) or sarcasm (I refuse to enter a battle of wits with an unarmed person . . .) to bolster its own forces and to deflate the opposition. When attacks devolve to the personal level, their goal rarely is to persuade the opposition, but rather to keep the troops in line. The implicit message of the majority's criticism of the out-group, that is, is directed to the in-group—don't do anything that puts you on the other side of the majority fence, or you'll likely receive the same treatment.

So the Minority Has the Advantage?

Not exactly. Despite the chinks in its armor, the majority still has the big guns. We can describe conditions that help ensure the minority's position will be considered. We learned from the prior chapter that the minority must be viewed as part of the larger majority group, an in-group minority, if this is to happen, but this can be done. However, just because a minority is accepted as a legitimate (if somewhat wacky) part of the group, and just because majority positions sometimes are vulnerable, doesn't guarantee that a minority will prevail. In fact, they rarely do. The majority's acknowledgment of a common social identity with the minority merely allows the minority a foot in the door, and the sometimes relative fragility of majority views gives the dissident group a shot to advance its goal, but it still has considerable work to do to effect change.

The overarching strategies the minority must use to take advantage of the majority's acknowledgment of their in-group status are discussed in the chapters that follow. They are concerned with the necessity for persistence and consistency of message and behavior, and with the recognition that initially, indirect changes are more likely to be seen than direct successes. The later chapters also emphasize the need to frame the argument appropriately and persuasively, and to avoid actions that could subvert years of patient efforts. These strategic features determine the majority's response to the minority, and ultimately, the minority's fate.

The majority's failure to obtain its members' willing acquiescence is the opening the minority needs, because it suggests the possibility that the majority may not be able to carry the day—and by extension, that the dissidents may. This kind of encouragement emboldens the minority to press its case. If the issue under consideration is not particularly relevant or central to the majority, but the minority finds it critical, it will have an advantage it can use to move others to its point of view. We'll see how all this works in the chapters that follow. For the moment, it is important to understand that the majority is not an immovable force. Although it may strive to create that impression, we have seen how the majority can be stalled, if not stopped completely. However, winning requires more than a stall. To prevail, dissidents must adopt a carefully considered series of actions that can result in its moving the larger group into its corner. There are many ways to bungle the process, to lose the game, but the necessary procedures, the rules of influence are clear. They are presented in the chapters that follow, along with the grisly details of failing to stick to them.

FIVE

The Holy Trinity (plus One) of Minority Influence

Persistence, Consistency, Unanimity, and Flexibility

Almost always, the creative dedicated minority
has made the world better.

—Martin Luther King Jr.

Clarence William Busch had been arrested for drunk driving four times, but had never served more than forty-eight hours in jail. On the night of May 3, 1980, Busch was drunk again. Just two days previously, he had been arrested for a hit-and-run, but was out on bail. Nothing unusual for Busch, but this time it turned out differently. This time, in a drunken fog in the middle of the afternoon, he lost control of his vehicle and ran down Cari Lightner, a young teenager, as she was walking on the sidewalk in suburban Fair Oaks, California. Cari was thrown 125 feet. Busch did not bother to stop, but it probably would not have mattered. The impact was so severe that Cari could not have survived even if Busch had tried to help her. When apprehended later, Busch's blood alcohol level was .20, well beyond the drunk driving limit. Ultimately, he was sentenced to two years in prison.

Cari's mother, Candy Lightner, was bereft but not paralyzed by this catastrophe. Just days after the funeral, energized by grief, she traveled to the office of the Governor of California to plead for laws that would stop the carnage on the state's roads. She had a good case—in the 1980s alone, there were more than 240,000 alcohol-related traffic deaths—but Governor Jerry Brown was busy and would not arrange to see her. Drunk driving was not a politically advantageous issue at the time, and the governor apparently saw no point in meeting with Lightner and possibly upsetting the powerful alcohol lobby. Lightner was not deterred. She told her story to anyone who would listen, and religiously turned up at the governor's office *every day*. She would not accept Brown's refusal to grant her an audience, and vowed that she would sit in his waiting room until he saw her or hell froze over.

In short order, the press picked up her story and its widespread distribution forced the governor's hand. Under intense media pressure, Brown met with Lightner and, to his credit, set up a commission to attack the problem of drunken drivers in his state. The movement grew so large and so fast that only two years later, President Reagan also decided to appoint a commission to study the problem. By this time, Mothers Against Drunk Drivers (later changed to Mothers Against Drunk Driving—MADD) was a political force to be taken seriously. In 1984, less than four years after Cari Lightner's needless death, the president's commission recommended, and the Congress passed, the National Minimum Drinking Age Act. During this time, Candy Lightner worked tirelessly to further her cause, which had become all consuming. Today, all fifty states have adopted the act's provision that requires alcohol buyers be at least twenty-one years of age (Busch was forty-six when he ran down Cari Lightner), and every state also has reduced the legal limit for blood alcohol to BAC .08 (from BAC .10).

Would any of this have happened without the efforts of Candy Lightner? Maybe. The catastrophic carnage characteristic of driving in America at the time eventually would have affected enough families that some remedies would have emerged. But they would have been delayed without the dogged persistence of one person, Candy Lightner, a single mother who was willing to take on established political and economic forces—the majority—to fight for a change in the society. Was her dedication worth the effort? There is little doubt of this. According to the U.S. National Institutes of Health, deaths attributable to drunk driving from the early 1980s up to today have been cut in half. Many of us are alive today because of Candy Lightner.

How could one person upset the applecart of the massive booze industry in the United States? What was Lightner's secret? Persistence, consistency, and selflessness were all at work, and all were necessary to ensure her success. These factors play a major role in minority influence, and make no mistake, Lightner was a minority of one when she started her campaign. She had little money, no political connections, no ready allies, and she was fighting the strong and powerful alcohol lobby and the politicians who were dependent on the industry's largess. But she would not quit, she refused to take a single step back, and she had nothing to gain from her efforts. Everyone profited from her work, except those using cars as lethal weapons. These factors combined to create a powerful group of dedicated crusaders that overcame the entrenched interests of a well-heeled and well-connected industry.

Persistence and Consistency

The traits that contributed to Lightner's success when she helped create MADD could have been anticipated from Solomon Asch's research, which was conducted years before Candy's daughter was born. Asch's studies demonstrated the critical importance of a unanimous majority in bending the minority to its will. But these findings told only half the story. The results highlighted the majority's power to affect people's judgments and behaviors and simultaneously underscored the majority's fragility by demonstrating that anything less than group unanimity compromised the group's capacity to exert influence. Asch did not explore the other side of the influence coin, the effect of internal dissent on the *minority's* capacity to influence the majority. He might have skipped this part of the story because the ending seemed so predictable. If a single dissenter can obliterate the majority's capacity to influence outsiders, just imagine the effect of internal dissent on the minority's power to persuade others. Even without doing the research, it probably seemed obvious to Asch that dissent within the minority ranks was the kiss of death. Why should the majority take the minority's message seriously if the dissenters themselves can't agree on their message? The logical extension of Asch's work implies that minority influence is utterly dependent on a consistent, united (minority) front—without it, the minority's cause does not stand a chance. As we'll see in this instance, logic prevails.

Why is consistency so important to the minority's outcomes? When a weak group advances a consistent message, its actions imply confidence and certainty. Would people risk the derision of a powerful antagonistic majority if they were not convinced of the validity of their message? Think of the sidewalk preachers who harangue innocent passersby with threats of eternal damnation unless they change their sinful ways. Some of us may agree with the preacher, some may disagree, but all agree that the speaker is convinced of the validity of his or her message. Inferred conviction can have a powerful effect on people's judgments, and often leads to persuasion. Sidewalk preachers usually fail to convert listeners (sinners) to their cause, because they usually violate the first rule of influence—most people do not consider sidewalk preachers to be a part of their in-group, and so their message can be discounted and dismissed. Those listeners who already know and accept the preacher's message may be moved by it, but they were on board already. At best, the preacher's homily reinforces established beliefs; it rarely changes them.

This was not necessarily true in Candy Lightner's case. Of course, not many sane people were in favor of drunk driving or selling alcohol to kids, but not many people had thought to do much about the issue either. Candy Lightner's persistent and consistent demands to reform the drinking laws, to raise the age limit for legal use and possession of alcohol, and to establish reasonable limits on drivers' blood alcohol levels formed the backbone of her power. Her message never changed and she never faltered, and although she did not have the financial resources of her opponents, her moral currency was sufficient to pay for her and our success. Her actions provide wonderful examples of the second, third, and fourth rules of influence.

Rule 2. Be Persistent: Don't Retreat and Don't Compromise

Rule 3. Be Consistent: Stay on Message

Rule 4: Be Unanimous: Everyone Must Be on Board

These rules are related but not identical. And although they are related, they are so important that each is given the status of a rule of influence in its own right. A close study of Candy Lightner's actions reveals that she was a model of persistence and consistency. She doggedly persisted in the face of massive rejection. Her message never changed, probably because she knew it was right. And, she insisted that those who came to her assistance and joined the cause stayed on message. There really was no room for "alternative interpretations" of her demands. And she prevailed.

Experimental research conducted more than fifty years ago in Paris by the great European social psychologist Serge Moscovici clearly anticipated Lightner's successful outcomes. In fact, Candy followed the implications of this research so closely that it seems she was reading a script Moscovici had laid down years before her crusade. The French minority-influence studies, which bear a strong resemblance to Asch's investigations of *majority* influence, laid the foundation for much of what we now know of influence by people and groups that do not have the power to force compliance to their wishes.

In one of his earliest studies, Moscovici and his colleagues brought people together in groups of six. The subjects' job was simply to judge the colors of slides that were displayed, one after another, on a movie screen. At the start of the study, everyone took a brief eye exam, which all passed with flying colors.

Suppose you were one of the participants. The first slide flashes on the screen. It's blue. *Unambiguously* blue. You are *certain* it is blue. The first three subjects, and you, respond accordingly. However, the last two participants (remember, there are six of you) respond green! You don't know this, but these two have been paid by the experimenter to lie, and they do on all thirty-six of the judgment trials. If this reminds you of the Asch setup, it should.

As the study progresses, you notice that the light intensity of the slides changes from trial to trial. What you don't know is that the wavelength of every slide you see is identical. So for all intents and purposes, the same color is flashed on the screen every time, over thirty-six consecutive judgment trials. The slides simply differ in terms of luminance, or brightness. What's the point? It's easy. The study's central question is whether you or the other real subjects ever report seeing a "green" slide.

Think about the conditions of this study, and try to estimate the proportion of "green" judgments subjects will report, but before you do, there's something else you should know. When people judged the slides without the confederates, they said "blue" 99.75 percent of the time. Like Asch's lines, the proper judgment was painfully obvious. Now, knowing that and knowing about Asch's studies, what do you think? What proportion of subjects' judgments were "green," a judgment that was clearly contrary to what they must have seen. Wait. Before you answer, think about this: The people you are responding with, your fellow subjects, look just like you. They are not from Mars. They do not have any apparent reason to lie. You have every reason to assume that they are reporting their true perceptions.

Okay, now, what is your estimate of the proportion of "green" judgments that real subjects made? The result might surprise you. Your fellow participants said "green" on 8.4 percent of all judgments. Analyzed another way, in one third of the thirty-two groups that were studied, at least one of the real subjects responded "green" at least once. These results might be understandable if the slides' colors were on the blue/green edge of the spectrum, but they weren't. As I've told you, almost no one in a preliminary study ever judged the slides as anything but blue.

Why would the judgments of a small minority (two of six subjects) have such an effect on judgments that were so obvious? After all, the two confederates' estimates were contrary to the majority of the subjects' reports, and to your own perceptions, and they obviously were wrong. The researchers answered this question in the following way. They reasoned that the minority's judgments created uncertainty and mental conflict in the larger group—that is, in the group of real subjects. If the real subjects were confused and uncertain as a result of the minority's wholly unexpected responses, they might have reasoned as follows:

> "How could they possibly say 'green'? What am I missing? We all passed the same eye test. They seem 'normal,' like me. What do they see that the other four of us don't? I think they're wrong. The slides look blue to me and most everyone else, but those two must really be sure of themselves to keep bucking the rest of us. Maybe I'd better look more closely at the next slide."

If these were the subjects' thoughts, the results make sense, because if any of these issues came to mind, they would bolster the minority's cause, dubious as it was, and undermine the larger group's consensus.

A second study further tested the importance of the influence group's consistency, persistence, and unanimity. The setup was largely the same, but this time, the confederates said green on only twenty-four of the thirty-six judgment trials. In this version of the study, though unanimous, the minority lacked consistency and apparent persistence, and this deficit had a clear and disastrous effect on compliance levels. Only 1.25 percent of the real subjects' judgments were green in this study—a marked drop from the earlier investigation, when the two confederates held firm on all thirty-six judgments in the face of the larger group that was, at least initially, resistant to their influence.

Asch's research showed how cracks in the majority's unanimity empowered defectors. Moscovici's blue/green investigations illustrate how the *minority's* consistency facilitated influence, and how its lack of absolute consistency, persistence, and unanimity undid its persuasive power. For the majority, the minority's inconsistency reaffirmed what they *knew* to be the right answer, whereas the consistent dissidents caused members of the larger group to reconsider their fundamental color perceptions. The take-home from this research was that to be effective, the minority must be consistent—and persistent, and unanimous. The necessity for persistence plays out over the course of the experiment. The minority did not influence the larger group on the first few trials. Their effect was seen after they had made their unexpected judgments and stuck with them across the length and breadth of the study. To be effective, the influencer must take a stand and not compromise or back away from it. And all members of the group must maintain unanimity of position. When these conditions were met, the minority had a strong effect on a very basic judgment.

Applying this result to the world outside the laboratory raises the question, "Wouldn't people like this—people who held unusual perceptions or opinions and were absolutely committed to them, who refused to compromise or respond to alternatives— prove unbearably dogmatic? Insufferable? Unendurable? Aren't these the kind of people most of us avoid at all costs?"

Yes.

It is difficult to tolerate such people, but they can avoid the negative connotations of their consistent and doggedly persistent positions if there is a rational basis for them. If we can see why the group or individual holds a strange or unusual belief, our tolerance for the position increases, though we do not necessarily adopt their views immediately.

The battle is not totally uphill. We spontaneously respond to people who consistently push a position in the face of strong opposition. They deserve a hearing, even if their position is outside the mainstream opinion and contrary to our own. From childhood, we have learned to like underdogs. We have a long tradition of cheering for the little guy, of not kicking the person who's down. This fundamental tendency to extend a fair hearing to the less fortunate, less numerous, or less usual is useful for dissident groups, because it opens the door to influence. Marketers know that the first step in persuasion is getting you to listen to their spiel, and so they do all they can to draw your attention to their message. In many circumstances, groups holding unusual positions, especially if they are in-group, have a built-in advantage, which is calculated in terms of others' curiosity or attention. These groups can enhance their power to influence the many if they combine persistence and consistency with flexibility.

Flexibility

Along with other researchers, Moscovici and his team demonstrated unequivocally that a minority group would be ineffective unless it presented a united front. The group must be consistent and persistent if it is to prevail. But there's more to it than mere consistency or repetition. James Carville and Paul Begala hit the nail on the head in their book on marketing political candidates with the intriguing title of *Buck Up, Suck Up . . . and Come Back When You Foul Up.*[xxiv] Their most critical advice to potential candidates was to stay on message, maintain a consistent position, hammer home the points they want to make, and refuse to be drawn into arguments that detract from them. This is good advice for anyone, progressive and conservative, Democrat and Republican, but it is most important for would-be persuaders who are members of minority groups, whose "face time" with the majority may be limited. Staying on message, however, does not mean that we mindlessly parrot the same old script. Lots of politicians today have missed this point, appearing to think that staying on message requires only that they repeat the company line over and over again, no matter the question. That is not what

Carville and Begala advised. Sure, consistency is essential, but mindless repetition is not consistency—it's mindless repetition. To stay on message, persuaders (groups or individuals) who have not yet secured the majority's agreement must fit the message to the specific circumstances in which they find themselves, all the while maintaining a consistent position.

This is a tough prescription, because circumstances change, and as they do, the persuader must be responsive to them while maintaining a consistent message. In the typical labor-management negotiation, for example, labor argues for higher wages, better benefits, and so on. When the economy is in a tailspin, however, these demands may be softened, and others put in their place— demands for more job security or better working conditions are substituted for the more immediately costly demands for wage hikes. This change in demand reflects flexibility *and* consistency, because the underlying motive of both bargaining ploys is the same, to improve the lot the workers. The shift from wage to security demands is not presented as a backward step, or as a change in fundamental position, but rather a flexible and reasoned response to the conditions that exist at the time of the negotiation.

This flexibility actually enhances the perception of the persuader's consistency. Far from detracting from influence, flexibility in our approach to influence boosts the likelihood of persuasive success. Flexibility indicates that we are in touch with the realities of the situation, and are willing to work within them. It does not signal a willingness to step back from our central positions. In our scheme, flexibility must be paired with consistency of purpose if the minority is to succeed. Persistence is understood, as are consistency and unanimity; the necessity for these virtues in all influence contexts cannot be oversold. These rules of influence are not up for debate, and the fifth rule reinforces and enlarges them.

Rule 5. Remain Flexible: Adjust Your Message to the Circumstances

Flexibility is critical, and it must be distinguished from wild swings from one position to another whenever the wind blows in a different direction. We saw what the tag of *flip-flopper* did to John Kerry's candidacy in the 2004 presidential campaign. When explaining a set of apparently contradictory funding authorization votes, he said, "I actually did vote for the $87 billion before I voted against it." This quote, which played a large role in his opponent's ad campaigns, did not serve Kerry well.

When the minority flips from one position to another, its perceived consistency is forfeit, and so is its power to influence. So what, then, is flexibility? In the context of outsider influence, flexibility implies that the group is willing to modify its arguments to take account of the circumstances that exist at the time of its interaction with the majority. In essence, flexibility means that when conditions change, so, too, do the minority's messages, expectations, and demands. However, the substance of their message is unaltered. The minority's position remains consistent—the thrust of its arguments is unswerving—but its demands *can and should* be altered if external circumstances change.

A 2010 lawsuit involving the Los Angeles Unified School District (LAUSD) provides a useful example of a flexible minority strategy. The plaintiffs, a small group of parents whose children would be affected, were attempting to block LAUSD's planned teacher layoffs at three of the city's worst-performing middle schools. The group's *original* demands were simply that the layoffs be stopped. Like most big cities, Los Angeles was under extreme financial pressure, and one of the city's solutions to a huge budget deficit was to fire schoolteachers and expand class sizes. The layoffs were to be made on a last-in, first-out basis. The least experienced teachers would be laid off; the more experienced teachers would be the last to go. This is a common and apparently reasonable strategy until you consider that new teachers usually have relatively little choice of school. They are compelled to vie for positions in the system's worst-performing, least-desirable venues. This system results in considerably less staff stability and considerably greater teacher turnover in the worst-performing schools. It also means that the worst-performing schools are almost always staffed by the least experienced teachers in the system. Usually, these teachers are not in the school for long, because they either are laid off (remember: last in, first out) or transfer to better-performing schools where their jobs are easier. This was the case in Los Angeles, where because of their lack of seniority, more than two thirds of the teachers in the three affected schools were to be laid off.

The small group of parents opposing the practice was supported by the American Civil Liberties Union, among others, but they were fighting the second-largest school district in the country, along with the district's lawyers, consultants, and other hired guns. The parents saw themselves as David facing the Goliath of the mighty L.A. school board, and they were not far from wrong. However, their argument was strong. They claimed that the last-hired, first-fired policy was discriminatory, and that layoffs should be spread equally across all schools in the massive L.A. school district. If layoffs were distributed equally among all LAUSD schools, then those schools with an abundance of newer teachers would not be unduly penalized. Ultimately, this compromise was judged reasonable to both parties, and so it was agreed.

As the debate progressed, however, it became evident to both the plaintiffs and the city administration that the issue was much larger than firing young teachers from three underperforming schools. As both groups recognized the larger problem, the discussion expanded to a consideration of educational quality in the public school system of Los Angeles. In this discussion, one side raised the possibility of using performance indicators to determine who would be laid off and who would keep their jobs. Better teachers would be spared, even if they were new and next in line for layoffs in the old seniority-based system. The quest for quality education became the theme underlying the plaintiffs' demands, and as this more general issue was considered, the parents expanded the argument to include a host of other issues, all of them related to the larger theme of quality public education. This more general discussion was considerably more expansive than the original dispute that brought the two groups into conversation, but it was focused on the general issue that was at the heart of the original dispute. The minority won on the teacher-layoff issue. Time will tell if the broader agreements designed to enhance educational quality in the school system will stand. There is a reasonable likelihood that they will, despite the union's disagreement with many of its provisions.[9]

The minority's effectiveness was enhanced by its willingness to remain flexible in search for agreement while *consistently* arguing for its central position, that educational quality in Los Angeles public schools had to be improved. Minimizing teacher turnover in low-performing schools was the precipitating issue, but it was only one avenue to enhanced children's school performance, and the conversation expanded from that point. Maintaining a consistent theme of high-quality public education allowed the minority to attack related issues without diluting their persuasive impetus on the focal teacher-layoff issue.

---

[9] The powerful teachers' union, the United Teachers of Los Angeles, was only minimally involved in the court's deliberations. It had always held out for the seniority system, and so the ultimate outcome of the more general agreement cannot yet be stated with certainty.

The Door-in-the-Face

A variation on the theme of minority flexibility makes use of a tactic of social influence that in social psychology has come to be called the door-in-the-face effect. (In business and negotiation studies, it is known as "adopting an extreme initial position.") The technique is most widely used by those in subordinate positions (for example, members of minority groups) who are in need of aid. The tactic calls for the requester to make an outrageous initial appeal. A teenager, for example, might ask, "Dad, I need the family car every day for the next two weeks. Would you give me the keys?" After Dad predictably responds, "Are you nuts?" the teen might modify his request to, "Okay, then can I have it just for tonight?" Research shows that the odds of receiving a favorable response to this second request are considerably better than if the teen had not made the initial (outrageous) request in the first place. This outcome has been found in many studies in the United States, and recently my colleagues and I extended the research into France, where we obtained the identical results. More important, we found that requesters who were part of the in-group fared much better with the second request than those who were not. Although the door-in-the-face worked even for needy out-groupers, it had a much greater impact when the requester was in-group.

The study was conducted on the campus of a large French university, the Université de Toulouse in the southwest of France. In the "extreme initial request" part of the study, a researcher approached random students on the campus and said,

We're currently recruiting students to help us as unpaid volunteers. What volunteers have to do is to spend two hours a week for a period of two years at the young delinquents' center, participating in the activities of a young boy [girl] at the center. Would you be interested in being considered for one of these positions?

When subjects refused the request (almost everyone did), the experimenter offered a concession:

Well, we also have another program you might be interested in, then. What volunteers have to do is to take a group of young boys [girls] from the young delinquents' center to visit the zoo. This visit should last for approximately two hours, and will only take place once. Would you be interested in being considered for one of these positions?

Sixty percent of those who had received and rejected the initial large request agreed to the second one. When the students were given the smaller request without first receiving the larger one, only 30 percent agreed. Put another way, twice as many people agreed to the lesser request when it appeared to be a concession.

The differences were even greater when the common social identity of the requesters and the subjects was emphasized. When the requesters wore clothing that identified them as members of the same school as the subjects, the door-in-the-face effect was much stronger than when their outfits identified the supplicants as students from a rival college.[xxv]

Many explanations have been proposed to explain the success of this influence tactic. The two most likely are contrast and politeness, or reciprocation of concessions. The contrast explanation suggests that the second request seems so much smaller in the context of the larger one that it is more often granted than when it is made without the outrageous one preceding it. The contrast between first and second requests fosters compliance.

Think of the baseball player waiting to come to bat. Usually, he (or she) will swing a couple of bats, or a bat with a lead weight attached to it, before going to the batter's box. Other than tradition, why do they do this? Whether they know it or not, they are taking advantage of the contrast effect. After swinging the heavier bats, the bat taken to the plate *seems* much lighter than it would otherwise. This is a perceptual distortion, but it works, and it helps explain why the second request in the typical door-in-the-face experiment seems so much less onerous when it follows an initially outrageous one.

The alternative, politeness explanation appeals to the fact that the norms of most societies demand that we reciprocate favors. If someone does a favor for us, we are expected to reciprocate. This expectation is built into the negotiation process, where reciprocation of concessions is an expected feature of the interaction. Think back to the earlier car example, where Junior dramatically reduced his initial request. He made a concession. When someone concedes a point in a bargaining situation, we have learned to reciprocate. Dad was fooled and fell into the reciprocation trap— unless Dad has read this book.

Which of these explanations is correct has not yet been established—in fact, they both might be right—or wrong. For our purposes, why the tactic works is less important than the fact that it usually does. People seem to have an intuitive grasp of how to use the door-in-the-face, and in this case, common folk intuitions seem to be right.[10] The relevance of the tactic for minority influence is that the second (more modest) request is not seen as inconsistent with the first. Rather, it is viewed as a concession, as a flexible response to the conditions on the ground, and in this way gains persuasive strength. When petitioners are flexible, when their

---

[10] They often aren't.

demands are tied to changes in external circumstances, their arguments actually gain strength, as we'll see when we consider some laboratory studies that implicitly manipulated the apparent rigidity of a minority group in its interaction with the majority.

A wonderful example of the simultaneous operation of consistency, persistence, *and* flexibility is evident in research conducted by Charlan Nemeth and her colleagues at Berkeley. When these researchers repeated the French blue/green studies, they found that the minority could maintain its effectiveness even when shifting their judgments from blue to green, *if* there was an apparent reason for the shift.

In the Berkeley study, as in the French investigations, researchers used colored slides whose wavelengths were identical across all judgment trials; however, they varied the *luminance* of the slides, so sometimes the slide was bright, while other times it was less so. Responding in order on each trial, the confederates sometimes judged the slides as blue, and sometimes as green. When their judgments were not associated with the slides' luminance, they had no effect on the other four respondents' judgments. But if the (confederate) minority's judgments were associated *consistently* with the slides' brightness, they had a powerful influence on the majority group's answers. When the minority always judged the bright slides blue, and the less bright slides as green (or vice versa), the majority subjects went along with them on 21 percent of the judgment trials! This is almost three times the proportion Moscovici found in his minority influence studies in Paris, despite the fact than in a control group that Nemeth conducted at Berkeley, almost no one ever reported the blue slides as green.

In the Berkeley research, the (minority) confederates' shifting responses from green to blue to green was viewed by the other subjects as *flexible*, because differences in judgments were *consistently* associated with differences in the slides' luminance. The influential confederates *always* reported that the bright slides were blue, and *always* judged dark slides as green.[11] These judgments had a powerful impact on the subjects in the majority because they were consistently associated with differences in the slides' luminance.

Selflessness and the Zero-Sum Game

Aligned with flexibility is the requirement that the minority position not appear to unduly disadvantage the majority, because if it does, the first rule is violated. Remember, to influence the majority, the minority must be accepted as part of the larger group. If the changes a minority requires will dramatically undercut the majority's position, it has little chance of success because it will not be perceived as in-group. After all, why would a person undercut the group that helps define his or her identity?

This does not mean that the minority must conceal its motivation when seeking to make its point. Unless persuaded otherwise, we naturally assume that a person or group arguing a particular position has a vested interest in the argument's outcome. This is an unwritten expectation of almost all negotiations. Otherwise, why bother arguing? A person's advocating for a position of advantage is acceptable; but we balk when the other's advantage works to our disadvantage. It's acceptable to me that you get your way, so long as my ox isn't gored in the process.

The requirement that the majority not be penalized if the minority prevails illustrates the distinction between what economists and psychologists call zero-sum and non-zero-sum games. In zero-sum games, the pot is fixed, so your wins are my losses. True

---

[11] In a variation of the study, this rule was reversed—the confederates always judged the bright slides as green, and the dark slides as blue. The results were the same—consistent and persistent minority responses proved persuasive.

winner-take-all poker tournaments are zero-sum games. The total buy-in is fixed, and the winner's gain comes at a cost to all the other players. In true zero-sum games, second place is no better than last. One player comes out on top, and everyone else loses. In the parlance of the racetrack, place and show are no better than also-ran.

In non-zero-sum games, the pot is theoretically limitless, so your good fortune is not necessarily my catastrophe. Almost all commercial transactions can be viewed as non-zero-sum games. If you are willing to pay $250,000 for your new Bentley, and the dealer is willing to part with it for that amount, most economists would consider this a non-zero-sum transaction, because both parties— buyer and seller—are satisfied with the arrangement and both feel that they benefit from it. The seller's gain is not your loss—after all, you're getting a new Bentley out of the deal. We are much more apt to go along with the minority in non-zero-sum circumstances—or when we're convinced that both groups gain from acceding to its request. When the University of Michigan was taken to court because it used race in its law school admissions practices to foster diversity, its lawyers argued that these practices helped white as well as black students. The society is increasingly diverse, the university's lawyers argued, and by ensuring this diversity in the classroom, the law school would produce better lawyers, and students of both races, white and black, would profit. Their argument carried.

This same non-zero-sum feature was evident in Candy Lightner's arguments to curb drunk drivers. In this case everyone wins— except the drunk. Lightner had much to gain from safer streets, but we all do. No one gained at another's expense. It is difficult to argue against an issue in which all stand to gain, and no one loses. Not surprisingly, a common communication tactic of weaker groups attempting to push their position is to demonstrate that all gain by acceding to their wishes—that the game is non-zero-sum, a win-win situation.

Moving the Majority

In combination these studies suggest that people can be influenced by a minority group even when the minority's position is clearly at odds with theirs. To do so, however, it cannot compromise or backslide. Consistency of message is essential, but at the same time, the message cannot be viewed as dogmatic or massively self-serving. If the minority can carry off this tough balancing act, it can succeed.

The influence results of the French and Berkeley researchers are compatible with the findings that Asch reported many years ago. Capitalizing on Asch's research, the influence studies advanced the reasonable idea that if disagreements within a majority group could destroy its power to influence, then disagreements within the minority would be even more ruinous. Research confirmed these suspicions. What's more, the findings suggest that a flexible minority can be extremely effective, if it is consistent in the general thrust of its arguments. It can modify its position to adjust to environmental factors, but it cannot modify its sought-for outcome.

The results of the research make perfect sense. If the minority itself is fractured, why should the majority bother listening? However, when the minority was consistent, it was influential, and when it was attuned to variations in the environment, it was even more influential. Nevertheless, for many readers, the question remains, do these laboratory-based findings transfer to the rough-and-tumble social world of the streets? Let's consider people's intuitions about the use of compromise by minority and majority groups.

Nine months before the 2010 midterm elections, the Pew Research Center for the People and the Press interviewed a nationwide sample of 1,383 adult American voters. They were asked a host of questions about their political attitudes, one of which involved the political party they favored. Another question asked them to indicate the most important issue in the upcoming election. Those leaning toward the Republican side were asked, "Should Republican political leaders be willing to compromise with the Democrats on this issue, or should they stick to their position without compromising?" When this question was asked in 2007, the Republicans held both houses of Congress. Sixty-three percent of the Republican respondents advocated compromise. In February 2010, when the Republicans were the *minority* party in both houses, only 52 percent advocated compromise, an 11 percent drop in openness to compromise.

Among the Democratic respondents, the opposite pattern held. Before the strong Democratic majority took over, 60 percent advocated compromise; by February 2010, when the Democrats enjoyed a majority in both houses, 71 percent felt that Democratic Congressional leaders should be willing to compromise. These results suggest that laypersons implicitly understand that the majority should be willing to compromise, but that this is a losing strategy for the minority.

Things did not change much after the election, even though the power in the House shifted from the Democrats to the Republicans. In a poll conducted just after the 2010 elections, the *USA Today*/Gallup Poll reported two startling results:

> Republicans are more than twice as likely as Democrats to say it's more important for political leaders to stick to their beliefs even if little gets done. Forty-one percent of Republicans put themselves at four or five on a scale in which five is the most unyielding. Only 18% of Democrats feel that way.

and,

> Democrats are almost twice as likely as Republicans to say it's
> more important for political leaders to compromise . . . to get
> things done. Fifty-nine percent of Democrats rate themselves
> at one or two on the five-point scale compared with 31% of
> Republicans. .

It is possible that the electoral landslide that swept the Republicans into power in the House emboldened them to repudiate compromise. The refusal to compromise is a minority tactic, but it did help turn around the fortunes of their party, which was in dreadful shape after Obama's electoral landslide in 2008. So perhaps they felt they should stay with the winning tactic. Or with their recent ascent so new, and their prior minority status still so fresh in their minds, the Republican respondents might not have switched gears into "majority mode." However, maintaining the old tactics is dangerous, because the new (Democratic) minority in the House can be expected ultimately to adopt a similar no-compromise approach, which we have seen is the only way the minority can prevail.

Although the Democrats may appear to believe more in compromise than the Republicans, this difference probably is attributable to their recent history as the majority party. Once they realize that they no longer run the show, the Democrats can be counted on to resist compromise as well. Pairing contending negotiators who refuse to compromise is the perfect recipe for gridlock, which is practically unavoidable if the majority is unwilling to bend and agree to some degree of cooperation with the minority.

Further complicating the picture is the necessity that the majority accept the minority as in-group, as a legitimate member of the overall group. If this acceptance is not forthcoming, if members of the Republican majority in the House do not view their Democratic peers as legitimate representatives of the people, if this common identity does not trump party identity, then it is unlikely that anything will be accomplished legislatively. The majority will not be moved by out-group minorities, no matter how cogent the minority's point of view.

Earlier instances of gridlock in the Congress bear the marks of a misapplication of the appropriate influence strategy. When the Republicans took over the House in 1995, their "Contract with America" attempted to pass a spending bill that involved massive cuts to social programs dear to the hearts of the Democratic legislators—Medicare, Medicaid, education, environmental controls, and earned income tax credits for the middle class. The House Majority Leader, Newt Gingrich, would not compromise, and neither would the beleaguered President Clinton. The spending bill was dead in the water, and the government essentially ran out of money. Whom did the American people blame? Gingrich, whose popularity fell through the floor while Clinton's rose to the highest of his presidency. We seem intuitively to know who should apply which tactic in a weak versus strong confrontation. When the outcome is positive, misapplications of strategies are forgiven. When the outcome is disastrous, those who violate expectations of appropriateness are punished. Gingrich resigned his seat in the House three years after the government-shutdown debacle.

What about Minority Selflessness?

It seems reasonable that the majority would be more open to the minority's requests if it was clear that the minority had nothing to gain from the majority's assent, and although it is indirect, research confirms this inference. In an early study of selflessness, for example, research subjects read a message that argued strongly for tripling the licensing fees on tractor-trailers. The author was said to be running for the Missouri legislature, and the message supposedly was a transcript of his speech. Half the subjects were told that the speech had been delivered to a local union of railway workers, who would be expected to approve, as the increase would escalate trucking costs and shift business in the railroad's direction. The remaining participants were told that the speech had been delivered to a local union of long-haul truck drivers, who were expected to reject an increase in their costs of doing business. Most reasonable people would assume that the truckers would be antagonistic to the speaker and the position he advocated. In fact, both groups of subjects read the identical speech—only the apparent audience differed between the groups.

After reading the speech, the subjects were asked their impression of its author, and their attitudes regarding the legislation he supported. The results strongly favored the speaker when it was clear that he was in a weak position. When presenting his ideas to a hostile audience, he was judged significantly more sincere, honest, and impartial, and less cynical, opportunistic, obliging, and tactful. In addition these subjects were significantly more persuaded by the speech than were those who read the identical message, but who thought it was being delivered to a friendly audience. Apparently, selflessly acting against one's self-interest pays dividends.[xxvi] Indicators of selflessness appear to have a powerful effect on people's judgments of credibility.

Mandela

A prime example of the selflessness effect is evident in the world's response to Nelson Mandela, who had been incarcerated for much of his adult life, yet soon came to lead the country as its president after being freed. How did he do it? As we'll see, almost everything Mandela did was consistent with the recommendations for influence outlined to this point.

Nelson Mandela was arrested and convicted of sabotage (which he admitted) by the apartheid government of South Africa in 1962. At the time of his arrest, Mandela was leader of the armed wing of the African National Congress, which had been fighting for an end of the country's racist policies for many years. He was sentenced to life in prison. Serving his sentence, Mandela had plenty of time to think seriously about conditions in his native country, and he put that time to good use. He rejected the usual calls for armed rebellion, and instead pushed for a moderate approach that involved people of all races coming together under the same flag, forming an overarching group—South Africans— that superseded racial differences. All citizens could be South African. Skin color simply did not matter. In making his argument, Mandela became the voice and conscience of reasonable South Africans, no matter their race. His stoic resistance made him a symbol of perseverance and defiance in the anti-apartheid movement.

The white leaders of South Africa recognized the growing power of this symbol and attempted to defuse his influence by offering him freedom—but only on the condition that he give up all political activity. In a letter that Mandela's daughter smuggled out of his prison, he eloquently refused the offer, writing that "Only free men can negotiate. A prisoner cannot enter into contracts." Despite the cost—remember, he was facing life imprisonment—he would not compromise. His actions were consistent, persistent, *and* selfless. By his actions, Mandela personified the qualities that a powerless minority must possess if it is to move the majority. As history would show, the powerless minority in South Africa moved and displaced the powerful majority.

It's Not All Good

You should understand that the necessity and consequent effect of a minority's united voice has nothing to do with the virtue of its message. In *Mein Kampf,* and throughout his adult life, Adolf Hitler showed amazing consistency of message, beginning long before the Nazi Party achieved power. The two volumes of his depraved book were published in 1925 and 1926, well before Nazism was a credible, or rather, potent political force. The blueprint for all that was evil in the movement was printed in black-and-white from the start for all to see, and the reprobates and fanatics who joined this cause used this book as their bible. They did not stray from its central themes until they were forced to do so, or were exterminated. And many of those who did survive ultimately died with the certainty that they had done the right thing—that God was on their side. As Hitler wrote, and many of his followers accepted, "I believe that I am acting in accordance with the will of the Almighty Creator."

Examples of the effects of consistency on the persuasive strength of messages are readily available. The big lie technique of the Nazis, which seems to have become quite popular in some American political circles, was not invented or pursued whimsically.[12] The technique works, especially with those who avoid thinking critically. It is primarily a tool of the majority, but it also can be a powerful weapon in the hands of the minority—unless the majority

---

[12] As Hitler wrote in *Mein Kampf,* long before he achieved the power to address even small assemblies of followers, "The great masses of the people will more easily fall victim to a big lie than to a small one."

knows how to combat it. We will consider the persuasive techniques most useful for minority groups in chapter 10, but for the moment it is sufficient to reflect on the examples presented here, which have revealed the manner in which a minority's communication strategy can move a majority. A consistent and persistent message can accomplish great things, for good or evil, if it is presented as a logical and rational response to prevailing conditions, and if the ulterior purposes of its originators do not conflict with the vested interests of the majority.

In addition to its consistency and the persistent way it is pursued, the manner in which the issue is framed determines the success or failure of the minority's message. Do you think it would be easier to change people's minds about subjective preferences or objectively verifiable facts? And would majority or minority status matter? If you reasoned that it would be difficult to change people's subjective beliefs, you're right. And if you thought that majority or minority status might play into the equation, you're right again. In the coming chapter, we'll consider some of the work that has been done to shed light on these issues, and the useful strategies that emerge from these investigations.

SIX

Making the Subjective Objective

The proper basis for marriage is mutual misunderstanding.

—*Oscar Wilde*

On October 14, 1962, a U2 aircraft piloted by Air Force Major Richard Heyser flew over the westernmost landmass of Cuba. The U2 was America's premier reconnaissance aircraft. Flying at nearly seventy thousand feet, the plane was practically invulnerable to the antiaircraft defenses of the day. Heyser's cameras took nearly one thousand pictures of the land below during the six-minute overflight of Cuba's sovereign territory. When the film was developed, the United States found itself on the edge of a nuclear abyss. The pictures indicated that the Soviet Union had begun constructing a string of nuclear missile bases on Cuban soil. The missiles had the capability of reaching almost every city in the continental United States.[xxvii]

For many, the Cuban missile crisis is at best a dim memory. The drama played out nearly a half century ago during the coldest winter of the long-past cold war. But the danger was extreme, and many at that time thought the world could be changed irrevocably by a single miscalculation by either of the contending parties. One serious mistake by the Americans or the Soviets would create a new world, a world vastly different, and vastly worse, than the one we knew. We have not, before or since, come so close to a major nuclear conflagration. The background of the crisis provides some indication of the major players' thinking and helps us understand how a minority's position can gain strength if its authors understand how the game should be played. We will see that the way an argument is posed—as involving objective facts or subjective preferences—can work to the advantage of the communicator. The central actor in this play, for our purposes, was U.S. Ambassador to the UN, Adlai Stevenson, but for the moment, let's consider some of the forces in play as the crisis evolved.

Some Ancient History

Just six months before the Cuban missile crisis was in full bloom, the United States had been involved in the disastrous Bay of Pigs invasion (see introduction), a simultaneously comic and tragic affair in which everything that could go wrong did. The new U.S. president, John Kennedy, had suffered a humiliating introduction to international politics. The Soviet leadership knew this and assumed he would be disinclined to reawaken memories of his recent embarrassment. He was new, they reasoned, and probably would not risk another major diplomatic disaster. They had seriously misjudged Kennedy's tenacity, one of the most prominent features of his personality.

When he learned of the appearance of Russian missiles on Cuban soil, Kennedy hit the roof. In response to their unwarranted actions (in his view), he threw the kitchen sink at the Soviets. He attacked on almost all fronts. Simultaneously, his counselors engaged the Soviet leaders in heated negotiations in Washington and Moscow. He called an emergency session of the UN Security Council. He imposed a naval blockade around the island of

Cuba, and publicly threatened to blow out of the water any ship attempting to run it. And he set Adlai Stevenson loose at the UN, allowing him to take off the diplomatic gloves and go after the Soviets in a bare-fisted manner that was completely uncharacteristic of this gentle man. Of all these frenetic responses to the Soviets' actions, which appeared clearly provocative and threatening to the security of the country, Stevenson's work was the most public. For our purposes, it clearly illuminates the persuasion tactics used by a group (in this case, the United States) attempting to sell a position to a reluctant and initially unreceptive audience (in this case, nearly everyone else).

The world was not keen to witness the two superpowers going head to head. It was clear to every thinking person that a nuclear storm would not, perhaps could not, be confined to the combatants alone—it would rain on the rest of the civilized world as well. Stevenson's job was to stir world opinion in a way the Soviets could not ignore, and ultimately would be forced to dismantle the missile sites and take their toys home. This was not an easy job, as a good portion of the world did not believe, or did not want to believe, the United States' assessment of the situation. And Stevenson himself was not held in particularly high regard by his fellow UN diplomats. Only months earlier, he had been caught in a series of lies when he unwittingly denied U.S. involvement in the Bay of Pigs invasion. His explanations were pale imitations of the truth, and this had lowered his stock considerably in the UN. To his credit, Stevenson had not consciously lied. He told the truth as he had been led to understand it. The tight-knit administrative group of the Kennedy Administration had hidden much of the Bay of Pigs subterfuge even from its own ambassador.

To add to his problems, the Soviets resolutely denied Stevenson's claims. The issue threatened to become a "he said, she said" confrontation with no clear resolution. In these cases we are free to choose whatever side of the argument is most convenient, and in this case the most convenient side for most of the world was the Soviet Union's. If indeed nothing was amiss in Cuba, there was no need for difficult negotiations or force to resolve the (non)problem. If the world's lack of action could convince the United States not to respond aggressively to Soviet actions in Cuba, the problem would go away. Moving the United States into the weak position on this issue would defuse the time bomb that was sitting in the middle of the room—at least, this is what most of the Soviets and the representatives of many unaligned countries seemed to think.

Stevenson would have none of it. His job was to change the game from one involving subjective opinions to one anchored in objective reality. He had to move the issue from "This is what I think" to "This is what I know." He did that in one of the most powerful and undiplomatic speeches ever delivered by a U.S. Ambassador to the UN, accusing his opposite number not only of being an out-and-out liar but a bad one at that. The tactics he adopted were clearly the tactics of the outsider, but of a strong outsider that could be seen credibly as soon moving to insider status. This is an interesting ploy, as it suggests that he possessed information that would unquestionably and irrevocably move the hesitant parties to his side of the fence. Stevenson signaled this strength by attacking his opponent directly and without moderation. This is a rhetorical strategy only the majority or large minorities can use, and even then, they must use it with great caution. Consider Stevenson's opening salvo:

> I want to say to you, Mr. Zorin [the Soviet Ambassador to the UN Security Council], that I do not have your talent for obfuscation, for distortion, for confusing language, and for double-talk. And I must confess to you that I am glad that I do not!

He followed his disrespectful introduction with an appeal to the Security Council that is noteworthy in his singular focus, his insistence on facts, not opinions, his unwillingness to back down or concede even the smallest point, and his persistent resolve to pursue the issue until, as he put it, "hell freezes over." These are the very features of minority argumentation that have been shown to be critical if it is to prevail—persistence, consistency, unwillingness to concede, and a new feature that we must consider very carefully, his insistence that the issue involved facts, not guesses or opinions. Considerable research has shown that a minority's chances are strongly improved if its spokesperson is dealing with objective reality rather than hopes or opinions.

> ... if I understood what you said ..., that today I was defensive because we did not have the evidence to prove our assertions that your Government had installed long-range missiles in Cuba. Well, let me say something to you, Mr. Ambassador—we do have the evidence. We have it, and it is clear and it is incontrovertible. And let me say something else—those weapons must be taken out of Cuba.

Stevenson left little doubt as to his position or his seriousness of purpose. He then proceeded to the coup de grâce. He had a small easel set up in the council chamber, where pictures displayed the incontrovertible U2 photographic evidence of the missile facilities being built in Cuba. The ambassadors to the Security Council intently studied the photos as Stevenson described them. His commentary on the picture left no doubt as to its interpretation:

> The first of these exhibits shows an area north of the village of Candelaria. ... A map, together with a small photograph, shows precisely where the area is in Cuba. The first photograph shows the area in late August 1962; it was then ... only a peaceful countryside. The

second photograph shows the same area one day last week. A few tents and vehicles had come into the area, new spur roads had appeared, and the main road had been improved. The third photograph, taken only twenty-four hours later, shows facilities for a medium-range missile battalion installed. There are tents for 400 or 500 men...there are seven 1,000-mile missile trailers. There are four launcher-erector mechanisms for placing these missiles in erect firing position.... It is identical with the 1,000-mile missiles which have been displayed in Moscow parades. All of this, I remind you, took place in twenty-four hours.

What had been a controversial, subjective issue became an objective fact after Stevenson revealed the U2 evidence. Speaking from the position of the minority (most of the UN's members did not want to engage this issue), the ambassador changed the game by making the subjective objective. After Stevenson's hatchet job, the presence of Soviet missiles in Cuba was no longer a matter of opinion or subjective guesswork—the photographic evidence proved beyond any reasonable doubt that the Soviets had begun to build a missile-launching facility less than ninety miles from American soil—and the Americans did not like it.

Stevenson made his case as good lawyers do, bringing evidence to the table and offering a bulletproof explanation that could not be resisted by any sane person. But there's more to it than making a strong case. His arguments also transformed the issue from subjective to objective, and this transformation played an important role in his success as a minority voice in the Security Council. He succeeded in making his case. The Soviets, under the weight of world opinion and obvious U.S. unwillingness to allow serious offensive weapons so close to its borders, were forced to withdraw. Of course, the United States made some backroom deals with the

Soviets, and these played out over the coming year, but the un-equivocal response of the UN Ambassador had a major role in defusing an exceptionally dangerous confrontation between the two superpowers.

Stevenson probably constructed his argument based on his ex-perience as a strong debater. He clearly was angry with his Soviet counterpart, and it showed, but the important feature of his address to his fellow United Nations' ambassadors was not his ir-ritation but his skillful presentation, which turned a matter of subjective guesswork into objective reality. In this case, his intu-itions about the proper persuasive strategy were completely cor-rect. Stevenson's actions anticipated the sixth rule of minority influence.

Rule 6. Make the Subjective Objective

The process of making the subjective objective is a crucial deter-minant of a minority's success or failure to move the majority to its position. Our research has shown that when minority group members attempt to bring the majority to their way of thinking, the subjective or objective nature of the issue under discussion strongly affects their odds of persuasive success. We have a much easier time of moving the majority when the issue involves objec-tive judgments. This makes intuitive sense, because trying to convince people that their subjective preferences are incorrect is a tall order for anyone, and an even taller order for a person of minority status.

Imagine a Windy City resident visiting Manhattan. Surrounded by a group of New Yorkers, the Chicagoan attempts to persuade the group that deep-dish Chicago pizza is the tastiest of all pizzas, despite the majority group's obvious love for the thin-crusted hometown variety. Because this judgment is a matter of taste, literally, convincing the group that their collective taste buds are wrong is foolish as well as being next to impossible, and the job's difficulty is aggravated because of the out-group minority status of the persuader. So, surrounded by a covey of New Yorkers, it's a good bet that the Chicagoan would not prevail. It is possible that some members of the group might try the Chicago variety, but it's unlikely they would be converted.

Now let's consider a slightly different situation. In this one, suppose you are in a group of people arguing about the capital of Guinea-Bissau. The majority of the group thinks it's Freeport. You are the lone holdout for Bissau. Unlike the taste of pizza, your position can be definitively verified—or invalidated. If you were to whip out your iPhone, you could bring the group to your side almost instantaneously merely by searching the right database and showing everyone that you are correct. It wouldn't matter if you were the only person in the group who thought that Bissau was the correct answer—it is—or even if you were a complete outsider. The objective nature of the judgment reduces the importance of group membership. With objective issues, in-group or out-group majority or minority status does not matter much.

Extrapolating from this example provides an important addition to the minority rules, because it suggests that under some circumstances, even members of the out-group can move the majority to their position. Once your position is self-evidently correct, you can win the game, and your in-group or out-group status does not matter, though even when you are demonstrably correct, the majority may refuse to bend, but this is an unusual response often reserved for the members of detested out-groups. Generally, when the objective evidence favors your (initially unpopular) position, the fact that all your audience thought otherwise at first also does not matter. And your initial minority status on this issue—after all, everyone else believed it was Freeport—doesn't matter either, because your view is verifiable, and you were verifiably correct.

The same process was at work in the Cuban missile confrontation in the UN Security Council. Many members of that august body were not positively inclined to the Americans. Along with the French, representatives of the nonaligned countries often found the United States acting in ways they judged contrary to their vested interests. No matter. When Stevenson unleashed his evidence, there was little to do but agree—the evidence was objective and incontrovertible. The Soviets had indeed tried to sneak a missile facility under the noses of the Americans. Some in the chamber might have thought this was a justifiable action, but they could not deny that the action had occurred, in contravention of UN rules.

This example stands in stark contrast with a parallel episode in February 2003, when the U.S. Ambassador to the UN, Colin Powell, attempted to sell the case that Iraq had created weapons of mass destruction, an action requiring the civilized world to step in and stop the threat that Iraq's ruler, Saddam Hussein, posed to the peace of the world. Powell had almost no credible evidence to present. The arguments he made were largely based on the reports of an Iraqi source, Rafid al-Janabi, who had a reputation as a habitual liar.[xxviii] In fact, his code name in the intelligence community was "Curveball." Imagine meeting a guy with this nickname.[13] If he weren't a pitcher or a spin bowler, how much faith would you put in anything he said?

---

[13] The nickname was wholly appropriate. In an interview with *The Guardian*, al-Janabi stated that he simply had lied: "I had the chance to fabricate something to topple the regime. I and my sons are proud of that." Reminded of the deaths he might have caused in the American war in Iraq, he simply stated that there was no other way to topple Saddam Hussein. "I did this and I am satisfied because there is no dictator in Iraq anymore." For Curveball, apparently, the ends justified the means.

Diplomat speak is sometimes hard to decipher, but in this case, the meaning was clear. This guy could not be trusted. The "hard" evidence he presented was anything but definitive. Powell was constantly forced to interpret satellite photographs, which he admitted even he could not decipher.

> The photos that I am about to show you are sometimes hard for the average person to interpret, hard for me. The painstaking work of photo analysis takes experts with years and years of experience, pouring for hours and hours over light tables. But as I show you these images, I will try to capture and explain what they mean, what they indicate to our imagery specialists.

The statement he made near the beginning of his speech revealed that Powell knew he had to make the subjective objective, but try as he might, he was unable to do so with the available evidence.

> My colleagues, every statement I make today is backed up by sources, solid sources. These are not assertions. What we're giving you are facts and conclusions based on solid intelligence. I will cite some examples, and these are from human sources.

Almost all Powell's assertions were interpretative, attempts to make others see what he saw, but he had nothing solid, nothing so obvious that even a person who was not on his side would be forced to acknowledge as conclusive. He needed a smoking gun, and all he had was a work of fiction created by a man no one in the chamber remotely trusted. Contrast Powell's speech with that of Stevenson's and you can see why one carried the day and the other, forty years later, failed.

We can draw three important conclusions from the examples presented:

First, it seems almost self-evident that people are difficult to persuade when they view the topic under consideration as involving opinions, or subjective preferences. Second, it seems reasonable to assume that the minority is likely to have an even more difficult time than the majority when dealing with people's subjective preferences. Finally, we note the surprising possibility that minority status might not prove a hindrance when the issue has (or is believed to have) an objectively correct solution.

This does not mean that the minority can influence the majority only when dealing with objective issues, but rather that the outsider group should always try to frame its persuasive arguments, if possible, as involving objective facts. The minority is most likely to succeed in persuading the majority by stressing the objective features of the issue under consideration, and is especially likely to succeed if the issue is not near and dear to the hearts of majority group members, or is one on which the majority has little knowledge or experience. Conversely, when combating an insistent minority group, the majority is likely to recast the issue as involving subjective preferences rather than objectively verifiable facts. If it can succeed, there is little reason to listen to the outsiders, as the issue under consideration then becomes a matter of preference, and who says their preferences are any better than ours?

Interesting social psychological research supports these deductions, and supplies some insights into why the subjective or objective nature of the judgment has such a huge effect in determining people's susceptibility to influence. In a study that a colleague and I performed not too long ago, we asked university students to assume the role of admissions officers at their university. "Charlie

Hewitt" had applied for admission to the university. The subjects were to read Charlie's file. Their job was to decide on their own whether to accept or reject his application for admission.[xxix]

Half the students were told that theirs was an objective task, and that they had all the information needed to make an informed, dispassionate judgment, and they were to use only the information provided in coming to an objective decision. They were told they had all the information the typical admissions officer had when deciding the fate of an applicant.

The other students were told that they couldn't possibly be supplied with all the information a typical admissions officer had available, and so they were not expected to form an objective judgment. Rather, the judgment they were to make was fundamentally subjective. They had to fall back on their subjective feelings and beliefs to judge Charlie's admissibility to their university.

In fact, all the research subjects received the identical materials, irrespective of the objective or subjective instructions we provided them. These materials included the applicant's grade point average and Scholastic Aptitude Test scores, a letter of recommendation from one of Charlie's high school teachers, Charlie's personal statement, and his reports of job and leisure time activities. Almost all good universities require this kind of information when deciding whether or not to admit a student to their incoming class. The information was written in such a way that the admissions decision was not easy or clear-cut. Charlie was on the bubble, in the borderland between acceptance and rejection.

After reading the dossier and making their judgments regarding the applicant's admissibility, participants in both the subjective and the objective judgment groups wrote short paragraphs detailing the reasons for their decision. After they finished writing their decision rationales, they were told, "In the usual circumstances, such decisions are rarely based on one person's verdict. Instead, they usually involve a discussion among a committee of admissions officers." The researcher continued, "The experiment doesn't allow for a full-blown discussion—that would take too much time and resources. However, to help you approximate the real admissions decision context, you will be given the opportunity to read the decision rationale of *one* other officer's judgment—if you wish to do so."

Everyone did.

The other officers' decision rationales were in manila envelopes, which were labeled ADMIT or REJECT. In this way, subjects knew that some judges' decisions were consistent with theirs, while others had formed judgments opposite to theirs. The subjects could read either one or the other. Which did they choose? Did the way the judgment was characterized—as involving subjective preferences or objective assessments—affect their choice of the paragraph they wished to review? There is no question that it did.

As shown here, the results of the study clearly demonstrated that the way the judgment was framed had a powerful effect on subjects' preferences to read

Subjects were told the judgment was:	Subjects' choices of others' decision rationales:	
	Similar	Different
Objective	8	35
Subjective	32	12

one or another admissions officer's views. Thirty-five of forty-three subjects who thought the task involved objective judgments opted to see the paragraph written by an admissions officer who held an opinion *different* from theirs. The opposite was true for the subjects who thought their decisions involved a subjective judgment. Of the forty-four subjects who thought the task was subjective, thirty-two wanted to see the judgments of admissions officers that were *similar* to theirs.

Why?

We reasoned that participants assumed that their subjective judgments could not be proved right or wrong—these judgments involved preferences, not facts, and could not be confirmed one way or the other. Some judges might weigh the student's GPA more strongly than work experience, others might do just the opposite, and both could argue that theirs was the better decision rule. In this circumstance there's little reason to believe that the conflicting judgment of another person would prove particularly informative or useful. Another person's subjective opinion may be different from ours, but it is based on personal preferences, just as ours is. Why should their preferences be any better than our own? This reasoning led the subjects to assume that conflicting information could be ignored safely. If the judgment involves subjective preferences, my opinion is as good as yours. On the other hand, confirmatory judgments of those who share our subjective preferences are reinforcing, they bolster our opinions, and so we expected that they would be sought out by most of those who believed the task involved subjective estimates—and that is precisely what happened.

The game changes when we deal with objective issues, however. On objective judgments, there is a commonly agreed upon, verifiable answer—this is a definitional requirement of the word *objective*. We might not know whether the capital city of the United Arab Emirates is Abu Dhabi or Dubayy, but we know that our choice of one or the other can be proved definitively as correct or incorrect. The judgment, in other words, can be verified, just as Adlai Stevenson verified the presence of Soviet missiles in Cuba.

If someone disagrees with us on a difficult judgment that involves an objectively verifiable answer, and if we are not completely confident that we are correct, then it pays to see what they have to say. Learning about the rationale of a person who agrees with us on an objective judgment is not nearly so informative. So in these objective judgment circumstances, we bite the bullet and listen to those who hold positions at odds with ours.

How does this apply to the study we've reviewed? Remember that in our research we structured the applicant's dossier so that the correct decision was not readily apparent. The students probably were uncertain of the soundness of their decisions. They had never decided a college applicant's fate, and the information made available to them was designed to be ambiguous. For these reasons, when the judgment was cast as objective, they sought out others who shared opinions different from theirs, to check on their own reasoning, and learn if they had perhaps missed anything when dealing with the question of Charlie's qualifications.

In planning this study, we predicted the subjects in the "objective judgment" part of the study would be prone to seek the information from people who were different from themselves, on the assumption that these "outsiders" might not share their own biases and shortcomings, and so might be able to produce a better solution to the problem than they themselves could. And this is precisely what happened—but only among the judges who thought their task involved objective judgments. In this circumstance, they were much more likely to opt for opinions that were contrary to theirs.

When the decision was cast as being subjective, the opposite preference was evident. Here, the subjects did not see much point in reading a position that disagreed with theirs. As the judgment was subjective, opponents were entitled to their opinions. But they were just that—opinions—and not any more valuable than one's own. In this case it made sense for them to read the opinions of other, like-minded admissions officers.

When the Minority Has the Advantage

Thinking back, you might realize that most of the examples of minority influence we've considered to this point have involved judgments that appear to have entailed objective answers or positions. We think that everyone sees the blue shirt we're wearing as blue and that grass is green—on *both* sides of the fence. Often, however, we must deal with subjective judgments. Furthermore, in almost all of the examples considered so far, members of the majority had already developed an attitude or a position on the issue in question, and as we know, the majority almost always had the upper hand in terms of number, status, or power. It could pressure people to go along with its decisions, and as we have seen, the minority had to conform to a strict set of rules if it hoped to overcome the majority's advantage. However, in some circumstances, the issue under consideration is one on which members of the majority have not formed a strong opinion. In those cases, the minority might actually hold a slight persuasive edge. Your telling most Americans that Canada's best curling rinks are to be found in Thunder Bay, Ontario, would be an easy sell, especially if you're a Canadian. This is a special case—it requires that the majority not have a dog in the race, perhaps not even to know that there is a race. In these rare circumstances, the majority is susceptible to minority influence.

Let's consider a study that met the requirements that the majority had not formed a strong opinion on an issue, and had no skin in the game.[xxx] This study was set up in such a way that it apparently involved a test of knowledge. We presented subjects with a series of really obscure questions, like the ones in the following examples:

An average of 50 ships entered or left New York harbor daily during the period from 1950 through 1955. What do you think was the largeast number of ships to enter or leave New York in a single day during this period?

1	2	3	4	5	6	7	8	9
	76 ships			115 ships			153 ships	

and

Weather officials report that during this century Washington, D.C., has received an average rainfall of 41.1 inches annually. What do you think is the largest amount of rain that Washington has received in a single year during this century?

1	2	3	4	5	6	7	8	9
	51.2 inches			66.8 inches			82.4 inches	

Obviously, there *are* objectively verifiable answers to these questions, but almost nobody on earth knows what they are. These facts played into our research plans. They allowed us to tell some subjects that the questions we were going to ask them were so esoteric that they would have to rely on their subjective feelings to answer them—take a guess, based on how you feel about it. In other words the judgment was essentially subjective—they couldn't rely on objective knowledge, because the information required of them was so esoteric that almost no one had the requisite knowledge base to answer the questions with any degree of confidence.

Following our earlier study, as you might have guessed, other subjects were told that there *was* an objective answer to every question that was posed, and their job was to figure it out. Strictly speaking, this was true, there was an objectively correct answer to every question, but the instructions counseling subjectivity made sense as well. The focus of the research concerned subjects' susceptibility to a person from the minority when they thought that the judgment task involved subjective versus objective estimates. Would a minority influence source be more effective under one or the other experimental condition? Would subjects reject the minority's influence under all conditions? Or was the minority advantaged only when the majority had taken no position on the issue and the obscure issue involved an objectively verifiable answer?

To answer these questions, the experiment was set up so that subjects were told that they had been paired with a partner who was in another room. Actually, the partner was a computer, programmed to make responses that usually were slightly higher, if possible, than the one the subject gave.[14] Half the subjects thought they were paired with someone who was in the minority of their in-group. The others believed they were paired with a respondent from their group's majority.

In the study, subject and "partner" answered a set of twenty obscure questions of the kind given in the examples, and communicated their responses via computer. Subjects could see the judgments of their partner on their computer monitors, and presumably, the subjects' partners could see theirs as well. The specific aims of the study were

- to see if the constant upward judgment pressure exerted by the computer would gradually influence subjects to make higher and higher judgments over the course of the twenty judgments required of them,

---

[14] Sometimes, the subject chose the highest choice possible, the extreme point on the scale. In that case, the computer matched the subject's choice. In all other cases, the computer's "estimate" was one to two points higher than the subject's. It never made estimates that were lower than the subject's.

- to learn whether the majority or minority status of the subject's partner made a difference, and

- to determine if the apparent objective or subjective nature of the judgment task affected judgments of the subjects paired with a minority (or majority) group response partner.

As we expected, given the obscurity of the questions, the subjects' computerized partner had a strong effect on their judgments, gradually pushing them higher and higher over the course of the twenty judgment trials—but it mattered how the partner had been portrayed. When described as an in-group minority, the partner was *more* influential than a majority group partner, but only when the judgment was cast as objective. As the questions were nearly impossible to answer with any degree of confidence, this result suggests that we are quite susceptible to minority influence on issues that we perceive as involving an objective answer or solution that we know little about, and that does not involve our self-interest or established beliefs.

But why were the in-group minority partner's judgments even more influential than those of the partner who allegedly belonged to the majority? We had reasoned that by virtue of their relative rarity, minority group members may draw our focus or attention even more than would members of our majority group. We are curious about minorities. We wonder about the opinions they express. They're noticeable, we listen to what they have to say, and when dealing with objective issues on which we don't have a strong position, we don't have much reason to resist their ideas. An old cowboy with long whiskers and scarred leather chaps probably does not fit into most readers' in-group. However, if he were to describe the best way to trap an armadillo, you probably would listen and accept his story. There's nothing to promote rejection of his view. The topic is not particularly relevant to you, you've probably never even thought about trapping armadillos, and he apparently has nothing to gain from your buying his story. Our results suggest that people may be more susceptible to in-group minorities than members of their own majority when they believe the issue is objectively verifiable and they, themselves, are uncertain of the verifiably correct answer.

It is important to understand that this result was found *only* when the subjects thought the obscure judgments admitted to an objective answer. The game changed completely when they believed their judgments involved subjective preferences. In this circumstance they were immune to their minority partner's influence—but they were strongly influenced by partners who allegedly came from the majority.

How would all this play out in the world outside the laboratory? Suppose you're complaining to the service attendant at your gas station about the high gasoline prices. A person with a big Green Party badge overhears your complaint and cuts in on your conversation. She describes the Acme Surefire Vapor Injector, a device that spews water and alcohol vapor into your car's cylinders when it's running. She tells you that it will cut your gasoline bill in half. You're not a member of the Green Party, but you don't have anything against the group—in fact, you think they might be doing some good for the environment although you realize that they're clearly a minority voice in the United States.

How would you respond to this pitch? She's not trying the sell anything, so there's no strong reason to question her motives. And she says she has the Surefire Injector on her own car. She seems to know a lot about gas mileage—and you know next to nothing about how cars work.

The research we just reviewed suggests that you'd probably believe her, assuming you know little to nothing about cars, and were bothered by high gas prices. Why resist good advice from a person who seems to be an expert, even if the expert doesn't share your political philosophy? Whether you would ultimately buy the product is another question, but you would be positively inclined to do so on the basis of your interaction.

If, however, our helpful intruder admitted to some subjectivity, if she stated that she used the vapor injector and *thought* it had improved her mileage, or that her husband owned the patent on the Acme Surefire Vapor Injector, the likelihood of your looking into the device would drop dramatically. Judgments involving subjective estimates are highly resistant to a minority group's persuasive pitches, and this is especially true when the issue is important to the majority group member. The take-home from this example should be clear. When attempting to influence others, even when you are not a part of their in-group, it is useful to frame the issue under consideration as involving an objective solution, and also to show to the extent possible that your position is not based on self-interest. Avoid qualifications. "This injector really works" is more effective than "I think the injector may help improve gas mileage." These conditions enhance the persuasive power of the appeal, along with the likelihood that your audience will adopt your recommendation.

Gender Equality in the Workplace

The studies we've considered to this point all imply that members of minority groups should try to skew their characterization of issues so that their solution appears to be based on objectively verifiable evidence, and this is precisely what *successful* minorities do. Most minority groups do not consider the subjective or objective character of the issues they are debating with the majority, and most fail accordingly. Consider, for example, arguments for gender equality that have been a part of the political landscape of the United States at least since the suffragette movement of the late 1890s. Often, proponents will go on and on about the unfairness of discrimination against women, and they're right. But this argument usually doesn't change anyone's attitudes or behaviors. The research we've just considered suggests that a more effective approach would focus on objective factors. For example, we could point out the differences in pay afforded men and women performing the same job. The National Organization for Women quotes statistics showing that women earn approximately seventy-eight cents for every dollar a male earns in the same job, and males earn more than women even in female-dominated professions. These statistics are objective, irrefutable facts produced by a disinterested Government Accountability Office, which has no political ax to grind.

Bringing the hard facts of pay inequality to the discussion of gender equality can transform the discussion of women's rights into an objective issue. The pay differential is not a matter of opinion or conjecture; it is a fact backed by powerful objective data. In addition to claiming membership in the majority group (remember Rule 1)—we're all American workers, we're your mothers, your wives, your daughters—the movement uses the objective pay difference to maneuver the argument for equality of treatment on the job onto objective territory, because it's here that the minority stands the greatest chance of prevailing. The rejoinder to the objective argument attempts to move the argument back into subjective territory: "Yes, but women are not dependable—they are too worried about the family or the kids," or "Right, but they can't meet the physical demands of the job," and so on.

The individual most skilled in moving the argument from subjective to objective, or vice versa, depending on the sought-after outcome, wins this influence game. Everything depends on the way the issue is presented. The mechanics of the persuasive approach assume critical importance in determining the success or failure of any attempts at persuasion. Remember, the research showed that the minority was most successful when the issue was presented as involving objective judgments, the majority had not established a strong position, did not know much about the issue, and did not stand to lose by acceding to the minority's demands.

Obviously, when arguing for gender equality in the workplace, meeting the requirements is difficult, especially when the entrenched group may feel that it could be disadvantaged by yielding to women's demands. The pay-equality position can prevail even in circumstances such as these, but as history has shown, the process is neither simple nor short term. With consistency and insistence, the minority can ultimately prevail in this contest.

Despite the law and the sensible position that people who do the same job should be paid the same for good performance, the battle for sexual equality in the workplace is far from won. The Equal Pay Act of 1963 made it illegal to pay men and women differently for the same job, and the Supreme Court has upheld the law, arguing that if jobs are substantially equal, even if not identical, the pay must be the same. The effect of the law has been felt, but inequities still are obvious. Women are paid approximately only about three quarters of the wage given a man for comparable work. This suggests that practice sometimes trumps the law. Those who seek pay equality, the minority in this case, must follow the rules of influence if they are to succeed. They must establish that they are a legitimate part of the larger group, in this case, the American workforce. They must fight to keep the issue on a factual, objective level. Subjective interpretations of women's relative strength, their capacity for heavy work, their devotion to children and family, which critics argue may detract from their commitment to the workforce, and other subjective judgments weaken the argument for equality. The battle should be fought on objective grounds. Having established in-group status and the objective nature of the argument, all the proponents of the "equal pay for equal work" minority must persist, remain consistent, and refuse to backtrack. Following these rules, and others that are presented in the pages that follow, will help ensure a positive outcome. Ultimately, this minority will prevail.

SEVEN

Things Are Not Always as They Seem

Leniency, Change, and the Indirect Nature of Minority Influence

Truth always originates in a minority of one,
and every custom begins as a broken precedent.
—*Will Durant*

WELCOME TO THE EXPERIMENT!

The following questions require you to estimate the likelihood that you would change your attitude on an issue, assuming that you changed your attitude on an earlier issue. Think about your feelings regarding the various issues presented in the questions below, and then estimate the probability that your having changed your mind on one topic would affect your attitudes on the other:

If you changed your mind regarding your position on SOCIALIZED MEDICINE, what is the probability that you also would change your position on CONTRACEPTION?

Probability (can range from 0 to 100%) _____

If you changed your mind regarding your position on ABORTION, what is the probability that you also would change your position on CONTRACEPTION?

Probability (can range from 0 to 100%) _____

If you changed your mind regarding your position on GAYS IN THE MILITARY, what is the probability that you also would change your position on GUN CONTROL?

Probability (can range from 0 to 100%) _____

If you changed your mind regarding your position on GUN CONTROL, what is the probability that you also would change your position on CONTRACEPTION?

Probability (can range from 0 to 100%) _____

If you changed your mind regarding your position on SOCIALIZED MEDICINE, what is the probability that you would also change your position on GAYS IN THE MILITARY?

Probability (can range from 0 to 100%) _____

Thank you for your participation. We will return to these answers later in the chapter.

Super Tuesday

February 5, 2008, Super Tuesday, a momentous day in American politics. The day on which twenty-four states held primaries or caucuses that would decide the Republican and Democratic standard bearers, their party's nominee for the president of the United States. By the end of this day, 52 percent of all pledged Democratic, and 41 percent of all pledged Republican Party delegates would be chosen. This was a day of high tension and even higher hopes. Major losses by any of the candidates, and there would be some, would sound the death knell of their campaigns.

For the Republican front-runner, the outcome was not terribly stressful. John McCain held a comfortable lead in his race for the nomination, so all he had to do was avoid a major upset, which he succeeded in doing. McCain's comfort level was decidedly not shared by the contending Democrats, Barack Obama and Hillary Clinton. Just as the primary campaign had been muddled from the very start, so, too, was the outcome of Super Tuesday. Senator Hillary Clinton claimed twelve states and a total delegate count of 834 to Barack Obama's thirteen states and 847 delegates. Both remained in contention for their party's nomination, though the smart money was beginning to run in Obama's direction, as he looked stronger in the remaining states and had loads more money to spend on his campaign. In his public response to the results, Obama tried to put the best face on what was, practically speaking, a dead heat when he stated, "Our time has come, our movement is real, and change is coming to America. . . . We are the change that we seek."

As usual, Obama took no personal credit for his capture of thirteen states—the victory was "ours," the movement was "ours," and the time that had come was "ours." He understood the First Rule. The feature of this speech that is particularly relevant for present purposes, however, was his emphasis on *change,* a word that resounded throughout his campaign from its very first days. Change was a watchword that referred not just to a replacement of the political party in power, but of a fundamental transformation of the political process in the American democracy. This was the promise. But the change processes used by a minority—be it a minority candidate for the presidency of the United States or the lone holdout in a partners' meeting of a major law firm (an opinion minority)—are different from the processes used by a majority to induce change. From the very beginning of the Obama campaign, the people running the show, including its leader, implicitly understood what was needed to secure the nomination for their minority candidate. He had to connect and become one with the mass electorate, had to stay on message, had to be flexible, and so on. In short, he had to follow the rules of influence described here. He did, and he won.

However, neither Obama nor his advisers switched persuasive gears once they had attained power. They did not understand that the processes by which the minority created change were not optimal once it had wrested power and, essentially, had morphed into the majority. Understanding the use of majority power after shifting from minority to majority eluded even this group of astute political operatives.

When they assumed power, the former minority attempted to use the same techniques of (minority) influence to move their agenda, even though they were no longer in a weak position, and even though the opposing team, which included almost all elected Republicans, pretended and acted as if they still were running the show. The use of minority tactics in a group that had carried both Houses of Congress was a strategic error of major proportion, and was to prove their undoing. It cost them the electoral advantages they gained and allowed the loyal opposition to stall their agenda immeasurably. Their understanding of the differences between minority and majority influence tactics was wholly deficient, and because of this, they forfeit the enormous gains they had made in their historic campaign. They maintained their minority influence strategies even though they were the new majority. By continuing with these minority-based strategies, the new leadership surrendered without a fight the massive advantages of their new (majority) status. Their failure to adjust was to cost them dearly. A campaign based on change was remarkably resistant to changing its own successful tactics of influence, even though its circumstances had changed immensely. *What they failed to realize is that although the majority can force the minority to submit, the minority is fundamentally incapable of directly changing the majority.* Keeping with the strategies of the outsider, they gave up the implicit threat of brute force, which the majority can use to its advantage.

Indirect Change

As this book is about the ways in which the minority can influence the majority, these observations perhaps require a bit of explanation, for if the minority cannot change the majority, then reading this far may represent a large waste of time for you. *Directly* is the critical word in the statement that minorities are "fundamentally incapable of directly changing the majority." Obviously minorities *can* change the majority. Examples salted through every chapter of this book have amply demonstrated that minorities sometimes can bring the majority to their way of thinking, though they fail to do so more often than not, because they do not understand the rules of influence. However, the processes by which the minority induces the majority to change are exceedingly different from the ones the majority uses to impose its will on the minority. When the majority seeks to change things, it can use brute force if it chooses to do so. Sometimes the majority will appeal rationally for change, it will advance strong and persuasive arguments to bolster its position, but force always remains a tactic of last (and sometimes, first) resort for the majority. The weaker group does not have access to this possibility, and if it attempts force, it usually suffers terribly for its miscalculation. Native Americans, the Black Panthers, the Tamil Tigers, the Red Brigades, the Baader-Meinhof Red Army Faction, the Ku Klux Klan, Spartacus—history is littered with the debris of weaker groups and their leaders who attempted to overcome the majority by force. They failed. If it is to make its way, the minority must persuade. In the long run, force is never a viable option for the weaker group.

However, even when it does persuade the majority, minority-induced change inevitably is indirect, and direct (or focal) change, if it comes, never comes immediately.

The majority sometimes, perhaps often, changes in the direction of the minority's appeal, but it almost never changes directly, and it never changes straightaway. Minority influence is fundamentally indirect. On issues that matter to the majority, the minority almost never exerts direct influence. Rather, the weaker group's influence is seen in changes on issues related to the central focus of their appeal. Although Dad might be unwilling to grant Junior's request to use the car on Saturday night, he might be more lenient and adjust the usual curfew. Junior's appeal has not succeeded directly (he's riding the bus), but indirectly it has induced a change related to the car's usage. The majority often will concede points that are *related* to the minority's petition or demand, but it does not give in to the minority directly. It rarely grants the minority everything it wants, and never as soon as it wants it. The minority's initial successes are counted in terms of indirect or partial gains, and this gives rise to the seventh rule of influence.

Rule 7. Do Not Expect Direct Focal Influence, but Be Attuned to Indirect Influence

What, then, explains the minority's victories, many of which have been chronicled here? Successes have occurred because the in-group minority has followed all the earlier rules, including persistence, consistency, unanimity, and flexibility of message, and casting the issue in objective rather than subjective terms. The changes on issues that matter, however, do not occur immediately, but after some time has passed. The route to minority influence is not straightforward or direct. It almost always comes about after the minority has induced changes on issues related, but not identical, to the focus of their appeal. Sufficient indirect change on a related issue can strain the majority's capacity to maintain its resistance on the position the minority initially attacked. The majority's moving on a position that is related, but not identical, to the thrust of the minority's appeal (let's call it the focal issue) can make it difficult to preserve its original position.

The process by which this occurs is fascinating, and strange as it may seem, lots of research has confirmed that minority group influence begins with changes that appear, at best, only peripherally related to the central focus of their persuasive argument. For example, a small group of parents may argue that the dress code in their children's elementary school should be revoked. The school authorities and most of the parents may balk at this request, but may allow a loosening of the rules in other areas, which would not have been permitted before the dissident parents raised the dress code issue. The complaining parents did not prevail in this instance, but neither did they lose. The indirect change process described here represents only the first stage of the process of successful influence, but if the minority cannot get past the first stage of inducing indirect change, it has no chance of winning on the issue at the heart of its dispute. However, it has a chance if it persists. Indirect influence is an indispensable prelude to full-fledged direct influence.

The indirect change process sometimes is extremely indirect, and because they appear to have little to do with the original request, the changes induced by the minority may be difficult to track. Returning to our school dress code issue, the majority may prove completely resistant to the call to revoke the code, but it may loosen the rules in the school cafeteria, allowing more choices in food and beverages and less constraint on students' lunchtime behavior. These indirect changes are remote—after all, what do school uniforms have to do with a greater variety of Pringles in the cafeteria? They often are difficult to spot, but if the minority is attuned to them, it may be able to bring even greater pressure on the position that was the original source of discontent—in this case, the dress code.

Because they often are so remote from the contentious issue, proving the linkage between minority pressure and indirect change is difficult in uncontrolled situations. However, research in the controlled confines of the research laboratory leaves little doubt, and we will get to that in short order.

Indirect Change: Automatic or Calculated?

Remote changes in response to an in-group minority's pressure have led researchers to question whether the majority yields on indirect issues to placate the minority, or if indirect change is a more or less automatic feature of minority influence. If the majority's accommodations do not appear related to the minority's demands, it would not seem that they were made for the calculated purpose of deliberately cooling off the strident minority. The headmaster in our dress code dispute is not likely to think, *If I allow pizza in the school cafeteria, maybe these bothersome dress coders will go away.* The issues are so unrelated that even Machiavelli probably would not consider using one concession to forestall another. If indirect change is not a calculated method to defuse a group of strident dissidents, then it may be an automatic feature of the interaction of contending groups. In other words, the ruling party's members might not even be aware of the link between dissidents' demands and their own (indirectly) accommodating responses. This possibility suggests that if minority group members are aware of this process, they may be able to use it to further their ambitions. In the case of our school uniform example, if parents realize that the administration has moved on their complaint by giving ground on lunchroom choices, they would be well advised to push for even more concessions—in the lunchroom! With sufficient change, their agenda on school uniforms will be facilitated. This may seem a stretch, but suspend disbelief for the moment. Some research findings will reward your open-minded patience.

Sometimes, the majority will compromise by giving the minority some, but not all, of what its members demand. In these situations, recognizing and gauging the extent of the majority's gesture is not difficult. When this happens, the minority's job is to expand the gap between the old status quo and the new one represented by the change. Ultimately, the greater the indirect or partial change, the more likely is the majority to accede to the original appeal. So the answer to the question, "Can minorities induce the majority to change?" depends on what is meant by change. Can the minority induce direct change? Can it cause the majority to respond more or less straightaway to its petition? Rarely, if ever. Can the minority ultimately induce the majority to give in to its appeals? Yes, but it does so by first inducing change on issues that are related, sometimes closely, sometimes remotely, to their original complaint. These concessions can destabilize the focal belief and open the door to delayed change on the originally contested issue.

The Swiss Connection

One of the first studies to describe this strange indirect change process was reported by two social psychologists from the University of Geneva, who remain among the leading researchers on social influence. In their classic study, conducted in the mid-1980s, they assembled a group of female high school students in Spain. It is important to understand that at this time abortion was illegal in Spain, and the students held quite negative attitudes toward its legalization.[15] The researchers learned of their subjects' attitudes in a pretest they completed immediately before reading a strongly persuasive message that argued *in favor* of legalizing abortion in Spain. The persuasive message contended that all forms of abortion should be legalized, and that it was essential that the law be changed to make abortion legal upon request. The procedure was to be completely free, its costs borne by the state. The statement was strong, unequivocal, and unyielding. In the authors' words, "The style of the text . . . emphasized the necessity of all demands, [and] served to make the text as conflictual as possible."

The same communication was delivered to all students, but it was attributed to message sources that differed in terms of their group status. For half the subjects, the message was attributed to an in-group minority, young high school women like themselves. For the remaining subjects, it was attributed to an out-group minority, young high school men. In both cases, the students were told at the end of the message that the majority of high school women (or men, depending on the source of their message) was completely opposed to the pro-abortion communication they had read.

The results of this study may prove surprising to you, or if not surprising, at least odd. Analysis indicated that the students were unaffected by the pro-abortion message. Whether the source was attributed to an in-group or out-group did not matter. The experiment failed to show differences in students' responses to the pro-abortion message. Apparently, the message did not convince anyone.[xxxi]

For many researchers this would have spelled the end of the story. The conclusion—it failed, so let's get on to some other research—is the reaction we would expect from most investigators.

---

[15] On February 24, 2010, the Spanish Senate legalized abortion on demand at up to fourteen weeks' gestation, and longer in cases of fetal impairment or threat to the mother's life. These changes were made years after this study was conducted.

However, these researchers (Juan Antonio Pérez and Gabriel Mugny) are known for their tenacity as well as their brilliance, and they did not stop with the obvious. As part of their study, in addition to measuring the students' attitudes toward abortion, they also had measured their attitudes toward contraception, and on this measure they found major differences between the two groups. Remember, both groups had read the identical message. The researchers discovered that the students who read the strongly argued pro-abortion message became significantly more favorable toward *contraception,* if it was attributed to the in-group minority (fellow high school women). The students who read the *identical* message showed no change in abortion or contraception attitudes when it was attributed to the out-group minority (high school men).

Fine, one might argue, the in-group minority had an effect. Anyone who has read this far knows that in-group minorities can be effective persuaders, and in this case, they were. The effect was indirect, and this result, though unexpected, is perhaps understandable. After all, both abortion and contraception have to do with reproduction, so a message concerned with abortion might well affect attitudes toward contraception. And we can assume that the Spanish high school women in the mid-1980s would resist this communication.

On the surface, this explanation may seem reasonable, but for two facts: First, the word *contraception* was never even mentioned in the persuasive message presented to the subjects, so why did they become more liberal about contraception (which, incidentally, also is banned by the Catholic Church, which may have been one of the reasons the young women rejected abortion, as most undoubtedly were Church members)? Second, although abortion and contraception clearly are associated, there is no theory of persuasion that would lead us to predict this strange pattern of attitude change. True, researchers sometimes see changes in associated beliefs. Change on one attitude (say, you become much more favorable toward a political candidate) often is accompanied by changes in others (you become more favorable toward his or her pet legislative initiatives). If you change your mind about gun control, for example, you might also change your mind about the NRA. However, the communication had *not* changed subjects' attitudes in the study—at least not on abortion, the (focal) issue that it was designed to influence.

If the experiment had changed students' attitudes toward abortion, a corresponding change in attitudes toward contraception would not have surprised anyone. But to obtain an indirect change on contraception without also seeing the direct change on abortion was highly surprising—at least to many researchers who had spent their professional lives studying the ways attitudes behave.

Despite this puzzling set of results, many researchers were willing to write off the finding, probably reasoning that because the two beliefs were so tightly linked, pressuring one might well have induced change in the other. *How* the indirect influence bled over from one attitude (which did not change) to the other (which did, even though it was not mentioned, not even once) was never explained satisfactorily, but not many lost too much sleep over this mystery.

Some did. To some researchers this unusual result seemed to hold the key to a much deeper understanding of how relatively powerless groups can successfully influence powerful ones. As time passed, researchers noticed that this unusual pattern of indirect change occurred with some frequency in research involving minority influence sources.

One consistent feature of this research was that the minority almost never succeeded immediately. However, this is not to say that the minority influence source always failed—in fact, minorities succeeded often, but they never succeeded right off the bat. Inevitably, their influence was delayed. Why did the minority stimulate such a weird response when it attempted to pressure the majority? How did it work?

The accepted theory was that the minority tickled the majority's curiosity bone. Majority group members confronted with an in-group minority's contrary ideas were thought to respond, "Why do they believe that?" To satisfy their curiosity, they attended to the minority's message. Suppose almost all the members of the quality assurance (QA) unit in your company believe that a particular process is sufficient to meet standards, but a small faction in the group finds it inadequate. You probably would want to know why. You would listen to what the minority had to say, and think about its position. Your motivation would be to understand why some of your fellow in-group colleagues hold beliefs that are markedly contrary to those of most of the others in the QA group. As you mulled over the minority's position, however, you were incidentally exposing yourself to the minority's arguments, and consequently might come to agree with their position. This is especially likely if their message was well reasoned and strongly stated. This mulling-over process takes time, however, and for this reason, theoretically, the minority's effect on the majority is delayed.

Of course, even if the majority group member is persuaded, it is dangerous to side with the minority—after all, even members of the in-group who hold unpopular positions can be targeted by the larger group. There may be lots of reasons why the quality assurance unit wants to stay with the standard operating procedures. Deviations from the majority's positions almost always result in the majority attempting to bring the deviant back to the fold, and if that does not succeed, sometimes more severe actions are brought online. Deviants can be harassed or ostracized or in our QA example, fired. Applied to the Swiss study, we can begin to understand why the students who were exposed to the in-group minority's arguments on abortion held firm on this attitude, but changed their position on the related issue of contraception. The pressure to change their attitudes on an unchangeable issue (abortion) spilled over to the related belief, contraception.

We also might expect that the young high school students in the Swiss experiment came to appreciate the in-group minority's courage in standing up to a potentially hostile majority. Admiration for the brave in-group minority might have colored some members' evaluation of this group, and we know that admired people are more influential than disliked ones. You may be persuaded by a person you dislike, but odds are, you will do your best not to be.

Earlier we considered the persuasiveness of an individual's speech delivered to a hostile audience. The research subjects liked this speaker more, and found his message more persuasive, than a person who delivered the identical speech to an audience that was thought to be largely in agreement with his message. The person delivering his speech to a hostile group was viewed as more courageous, more committed, and more willing to go stand up for his beliefs. This person was an underdog, and we admire those who are willing to argue for their positions.

Lots of other factors could help account for the strange but consistent pattern of minority-induced change, but none was supported unequivocally. No matter the explanation, the consistent research finding is that we do not immediately jump into bed with the minority, but sometimes its message does have a powerful effect, just not on the focus of their complaint. When direct change occurs (that is, change in direct response to the minority's appeal), it happens after a delay.

The Second Generation of Minority Influence Research

Delayed focal change was novel in research on persuasion, and stimulated considerable interest in North America and Europe. To be fair, I should tell you that these delayed effects were not a sure bet. In many studies the minority's influence was neither immediate nor delayed. It just wasn't. This complicated matters, but it made the study of minority influence almost irresistible to some of us.

Understanding the strange pattern of attitude and behavior change caused by an outside group's influence attempts seemed imperative if we were to grasp a phenomenon of true importance—a weaker group's capacity to persuade a stronger group. The questions that were addressed in this "second generation" of research were many, interesting, and related to the unusual pattern of results that had been uncovered in the first generation:

- Why were direct minority effects almost always delayed?

- Why did the minority sometimes fail entirely to influence the majority?

- When the minority did affect the majority, why were its effects seen on beliefs that were related to the central core of their argument, but never the focus of the argument itself?

- Was this "indirect" change really a result of the majority's accommodating them, making the minority group members feel loved and appreciated by conceding on issues they did not care about?

- Would indirect changes occur on issues that no one in the majority thought were related to the focal issue of the minority's complaint? In other words, could indirect changes occur even if majority group members did not consciously attempt to use them to defuse the minority?

These last questions were critical. If we are to understand minority influence, it seemed crucial to know if the indirect influence effect seen in the Swiss research on abortion and contraception was the result of the majority throwing some crumbs to the minority to pacify them, or whether this process occurred beneath the majority group members' conscious awareness. Did the young women who rejected the in-group minority's pro-abortion appeal try to ease the apparent rejection by conceding on contraception? Or was the change to a more liberal position on contraception an automatic, unthinking reaction to the in-group minority's appeal on abortion reform? Answering this question seemed to my colleague and me to be a key to unlocking the mystery of minority influence, and we mounted a concerted effort to come to grips with it.

Two Experiments

To study indirect influence, and to determine whether it was the result of the majority group's conscious attempt to appease the minority, or an unintended and largely automatic process, we needed to identify two attitudes that were strongly related, but whose strong connection was not immediately obvious even to the people who held the attitudes. We needed to identify such issues because we theorized that the indirect changes that minorities sometimes induced might be the result of a strong link between two beliefs, combined with the research subjects' resistance to giving in to the minority. For example, in the abortion-contraception study of Pérez and Mugny, the changes in subjects' attitudes toward contraception might have occurred through a process in which they were somewhat persuaded by the in-group minority's pro-abortion communication, but they resisted showing any change on this explosive attitude. To move to a favorable position on abortion would place them in an extremely uncomfortable position with their teachers, parents, and friends. Changing on the less inflammatory issue of contraception might have been their way of appeasing the minority without changing on the more dangerous issue of abortion.

The Swiss study, however, did not address the question of the majority's conscious awareness of this pacification process. Were the high school students in the majority group so calculating that they sought to mollify the young women in the minority by throwing them a bone, by changing on one issue to short-circuit the need to change on the other? Certainly this is possible, but so is the alternative, that indirect changes occurred below the majority group members' conscious awareness. This possibility not only appeared plausible, but was considerably more intriguing than the first, and clearly worth investigating.

To study this question, we needed to find two issues that were strongly related, but of whose relationship people were largely unaware. We completed a series of preliminary studies that asked subjects to express their attitudes on a variety of issues of contemporary interest, including, among others, abortion, contraception, gays in the military, euthanasia, gun control, and university tuition. Then we calculated the statistical associations between these issues. In the last of our preliminary studies, we had four hundred University of Arizona students complete a set of attitude measures on eleven issues of contemporary interest.

Some of these issues were included in the survey you encountered at the beginning of the chapter. Responses were analyzed to determine the strength of the association between subjects' attitudes on the various issues. We expected that people's attitudes toward some issues would be strongly related to their attitudes toward others. For example, it seemed likely that people who thought abortion was a terrible thing also would have a negative attitude toward contraception, and vice versa, as the Swiss research suggested. This intuition was confirmed by the data, as many might have guessed.[16]

Given this strong relation, we expected that the subjects would report that if they changed their attitudes on one of these policies, they would predict that they probably would change their beliefs on the other. This result, too, was found in the case of abortion and contraception. The Arizona students reported a 36 percent probability that they would change their attitudes on contraception if they had changed their attitudes toward abortion. (You might want to check your own estimate on the second item of the small survey conducted at the beginning of the chapter.) This pattern is perfectly sensible. It suggests that the subjects believed that their beliefs about abortion and contraception were associated, and if they were to change their attitude on one of them, their attitude on the other probably would follow suit.

These results were reasonable and lent confidence that our measures were appropriate, but they did not serve our main purpose, which was to identify two strongly associated attitudes of whose relation the subjects themselves were unaware. In this study we found what we were looking for, because the strongest statistical association between any pair of attitudes involved the relationship between gays in the military and gun control. Subjects who did not like the idea of gays in the military also disliked the idea of gun control, whereas subjects who favored the idea of

---

[16] We also found that euthanasia was associated in our subjects' minds with abortion and, to a lesser extent, contraception.

gays in the military favored gun control. We could speculate about why this association emerged, but that was not the point of the study. We needed to identify two attitudes that were related unexpectedly, and we did. In doing this, we analyzed students' estimates of the likelihood they would change their attitudes on gun control if they had changed their attitudes on gays in the military. This was the same question you encountered on the third item of the survey that opened the chapter. When they were asked about the likelihood of their changing their attitude toward gun control if they had changed their attitude toward gays in the military, the average estimate across all the students was only 11 percent. Despite the analysis that showed a strong association between these issues, the students themselves indicated they did not realize that the attitudes were associated. We knew they were.

This was the information we needed to test the competing explanations of the indirect minority influence effect that was commonly found in this research. To capitalize on the finding, we gathered a new group of 225 University of Arizona students to serve in our study. The question we investigated was unusual, but it flowed directly from the results we had uncovered: "If an ingroup minority attempts to persuade majority group members to change their attitudes on gays in the military, knowing what we know from our earlier study, will they reject the attempt, but change their beliefs about gun control?" You're right, it's an awfully strange question, but given our discussion to this point, you should understand why we asked it.

This study was designed to allow us to determine if indirect attitude change was a deliberate tactic used by the majority to placate the minority, or whether it occurred automatically, below the subject's conscious awareness. If the indirect change effects sometimes found in research on minority influence were the result of conscious (perhaps even cynical) attempts on the majority's part to pacify the minority, we would not expect the majority to try to placate the minority arguing for a ban on gays in the military by apparently changing their views on gun control. If subjects were only dimly aware of the linkage of their attitudes on these issues, a change of this sort would not be considered useful. However, if the majority's indirect change was an automatic response, then given the strong association of the two attitudes, the majority group subjects *might* show a change on the indirect issue.

On a pretest, the experimental subjects showed a strong association between the two crucial attitudes, gun control and gays in the military, just as we had found in the preliminary study. So far, so good. As expected, almost all the undergraduates were in favor of allowing gay people to serve in the military. We anticipated this result. As this was a study of influence (that is, changing people's minds), we had constructed an influential message that argued strongly that gay people should *not* be allowed to serve in the military. This was a reasoned and well-constructed communication, not the rant of a group of homophobes based on their own sexual identity insecurities. Each student read the same message, titled "The Case Against Gays in the Military." However, the source of the message was attributed to one of three different groups: Some subjects were told that the communication was written by "representatives of the University of Arizona's Student Union Association (ASUA): "On the basis of a large and comprehensive survey of students, the ASUA has determined that the majority of students at U of A strongly oppose any law that would allow gays in the military. We would like you to read and consider their statement." The description attached to the message was intended to indicate that the source was of (in-group) majority status.

A second group of subjects received the same message, but for them the communication was attributed to the "University of Arizona Students for Sanity in the Military," which was described as "a small radical organization of fifty University of Arizona students who strongly oppose any law that would allow gays in the military." This description was meant to suggest to our subjects that the source of the message was an in-group minority. The source was in-group because its members were all fellow students at the University of Arizona. It was a minority because it consisted of a small radical group of only fifty students who held beliefs strongly at odds with those of most other students.

The final group of subjects received the same message, but it was attributed to students from a local community college in the vicinity of the University of Arizona. This description was designed to inform students that the message source was out-group—they were students from a neighboring school that University of Arizona students did not evaluate highly. To emphasize the minority status of both in-group and out-group minority sources, participants read, "Although the [source's] position is contrary to the beliefs of a majority of students, we would like you to read and consider their statement."

After reading the statement, we again measured subjects' attitudes toward gays in the military, using measures slightly different from the ones we used in the first part of the study. The central questions of the research were, "Did the subjects change their attitudes on either issue?" and, "Were there differences between the three groups?"

The results of the study were enlightening. Students exposed to the anti-gay message agreed with it, if it was attributed to the majority. They showed clear evidence of complying with the majority group's position by changing their initial attitudes in the direction of opposing gays in the military. When the message was attributed to the students in the community college (the out-group minority), no change was evident. The out-group's opinions did not matter.

These patterns were quite different among the subjects exposed to the *in-group minority,* the small radical group of their fellow students. In this circumstance, there was no evidence of the students having changed their attitudes on the focal issue, *gays in the military.* However, these students changed their attitudes on *gun control* in a conservative direction, consistent with the politically conservative thrust of the anti-gay message that they (and all the other subjects) had read.

The results of this study were exciting, unusual, and expected. To make sure that they were not the result of a fluke or extraordinary luck, we reran the same experiment, but this time switched the issues and used a new set of research subjects. In this second study, gun control became the focus of our persuasive messages, and gays in the military the indirect issue. The pattern of results we obtained in this experiment was completely consistent with the earlier findings. These two studies, and others that have followed in our lab and others', confirmed our hypothesis that the minority's influence often was felt on issues it had not even raised, but that were related to the focus of its arguments (which we have called the focal issue). In resisting the minority's direct demands, the subjects appeared to give ground on "indirect" issues. Analysis indicated that they probably were not aware that they were doing so. Why? Because our earlier study showed that students were not cognizant of the association between the two. This being the case, it is unlikely that they would consciously try to pacify the minority by giving ground on an unrelated issue. The results showed that the minority could influence the majority on issues that were never even mentioned in its persuasive appeal.[xxxii]

How It Works:
The Leniency Contract

The pattern of these studies' results may appear anomalous at first glance, but the findings fit well with the literature on groups and group influence. First, the finding that the majority had an immediate effect on subjects' attitudes is consistent with years of research findings. People's response to majority pressure is almost always immediate and direct, and this is precisely what we found.[17]

The subjects who received the persuasive message attributed to the out-group minority also responded as expected. They appeared to ignore the out-group and acted as if their message never arrived. This result, too, is in keeping with years of research. The out-group minority apparently does not get on the majority's radar—unless it attacks a belief or practice that is important to the majority's identity. In that case, the minority can expect a swift and unkind response.

Subjects' reactions to the in-group minority are the most exciting and novel of all the findings in these studies. Remember, all students read the same persuasive communication; it simply was attributed to different sources. Those exposed to the message attributed to the in-group minority showed an unusual response. They seemed to ignore the anti-gay message, just as did those who read the same communication attributed to the out-group minority; however, they showed a strong change on gun control, an issue our earlier research had established as being related to the focus of the in-group minority's message (gays in the military). Was this result a fluke? Not likely. In the second study, in which we switched the two issues and used a new group of subjects, we

---

[17] Students who were alienated from their university did not show this majority influence effect, suggesting that people who are disaffected with their majority group may resist its influence.

found a strong in-group minority message on gun control resulted in changes in attitudes toward gays in the military.[xxxiii]

All You Ever Wanted to Know About Groups

To appreciate these results and understand why they are not as weird as they might seem initially, we need to understand some facts about groups. The first thing to know is that groups are weakened by defections, and so group leaders try hard to retain members. Except under high provocation, groups are extremely reluctant to banish or exclude members, because this weakens the group. Unless the member or in-group minority threatens the group's continued existence and refuses to be brought into line, the majority does all it can to keep its sheep in the fold.

What happens when an in-group minority proposes an idea that is contrary to the group's standard beliefs or practices? The majority's response almost never is instantaneous banishment. Rather, the larger group determines if the minority's proposal represents a threat to the group's continued existence. If it doesn't, then ostracism is off the table. However, we know that the majority almost never gives in to the minority's wishes, at least not immediately. So how does the majority maintain the goodwill of its minorities? It does so by allowing the minority to have its say, to express its issues freely, usually without fear of strong retribution. The majority will attend to the minority group's position and usually will not demean its members. Derogatory responses are dangerous in this circumstance, because the minority members are in-group. They share a common identity with the majority— we're all Brits, or teetotalers, or Green Party members. To demean a person who shares one's identity is to demean oneself.

This benevolent and open-minded response would seem to be

the ideal breeding ground for social influence. An attentive and non-defensive reaction to the minority's message, coupled with little if any defensive debunking of its source, is the stuff of which attitude change is made. So why then does the majority almost never change directly and immediately in response to a persuasive minority? We theorized that it does not do so because the process of minority influence works very much like a formal contract.

The majority extends many benefits to the in-group minority. The minority is allowed to make its case without fear of being demeaned, and with the confidence that the majority will hear it out respectfully and attentively. In return, the majority requires certain considerations as well—remember, all contracts contain a quid pro quo, a "this for that" which involves an exchange of fair value. The majority's demands are minimal: "We will give our open-minded attention to your petition without fear of reprisal, but in return, you must give the group your continued allegiance. And you must accept that *we will not change*."

We have termed this understanding *the leniency contract*. It is an implicit agreement that I believe operates in all groups, a contract to which all must subscribe in one form or another if the group is to survive. It allows the minority to have its say and to vent its dissatisfactions. The majority can make an apparent conciliatory gesture by offering a safe haven for the in-group minority's complaints, while maintaining the status quo on which all groups thrive. This agreement precludes rapid change from one position to another and then back again, which usually is the sign of a group in its last stages. Groups attempt to maintain their equilibrium, the status quo, by responding to changing conditions while simultaneously moderating change in important beliefs and behaviors as much as possible.

There is a snake in this woodpile, however. Even though the majority does not grant the minority its wishes immediately, their open-minded reaction to the minority's message supplies the ideal opportunity for change—but change has been repudiated by the leniency contract and so immediate changes in response to the in-group minority are rare. However, considerable change pressure has been introduced into the system. If you process a strong in-group minority's appeal to change your position on, say, a political candidate, and do not defend against it or call the persuader's credentials into question, you have a lot of pressure to deal with. Where does it go? The force for change will not simply dissipate into thin air. The leniency contract theory holds that this pressure will spread to other, related attitudes. As these related beliefs are not well defended (why should we defend our beliefs on gun control in response to a message on gays in the military?), they are vulnerable. This is why, according to the leniency contract, indirect changes are common in research on minority or outsider influence. If we have identified these related attitudes, we'll have a good idea of where the indirect changes are most likely to occur. The theory holds that it is for this reason that an in-group minority's communication on abortion caused changes in attitudes toward contraception, and why an anti-gays in the military message attributed to a majority caused changes in this attitude, but changes in beliefs about gun control were found when the same message was attributed to an in-group minority.

What's the Rush?
Why Focal Change Is Delayed

Although the results of these studies were strange, exciting, and enlightening, they said nothing about another odd feature of minority influence, namely the common finding that when the minority *did* have a direct persuasive effect on the majority, it almost always occurred after some period of time had passed. Could the results uncovered in our indirect attitude change studies shed light on this result as well?

To address this question, a colleague of mine and I performed another minority influence experiment. This study was similar to the first ones, but the issues were changed to ensure that the earlier studies' results were not attributable to the specific attitudes that were examined—gun control and gays in the military. In this new research, again conducted at the University of Arizona, subjects were asked their opinions on a number of topics of interest to university students, including an increase in tuition (not a single student liked the idea), a proposal to require ten hours' free mandatory university service of all undergraduates (no one liked this idea much either), mandatory student health insurance, senior comprehensive examinations, a double foreign language requirement, and so on. We found that attitudes toward mandatory service and a tuition increase were strongly related, and so decided to write a persuasive message advocating university service, with the intention of indirectly changing students' attitudes toward a tuition increase in a favorable direction. This study seems to stack the deck against a positive result. After all, what students in their right mind would become more favorable toward a tuition increase? This is precisely what transpired when students had read a strongly written and well-argued message that made the case that they should volunteer ten hours of their spare time, weekly, to work on projects for their university (such as filing, typing, other forms of office work, grounds keeping, and so on).

When the mandatory service message was attributed to a majority of one's fellow students, it created significantly more positive attitudes than when attributed to an in-group minority, for whom the message had no apparent effect. However, students who read the mandatory service message became considerably more amenable to a tuition increase when the message was attributed to an in-group minority. Remember, we had identified tuition as associated with mandatory service attitudes in earlier research, but tuition was never mentioned in the persuasive message. When this same message was attributed to the majority, indirect effects were not found.

These indirect change results were entirely consistent with our earlier findings and bolstered our confidence in the leniency contract interpretation. However, we also were interested in gaining a better understanding of the delayed attitude change effects that sometimes occur in minority influence research—and sometimes do not. Remember that in-group minorities sometimes have a delayed, but never immediate, direct influence on the majority. When the majority is influenced by the minority, the change is evident only after some time has passed. We thought that we might find a delayed influence effect in the study if we retested the subjects a week or so later on their attitudes toward a ten-hour mandatory university service requirement. So we retested the same students, but under quite different auspices. In an apparently unrelated study, they were brought to the laboratory a week after the initial experiment and asked to express their attitudes on a number of issues, only one of which was relevant for our purposes, the university service requirement. They were not reminded of the earlier study, which was never mentioned, and different experimenters were used.

We assumed that the students who had been exposed to the in-group minority's position on the university service program, and who had subsequently become more favorable toward a tuition increase, would show a change in the direction of the minority's arguments on the focal issue (the mandatory service program). And we expected those exposed to the argument attributed to the majority to show no effects. The results were not what we expected.

Neither group showed evidence of change on the university service issue, the focus of the persuasive message that had been delivered to them one week earlier. Apparently, we were wrong.

Or were we? Further analysis revealed that the subjects who had shown the greatest indirect change on the tuition issue in response to the in-group minority's message showed a significant delayed change on the focal (university service) attitude. In other words, they did change in the direction of the persuasive communication. Although this change did not occur immediately, it was evident a week after the message was delivered to them. However, those who did not show a strong indirect change in response to the initial message did not show a delayed focal change. This result helps explain why some earlier studies found delayed change effects, whereas others had failed. If the indirect change is large, a delayed focal change will occur. If the indirect change is not substantial, delayed direct (or focal) change is unlikely.[xxxiv]

How and Why Does the Leniency Effect Happen?

The leniency contract model and the curious pattern of changes it predicts when an in-group minority presents a strongly argued and logically sound persuasive communication are understandable if we are willing to make just a few easily accepted assumptions.

First, we need to assume that our beliefs do not exist in a vacuum. That is, my attitudes toward a person or an idea may be related to my attitudes toward other persons or ideas. For example, my attitude toward Barack Obama probably is related to my attitude toward mandatory health care. The more I like one, the more I like the other. The association is not perfect, of course, but it is strong. The alternative, that each of our attitudes is held independently of all the others, does not make much sense in light of considerable research on human thought and cognition. A mental system in which every belief is held independently would quickly be overloaded and overwhelmed. We're just not that smart.

The second assumption is that the associations among our beliefs may vary: Some attitudes are closely linked, others are only weakly associated, and still others are relatively independent of one another. This structural conception of the ways in which our beliefs are arranged in our minds is easily accepted, and also is consistent with considerable research. It suggests two interesting extensions, the first of which is that change pressure put on one attitude may affect other attitudes with which it is strongly associated; the second is that if we dramatically change one attitude, those with which it is most closely related are put under pressure to change as well, because massive change in one will unbalance the relationships among related attitudes. Think of an architectural structure—or, better yet, a building you might have created with an Erector set long ago. Pulling on one structural component causes all the others to move, and the more critical component, or the greater its deflection, the more the entire structure will move to adjust to the change.

These two assumptions are the basis of the leniency contract. They explain why pressure on an attitude by an in-group minority may affect related beliefs without affecting the focus of the persuasive message. In addition, they suggest that indirect change may affect the focal attitude, but that some time must pass to allow these structural adjustments to occur. Understanding the ways in which attitudes are related to one another is the key to understanding the apparently bizarre changes in beliefs that in-group minorities can set in motion.

Before you attempt this at home, we must reemphasize that successful minority persuasion (or almost all persuasion, for that matter), presupposes a strong, logical, and well-argued message.

If the in-group minority's message does not hold water, all bets are off. Their appeal will go unanswered.

Outside the Laboratory

The examples used throughout the chapter so far have all been drawn from the experimental laboratory. How would this work in the world of everyday life? In-group leniency would work in the same way. However, without focused research that uncovers the relationships between apparently independent beliefs in advance, it is nearly impossible to point to a change in public perceptions and unequivocally prove that it was attributable to a minority's pressure on another issue, so illustrations of remote or indirect change in settings outside the laboratory are difficult to conjure credibly. However, more tightly linked indirect change effects can be imagined.

An interesting recent change on the American political scene that might be a result of indirect change is seen in the recent policy change on gay military personnel. In December 1993, President Clinton published Defense Directive 1332.14, which became known as the Don't Ask, Don't Tell law. It allowed gay service personnel to serve in the U.S. military, but required servicepersons not to publicize their sexual preferences. It also ordered superior officers not to ask their subordinates to reveal their sexual orientation. And it required certain bars be passed before prosecutions were mounted in cases where the directive was violated.[18] This change in policy was not particularly popular on either side of the political divide, but most thought it better than the status quo, and so it enjoyed a somewhat rocky existence for a number of years.

---

[18] Later, a "Don't Harass" feature was added to the directive.

Seventeen years after the directive was enacted, its repeal was signed by President Obama. The reasons given for the repeal are many, but one factor that made a major difference was the changing attitudes of the American public. When the directive was enacted, 44 percent of the respondents of a national poll thought gay servicepeople who disclosed their sexual orientation should be allowed to serve; by 2010, the figure had jumped to 75 percent. Public opinion had moved in favor of gay servicepersons simultaneously being allowed to serve and being out of the closet.

There is no direct evidence of this, but it is arguable that a factor that might have made a difference in the Don't Ask, Don't Tell repeal was the changing attitudes of the American public to the rights of gay persons in general, brought about by indirect minority influence. From 2008 onward, twenty-four states banned same-sex marriage. In the election of 2008, millions were spent on both sides of California's Proposition 8, which would ban same-sex marriage, even though the practice had been upheld as legal by the California Supreme Court. The proposition passed, and the right of gay people to marry was revoked. In every other case in which same-sex bans were involved in referenda throughout the country, opposition to same-sex marriage carried. Obviously, the (gay) minority failed. Or did they? Were the arguments of the proponents of same-sex marriage, an unsuccessful but arguably in-group minority, persuasive, at least on some level? Was the minority able to help stimulate a change in attitude on the part of the populace toward related issues, like the rights of gay people to serve in the military? Possibly, and these indirect changes may be reflected in the population statistics, which have moved steadily in the direction of extending rights to gay people, and which had much to do with congressional reactions to Don't Ask, Don't Tell.

This linkage of same-sex marriage with gay rights in the military need not be consciously recognized by the populace. As was shown in our earlier laboratory studies, related attitudes that are not recognized as being linked nevertheless can be strongly interdependent. A minority agitating for change in one policy may have success in moving votes on another. Did the failure of a highly visible proposition in California affect congressional votes on a related issue? We do not have adequate information to answer this question, but the research that has been peppered throughout this chapter suggests that the question is not completely unreasonable. This is not to suggest that the rules of influence are certain to produce positive outcomes. There are many ways for the influence agents themselves to short-circuit in the process, and we'll review some of them in the coming chapter.

The Majority's Tests

Whether the majority is affected by the minority's appeal depends on many factors, which have been discussed throughout this book. The process the majority follows when it succumbs to minority influence is identical, no matter who constitutes the majority *or* the minority. Understanding this process will allow the minority representative to navigate the uncertain shoals of social influence. If the proper steps are followed, the weak *can* prevail, at least some of the time. It will not prevail every time, because as we will see in the coming chapter, the requirements for minority influence sometimes cannot be met. But when they are, understanding the *rules of influence*, the necessary steps that must be followed, will help ensure success. Knowing the various tests the larger group applies in responding to a minority's message is the first step in this process. Although it has taken many years, these tests now are well identified. The majority's first test concerns the in- or out-group status of the minority agitating for change. If the minority is not in-group, if it fails this first and primary test, all bets are off. The majority generally will reject the minority out of hand. A minority that is out-group is not relevant to the majority, unless it poses a significant threat to the status quo. In that case, the majority will attempt to squash it.

Assuming the minority is deemed in-group and so passes the first, critical test, its message then is scrutinized for threat in the second test. Does the minority's petition imperil the larger group? Is it a hazard to the group's continuance? If so, the minority is redefined and cast into the black hole of the out-group. At that point, its message is no longer evaluated as credible, and so need not be considered seriously. A corollary feature of expulsion from the in-group is that the minority, now an out-group, is evaluated in a very harsh light. These "black sheep" often become a target of the majority's ire. This is a common reaction to turncoats of all stripes.

The third test, assuming the first two are passed, concerns the content of the minority's message, and its persuasive power.[19] Owing to the leniency contract, the majority will seriously consider the message of the minority group that has passed the first two tests. Therefore, in this third phase, the quality of the minority's message becomes critical, because it will determine the majority's response. If the message is strong and cogent, the majority might be persuaded by it, but no matter how well constructed its message, the minority should not expect immediate acceptance of its proposals. Rather, a strongly argued persuasive message will cause the indirect change effects that have been the focus of the

---

[19] Of course, I assume that Rules 2 through 5, which guide presentation style have been followed. These rules are not negotiable.

discussion in this chapter. If the message is weak, you have blown your chance.

The majority will be influenced by strongly and expertly argued messages. The influence will not be evident on the focal attitude itself, but related attitudes will be moved in response to the minority's arguments. Some of these changes may be readily evident, if the indirect attitude is obviously associated with the direct thrust of the minority (as, for example, in the case of abortion and contraception). However, at times the linkages among beliefs are not at all obvious (as in gays in the military and gun control), and so the minority should be sensitive to indirect associations that might signal successful influence that could open the door to later direct changes. The diagram summarizes the tests the majority applies in responding to a minority group's appeal.

If the indirect change is substantial, the minority may expect delayed changes on the issue that is the focus of their initial battle with the majority. If the indirect change was not particularly large, it will not persist. This is the process the majority employs when responding to a minority's campaign for change. The ways the minority manages the majority's tests determine its

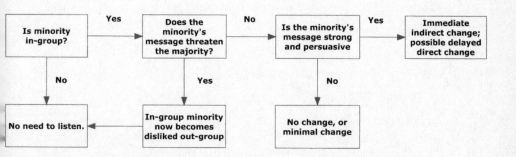

The "Tests" the Majority Applies in Responding to a Minority Group's Persuasive Communication

success or failure. Understanding the rules of influence, which I will summarize in the final chapter, is the essential step along the influence road. Groups that have internalized the rules have a chance to succeed. For groups that have not, there is no option but failure.

Getting It All Wrong

In politics, an organized minority is a political majority.

—Jesse Jackson

Just about anyone who has survived being born in a hospital owes a debt of gratitude to Ignaz Semmelweis. If your mother survived your birth, she owes him, too. And if you, yourself, have given birth and lived to brag about it, you owe him as well.

Who is Ignaz Semmelweis, and why these debts?

Semmelweis was a Hungarian, born on the first of July in 1818 on the Pest side of Budapest, Hungary, which then was a (minor) part of the Austrian Empire. He received his high school education at the Catholic Gymnasium of Buda, and matriculated at the University of Pest in 1837. He then traveled to the big city, Vienna, the capital of the empire, to continue his education in the study of law. Before the year was out, however, he had transferred to the medical college there, receiving his doctorate in medicine and a certificate in practical midwifery in 1844. He was a very bright student, and despite being Jewish in an anti-Semitic state, he attracted the attention of some of the leading medical professors at the university. Soon after graduation, he was appointed assistant in the First Obstetrical Clinic at the Vienna General

Hospital (the *Allgemeines Krankenhaus*), the university's teaching facility. Today his position would be called chief resident. Because of its size, the obstetrics clinic was divided into two nearly identical wards.

The problem of many obstetrics wards at that time was the high incidence of puerperal fever (a form of septicemia, or blood poisoning), which led to death rates sometimes as high as 40 percent in new mothers and their babies. Today, we know that puerperal fever is caused by the staph bacterium, the same germ that wreaks such havoc in many of today's hospitals, but at the time the cause was a vexing mystery. At Vienna General, the obstetrics clinic traditionally had been staffed by a mix of medical students and midwives, but it was split in two in 1841, three years before Semmelweis's appointment. The first obstetrics ward was run by Professor Johann Klein, Semmelweis's boss. It was staffed by medical students. The other, directed by Professor Franz Bartsch, was run by students of midwifery. This distinction was ultimately to prove crucial, because far more women were dying in Klein's (first) ward than in the second ward of Bartsch.

Why?

Childbirth in the 1800s was a risky proposition, but the discrepancy between the obstetrics wards at Vienna General was remarkable and to many pregnant women of the city, terrifying. Why were the odds of women assigned to the first ward so much worse than those assigned to the second? The disparity in death rates of newborns and their mothers did not go unnoticed. Sometimes women tried desperately to delay labor, as assignment to the two wards alternated from one day to the next. Proper timing would land a woman in Bartsch's second ward, rather than the deadly first ward of Klein and Semmelweis. Take a look at the mortality rates of the two wards in 1841, when the wards were staffed either by medical students or midwives. The figure shows the gravity of the problem. In the first ward, the childbirth mortality rate often was twice that of the second ward. Women were safer giving birth on the street than in Klein's ward. Semmelweis himself was horrified by the loss of life in his ward, admitting it "made me so miserable that life seemed worthless."

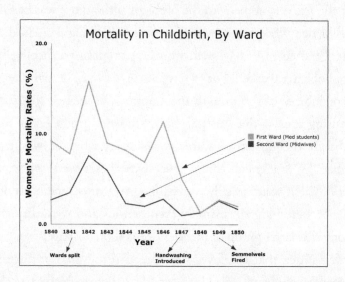

The doctors and medical students of the hospital were not indifferent to this problem, and they advanced and tested many theories to account for the disparity in mortality between the wards. One physician proposed that overcrowding in the first ward was responsible for the problem. This seemed a promising guess, but a quick check of the hospital records showed that the second ward was usually more crowded than the first. Furthermore, Semmelweis analyzed the birth rates and found a strong negative association between number of births and mortality. In other words, the hospital's own records indicated that as births increased, deaths decreased. So much for that hypothesis. Semmelweis's use of the data available to him in the hospital records should have alerted his superiors that his ideas were considerably more than mere conjecture or flights of fancy, but it did not.

Other researchers proposed more socially based theories. Some, for example, believed that the high mortality rate in the first ward was attributable to the fact that many of the medical students were foreigners, and this was responsible for the tragic state of affairs. Why their presence accelerated puerperal fever was never explained. The easy remedy to the problem, although it was based on no evidence whatsoever, was to dismiss all foreign medical students. Strange as it may seem from our modern perspective, this xenophobic fix worked. For two weeks. After that, despite the general prejudices of the time in the empire—"It seemed like such a promising idea"—the Austrian-born students produced as many deaths in the obstetrics ward as occurred when it was partly manned by foreigners. Many other hypotheses were raised, and most of them were quickly proved incorrect or on the basis of no evidence were judged as simply preposterous and were dismissed. Among this latter group of theories deemed preposterous was Semmelweis's idea that the fever was spread through "the fingers of the medical students, soiled by recent dissections, which carry those death-dealing cadaveric particles into . . . women in childbirth."

Why would this problem differ in the two wards? Because the medical students in Semmelweis's ward were called upon to dissect cadavers as part of their training, just as medical students do today. However, the midwives-in-training in Bartsch's second ward did no autopsies. Dissections were not seen as a necessary element of their education. This stark difference in educational practice meant that none of the midwives was dissecting cadavers, but all the medical students were.

Semmelweis deduced—incorrectly—that the *odor* of the dissected cadavers clung to the surgeons' hands. When they went immediately from the anatomy lab to the delivery room, he proposed that this odor infected the women in labor. To solve the problem, he insisted that all medical students wash their hands in a chlorinated lime solution (much like today's chlorine bleach) before getting near the patients. This was a major innovation at the time. No one did this as a matter of course. However, when they did, the death rate dropped like a stone, as is shown in the figure. In April 1847, the death rate in his ward was 18 percent! In May Semmelweis insisted on hand washing, and by June the rate had dipped to 2.2 percent. In August the rate was 1.9 percent. In January of the following year, Semmelweis strictly enforced his hand-washing order, insisting that his medical students "chlorinate" before every procedure, and in two months that year, no woman or baby died from puerperal fever.

You would think that Semmelweis would be on the receiving end of mass adulation from the medical establishment of Vienna, but more often he was the target of tomatoes and rotten eggs. At this time, medicine had not yet developed the germ theory of disease, so no one could fathom why hand washing could possibly have any effect on the horrific mortality rates in the wards. For most of the Viennese medical establishment, Semmelweis's conclusion was not based on objective facts, but rather on his ludicrous subjective opinion, and we know from Rule 6 the difficulty of influencing people on issues they believe rest on subjective beliefs rather than on hard evidence. Semmelweis did not have a microscope that could make the subjective objective, so he could not show the basis of his theory. And because the ways microorganisms functioned would not be understood for another twenty years, when Louis Pasteur developed his theories and interventions, he had no established wisdom to fall back upon. True, the results in Semmelweis's ward seem to us difficult to contradict today, but he did not publish his work for many years, and so it was easy for critics to throw stones, to disparage his procedures, and to offer alternative theories that did not appear any more ridiculous than his—and they did.[20]

This rejection of an obviously successful medical intervention can be understood in light of our understanding of the minority rules. First, and perhaps most important, though Semmelweis's work was attracting attention overseas, he was not a part of Vienna's medical establishment. He was an outsider, and hence automatically the target of dark suspicion. His primary language was Hungarian. His German was not particularly fluent, and he wrote poorly in this language, which may be why he failed to publish his work till near the end of his career. A young and unproven outsider, he was attempting to influence the medical establishment to adopt his ideas, but by all accounts, he was extremely autocratic. This personality feature was not likely to endear him to the men in power, and they remained his enemies throughout his career.

Semmelweis was completely devoted to his work, a good feature, but he also was completely unconcerned about the consequences of showing up his boss, who did not like him to begin with, despite the drop in mortality rates in his ward after he initiated the hand-washing regimen. This was not a good feature. And he pushed his luck. It had to be clear to Professor Klein, Semmelweis's immediate boss, that he would look stupid if not criminally incompetent if the world were to accept Semmelweis's hand-washing solution to puerperal fever, and he was determined to derail Semmelweis's train. As a member in good standing in the medical hierarchy of Vienna, Johann Klein was in a great

---

[20] This is more than an academic quibble. Had Semmelweis published his ideas, including his procedures and results, his work would have reached a wide audience of research scientists who could have repeated his studies and undoubtedly would have duplicated his results. This would have quashed many of the objections to Semmelweis's research, many of which were based on irrelevancies—his autocratic nature, ethnicity, place of birth, accent, religion, and so on.

position to ruin Semmelweis's career and reputation, and he did—and many women and their babies died as a result.

To top it off, Semmelweis also was not popular with the medical students whose work he directed. They felt unduly put upon by his demands. Why should they be forced to wash their hands before delivering babies? Nobody else did. Semmelweis insisted on it because he believed the odor from the dissections was responsible for the higher mortality rates in his ward.[21] Hand washing was viewed as an unfair imposition on their normal, tried-and-true routines. As they could not accept the link between hand hygiene and infection, the practices Semmelweis vehemently insisted upon seemed arbitrary and capricious. Hand washing wasted valuable time, and there was a lot to do on the ward. Of course, the students could not know the importance of proper hygiene, and so their resentment grew in proportion to Semmelweis's insistence.

The real power in this fight was the medical hierarchy in Vienna, which was strongly influenced by Professor Johann Klein, one of their own. Semmelweis was Hungarian, not Austrian, and Hungary was considered a quaint backwater by sophisticated Austrian standards of the time. He was known to be rigid, intolerant of even minor deviations from his orders, undiplomatic, and arrogant. He spoke with an accent. He couldn't write well, was not a good debater, and so could not defend his ideas well in public forums, and he had never published his results. Because of all these factors, Semmelweis could not sell his ideas to the people who could put them into play. In some twisted way, however, probably

---

21 In this sense, he was wrong. Odor had nothing to do with it, but he was wrong in the right way, because when students washed in a chlorinated solution, they effectively sterilized their hands and radically reduced the chances of infecting their patients. Of course, staph can be transmitted in lots of other ways as well—no one used surgical masks at the time, for example—but the simple expedient of hand washing was to prove a godsend for many women in the Krankenhaus's obstetrics clinic.

none of this mattered much to him. As we may deduce by his failure to publish his groundbreaking results, he apparently felt no need to explain himself, his ideas, or his theories to anyone. In Semmelweis's autocratic world, he knew he was right, and you did what he required or you found a new job. This approach worked on the medical students he directed, but it did not work on his boss.

Under these circumstances many of those who worked under him were in a state of more or less constant rebellion. He was an outsider from a backwater town, a minority voice in the hospital hierarchy, and on thin ice with his boss and his boss's bosses, the power structure of medicine in the greatest hospital in the greatest city in the world. He pushed his ideas without an explanation that seemed even remotely reasonable to most of his students and peers, and he was unpleasant to boot. In these circumstances, we would not expect this minority voice to prevail, and Semmelweis's did not, despite evidence that clearly attested to the validity of his medical insight.

Despite his success in largely conquering a deadly problem, he was dismissed as soon as his contract expired, his job given to a less qualified man who had been his subordinate. This dismissal was deeply insulting to Semmelweis, who was said to suffer from depression later in life, but it did not deter him in his work. Although Bartsch offered him a position in his ward, Semmelweis refused and returned to Budapest, where he again worked his magic, this time at St. Rochus Hospital. When he finally published his research in book form, it was met with considerable opposition from the Viennese medical establishment, who simply could not believe that the same underlying cause (germs) could produce the many different manifestations of the fever that was associated with so many deaths in their obstetrics wards. He fought back with characteristic venom, won no new friends, and failed again to persuade the Viennese, even though his work excited considerable interest in other medical centers throughout Europe. His ideas are credited by many historians as the foundation of modern antiseptic medicine. The European reaction was not enough, however. Eventually, his spirit broken, he died tragically in an asylum to which he had been committed by his wife and family. Ironically, he died from a wound that had become infected with the staph bacterium, the organism he had fought all his life.[xxxv]

Not more than twenty years later, Louis Pasteur produced a series of studies that showed conclusively that microorganisms were responsible for many diseases. Joseph Lister saw the relation of Semmelweis's and Pasteur's work, and demonstrated that chemicals could inhibit infections during surgery. He is considered the father of modern surgery, just as Semmelweis is considered by many as one of the founders of epidemiology. It would be an exaggeration to say that none of this medical progress would have occurred without Semmelweis, as a number of other researchers in Europe were beginning to think about the problem of infection in ways consistent with Semmelweis, but there is no question that the rate of progress certainly would have been slowed without the pioneering efforts of this complex man, whose contributions were never fully appreciated during his lifetime. This is no longer true, as one of Hungary's most renowned institutions of higher learning now bears his name, Semmelweis University. It is the oldest medical university in Hungary.

A Contemporary Failure of the Minority to Achieve In-group Status

Semmelweis's flair for snatching defeat from the jaws of victory is not an isolated occurrence in the annals of minority influence.

Although it is true that many factors worked against him, it also is true that he had the goods. His intervention worked, and although nobody believed his explanation, neither could anyone come up with an alternative explanation of his extraordinary results that made any sense. He *could* have prevailed, but he made a number of serious mistakes from the standpoint of the rules of influence, as they have been revealed, and these mistakes were to prove fatal to his chances. He was never accepted by the majority as part of their group, because he was rigid, and because he was dogmatic and arrogant. He made no attempt to become part of the in-group, and so he failed. Like Oscar Wilde, he might have thought that his "play was a great success, but the audience was a total failure," but the fact remains that the impact of his work was delayed and people died because of his inability to convince others of the validity of his thinking. Sadly, he was partly to blame.

A contemporary example of a minority violating the influence rules to their great disadvantage was evident in the 2008 election in California, where Proposition 8, which prohibited same-sex marriage, was passed by a majority (52 percent) of the voters. From June 6 through November 5, 2008, same-sex marriage had been legal in the Golden State, its State Supreme Court having ruled that gay people enjoyed equal protection under the law and thus were entitled to the somewhat debatable privilege of marriage. Prop. 8's principal sponsors were the Mormon and Catholic Churches.[xxxvi] Mormons constituted 80 to 90 percent of the campaign's early door-to-door volunteers, and were said to have contributed more than half of the $40 million dollars raised to support the proposition banning same-sex marriage.

The gay community went into the election with some reasonable degree of confidence that they could defeat the proposition and that same-sex marriage would be upheld as legal. After all, as many past electoral contests had shown, the state was progressive in its politics; it strongly supported Democratic candidates in 2008, and later bucked the national trend in the 2010 election by selecting only Democrats to its most important positions, including senator, governor, lieutenant governor, and attorney general. Both senators from California were Democrats, and Democrats held a 34–19 edge in congresspersons in the 112th Congress.

Although they were confident, the opponents of the same-sex marriage ban understood the pitfalls of an election of this kind. Opposing the ban was a loose alliance of spokespersons— California's two Democratic senators, Feinstein and Boxer, all of California's Episcopal bishops, the ten largest newspapers in the state, and some unexpected support from the right wing, including California's Republican governor, Arnold Schwarzenegger. With this kind of firepower, and approximately equal financial backing, it would seem that the same-sex marriage ban had little chance to pass. The election proved otherwise.

To understand this outcome, which many political analysts are still puzzling over, given the liberal bent of the state, it is necessary to determine who the real minority was. Most of the early polls suggested a very close race. If anything, the electorate seemed slightly to favor allowing same-sex marriage, but history suggests that this issue has always been a tough sell in the United States. In the 2004 election, for example, thirteen states passed ballot measures that banned same-sex marriage. In light of the national trends, it was important that those in favor of allowing same-sex marriage realize that they were in a precarious position, despite the nearly even poll reports, and to act accordingly. They did not.

As I have insisted throughout, it is imperative that the weaker group establish its in-group credentials. So logically, we would expect those fighting the same-sex marriage ban to work hard to establish the fact that gay and lesbian people were, first and foremost, *people,* just like everyone else. Their sexual preference may have differed from that of the majority of people in the state, but they shared many more similarities than this one difference. It was incumbent on the opponents of the marriage ban to convince the larger population that their differences were trivial when compared with their many similarities.

How would one do so? It seems self-evident that the ban's opponents would show gay people living like most heterosexual people did: going to work, church, or school; playing with their kids; behaving like everyone else. Surprisingly, however, reason and logic did not hold in this campaign. The ads of those arguing in favor of legal same-sex marriage almost *never* featured a gay spokesperson, never presented a picture of gay people acting just like everyone else. Given this approach, why would a voter who did not know any gay people decide that they were "just like me"? In attempting to sway a largely straight electorate, those opposing the ban on same-sex marriage never tried to convince those voters who might be on the fence that the gay community was, with the straight community, part of a larger whole—Californians and Americans. The campaign bragged that the massive Los Angeles Unified School District opposed the ban. Later in the campaign, it aired commentary from Democratic Senators Boxer and Feinstein, and the Republican Governor Arnold Schwarzenegger, all of whom also voiced their opposition it.

Presumably, none of these people is gay. From *the rules of influence* perspective, it is difficult to see how the stated opposition of a bunch of heterosexuals would do much to establish gay people's in-group position in the larger heterosexual (majority) group of Californians. It was as if the campaign did everything possible to interfere with the impression that gays were in-group, indistinguishable from other Californians on everything that really mattered. This is not to say that everyone would have accepted this proposition, far from it, but the campaign's failure even to attempt to persuade the electorate of this position was almost a guarantee that it would fail. They might have learned from Semmelweis's example; he also was unable or unwilling to show that on issues that mattered, he did not differ at all from the people who were situated firmly in the majority.

If the opponents of the ban on same-sex marriage did not attempt to persuade voters of the gay community's similarity with the larger majority, what *did* they spend so much money doing? Well, we learned from the television ads that an older married couple, Sam and Julia Thorons, didn't want their daughter's right to marry someone else's daughter abridged: "We have become very deeply committed to the principle that our daughter deserves to be treated in every aspect of her life with the same respect and dignity as her two . . . brothers." There's nothing wrong with these sentiments—they are probably the same hopes that most caring parents would express when talking about their children. Any parents worth their salt wish only the best for their kids. But that really was not the issue in the election.

The problem that proponents of same-sex marriage faced was establishing the in-group status of the gay minority, and this ad, like almost all the others they ran, did nothing of the kind. We never heard a single word about the proposition from the Thorons's daughter herself, for example, or from almost any other gay person. Except for a brief moment when a family photograph was shown, the daughter never even appeared in the ad. One would think that the person who was most affected by the ban would want to stand up and say something about it, but this never happened. Some of the ads run by those opposed to the marriage ban failed even to use the word *gay*. Were the opponents of the ban ashamed of their opposition to the marriage protection act, as it was termed by some of its proponents? An editorial in the *L.A. Times* noted this strange approach to persuasion, an approach that almost anyone familiar with the past fifty years of research on beliefs and attitudes found mystifying.[xxxvii]

> These days, it's pretty hard to walk the streets of a California city without seeing same-sex couples—shopping, strolling, holding hands, sometimes accompanied by children. What used to be called, self-consciously, "public displays of affection" are now merely public displays of ordinary family life. For gay folks, then, it is all the more stinging an irony that the one place where same-sex couples are invisible is in the advertising war over Proposition 8.

The decision to put gays back in the closet in the campaign opposing the same-sex marriage ban was disastrous. From everything discussed to this point in our consideration of social influence, it is clear that bringing the gay community into the larger camp was essential if they were to prevail in this referendum. Unless this requirement (Rule 1) was met, the campaign was doomed from the start, and the campaign failed to meet it. The strategy opponents of the ban adopted was so egregiously off base that some gay rights activists filmed their own ads, independent of the main campaign. Ellen DeGeneres, for example, bought $100,000 of television airtime to broadcast an ad in which she called her marriage to Portia de Rossi "the happiest day of my life." Margaret Cho and Molly Ringwald (and husband) also appeared in a series of humorous and effective ads, but they entered the ring so late that their effect was muted. Most people had formed their intention to vote one way or the other long before these more effective ads were aired.

Given the liberal or progressive voting record of the state, defeat of the proposed ban on same-sex marriage should have been easy. Instead, it was a disillusioning message to a large minority group that they really were less worthy, and different, from every-one else. This result was a direct outcome of the campaign directors' failure to understand the rules of influence that we have considered throughout this book, the first of which is that the minority *must* become recognized as a legitimate part of the larger group. Unless the campaign accomplished this, the opposition to the marriage ban was destined to fail—and it did.

Inconsistent Messages

Many other persuasive failures were evident in the campaign op-posing the ban on same-sex marriage. The campaign could never seem to agree on a consistent message that was to be a part of every ad that was aired. It never developed a "brand." Certainly the argument that all people should have the right to marry was in the forefront of the campaign, but many ads were focused only tangentially on this pitch. Some never used the word *marriage*. We know that if a minority is to prevail, after gaining acceptance by the majority as in-group, it then must push its agenda single-mindedly. This means that the minority has to avoid pressures to expand the argument, because if it succumbs to the temptation, its primary message will be diluted.

The proponents of the ban on same-sex marriage seemed in-stinctively to understand these facts, and took advantage of them. They developed a diverse set of quite incendiary ads in which they argued that should their referendum fail, gays would infiltrate all facets of society and turn it to their nefarious purposes; the very institution of marriage (currently only 50 percent of which survive divorce) would be threatened; churches would lose their tax-exempt status; arrogant, overbearing politicians and judges would take over the society; and the public education system would become a boot camp for the gay lifestyle. All these issues were raised in a scattergun strategy that seemed only tangentially related to reality.

The ban's proponents ran a much more persuasive campaign, strategically and tactically, than their opponents, whose response was scattered and ineffective. The opponents of the same-sex marriage ban consistently were put on the defensive, and rarely assumed the initiative necessary to push its own point of view in the most effective manner. The ban's proponents aired all manner of ads, and succeeded in forcing their opposition to respond to the many different thrusts of their persuasive onslaught. This strategy diverted the ban's opponents from what should have been the central thrust of their campaign, which is that gay people are part of the fabric of Californian and American society, they are a legitimate part of these larger groups, and to treat them differently is senseless as well as unjust. Opponents of the same-sex marriage ban watered down their message and failed to stick to a common theme that would have had considerable traction in the state—"We're just like you, we hold the same important values, we bleed the same blood, our differences are not important enough to deny us the right to marry"—and this diversion from what should have been a single-themed campaign effectively killed their chances. They bit the poisoned apple and paid the price for doing so.

Many morals can be drawn from this campaign, but we know most of them already. First, it should be clear that failing to be recognized as part of the larger group is disastrous. Influencing the majority from the outside is nearly impossible. Second, the necessity of staying on message is essential. Same-sex marriage proponents were answering new charges that seemed to pop up every day, even those that seemed absurd, rather than hammering their message home. They failed even to try to move the issue onto objective ground, allowing it to remain a subjective preference. Given their performance, it is a wonder that they did not fare even worse than they did.

Lies, Damned Lies, and . . . More Damned Lies

An interesting strategy of proponents of the same-sex marriage ban was their apparent lack of concern for valid evidence backing their claims. You might think that lying is a weak persuasive technique, but it can be highly effective. If the big lie is employed by the majority group consistently, and without capable minority response, the tactic can work wonders. It had a fatal effect on the fortunes of the proponents of same-sex marriage. We'll consider the big lie technique in chapter 9, but for now it is sufficient to understand that the strategy works if it is not counteracted rapidly and decisively. Those opposing the ban on same-sex marriage did neither, and simultaneously failed to establish their in-group credentials with the majority of Californians.

By their tactics, the opponents of same-sex marriage suggested that the issues at hand were not amenable to the usual rules of evidence. Rather, they implied that the issue involved preferences, not objective facts. When that happens, as we saw in chapter 6, the opposition does not have much chance to bring others to its side. The "no evidence" approach, which seems so misguided from a persuasive standpoint, in fact worked perfectly for the marriage ban's proponents, because it suggested to voters that the issue was a matter of subjective feelings rather than objective facts, and the insipid influence campaign run by their opponents played into their hands.

So the minority doesn't always win, even when the stars seem to be aligned in its favor. The common temptation that influence agents in weak positions must overcome is ignoring one or another of the rules, because doing so can kill their chances for success. Those in favor of same-sex marriage violated almost all of them. And they lost. The proponents of same-sex marriage thought that keeping gays off the TV screen would help their chances of winning the electoral battle. They thought that showing gay people in a family setting with their kids might threaten potential supporters. They thought they would play it safe, and the social and political climate of the state would save their cause. In reality, their approach ensured that they could not foster a common identity of gay people with the straight world, and they successfully surrendered the possibility of persuading the straight majority that gay people were very much like everyone else—working the same jobs, worrying about the same problems, and dealing with the same vexing issues of contemporary American life.

The opponents of the ban needed to show that gay people's hopes, fears, attitudes, and values were the same as everyone else's. They failed to do so, and the stereotype of the promiscuous gay world of the 1960s and 1970s was allowed to fester, a stereotype that was implicitly and explicitly amplified in church pulpits and across the airwaves in advertisements pushing for the ban's passage. In fact, Pastor Rick Warren of the Saddleback megachurch, who gave the invocation at Barack Obama's inauguration, had associated gay relationships with bestiality, polygamy, and pedophilia.[xxxviii] In answering these wild and wildly varying charges, the same-sex marriage proponents failed to come up with a consistent theme from which they would not diverge. They never kept on message because they never developed one.

What could they have done? Opponents of the ban needed to respond to their critics, but veering from one issue to another without a common theme did them no good. Politely answering incendiary charges does not work either. Even if they felt forced to answer the sometimes outlandish charges of the ban's proponents, they always should have steered the response back to the central theme of the campaign—We're just like you. If you deny these rights to us, you weaken everyone's protections under the law.

The proponents of the ban, on the other hand, played their cards just right. They won not only because the minority failed to follow the rules, but also because they assumed the majority role, and the majority has strong advantages it can use in opposing the minority. But, one might argue, in a tight election, there's no clear majority—after all, until the very end, the vote seesawed between passage and rejection. This is true, but it also is true that the framers of the ban *acted* as if they were the majority. And the opponents of the proposition *acted* as if they were the minority, and a disorganized one at that. Adopting a majority stance works if not counteracted. In chapter 9, we'll consider some of the ways the majority proactively defends its turf. We'll see that it's not just minority failure that allows the status quo to reign supreme, but it also is the majority's direct opposition to the minority that must be overcome if it is to prevail.

Why Is Consistency of the Minority's Message So Critical?

Considerable research has demonstrated that the minority will have little chance of bringing the majority to its way of thinking unless it presents a consistent message and sticks with it through thick and thin. This research was reviewed in chapter 5, and will not be hashed over here. However, the presentation to this point begs the question: *Why* are consistent minorities so much more effective than inconsistent ones? The failure of inconsistent minority messaging was demonstrated vividly in California's same-sex marriage battle, but the presentation to this point has not addressed the reason why consistency is so important when the minority seeks to move the larger group.

The most obvious reason is that majority group members' perceptions of the consistent and persistent minority are very different from their perceptions of an inconsistent and wavering minority. Clearly, people who are willing to stick their necks out for an unpopular cause in the face of threats and ridicule believe in what they say. This attribution that the minority message source believes its message does not necessarily convert the majority, but it may stimulate its members at least to consider their message. Think back to research in which subjects learned that a speaker was to give a speech to a hostile audience. The message he delivered was significantly more persuasive than the same message that was to be delivered to a friendly audience. We learned that subjects in the "hostile audience" condition of the study were more positively disposed to the speaker. They considered him significantly more sincere and honest, and less cynical and opportunistic, than subjects who heard the same speech that speaker was allegedly to give to a group expected to agree with him.

When we listen to a persuasive message from someone we admire, even if that person is a member of the minority, there is a reasonable chance that we will be moved by the message. This is especially so in cultures that value underdogs. We seem to assume that if people are willing to take a beating for their beliefs, then at a minimum their beliefs must be strong. Usually, this response triggers our curiosity—"Why are they saying the things they're saying? Why are they so convinced?"—and this curiosity leads us to consider their words carefully. These kinds of responses are expected when the speaker is part of our group. With out-group speakers (say, Sarah Palin at the Democratic National Convention), we often prove to be considerably less interested in their rants, and considerably more willing to reject whatever they have to say. According to this reasoning, the positive effects of in-group minority consistency occur because message recipients like or trust the source as a result of consistency, which suggests that the speaker is telling the truth. The majority enjoys a distinct advantage, as it is generally assumed that one's majority group is acting in one's behalf. However, the minority can enhance the audience's perception that it is trustworthy by promoting a consistent and strong line of argumentation. A wavering or weak message is the kiss of death for the minority, because its arguments will not be seen as credible or worthy of trust.

Obviously, it's more difficult for the minority than the majority to prevail. But we already knew that. The majority has the advantage, even if the minority follows all the rules carefully. But the minority can avoid stepping into many of the common traps that often prove so attractive. The minority has enough trouble making its case without helping the opposition.

We will consider how the majority protects its position, its persuasive strategies, and the many tools it can use to maintain the status quo in the next chapter. The defenses it brings to the ring do not always follow the Marquess of Queensberry's rules, but they usually succeed. Understanding the ways the majority defends itself against minority influence is both interesting and informative. For influence agents, this understanding is essential.

NINE

The Empire Strikes Back

Strategies and Tactics of Majority Resistance

Individual rights are not subject to a public vote; a majority has no right to vote away the rights of a minority; the political function of rights is precisely to protect minorities from oppression by majorities.

—*Ayn Rand*

The Augusta National Golf Course is one of the most beautiful sporting venues in the world. Built in 1933 on the site of a former indigo plantation, it reeks of Southern courtliness and charm. Since 1934, the course has hosted the Masters Tournament, one of the four crown jewels of professional golf. Even non-golfers find the course and its tournament enchanting. The Masters typically ushers in spring, and for many living in the northern United States, provides hope they just might make it through another winter. Behind this idyllic picture, however, is an unpleasant reality, for although the Augusta club's membership numbers many of the country's most influential men, it admitted its first black member 127 years after the Emancipation Proclamation, and women have fared even worse. As of 2010, there had never been a female member of the Augusta National Golf Club.

Martha Burk, chairwoman of the National Council of Women's Organizations (NCWO), took the club to task for its exclusionary policies. In a letter to the club's chairman, Burk wrote, "Our member groups are very concerned that the nation's premier golf event . . . is hosted by a club that discriminates against women by excluding them from membership." She went on to say that the NCWO, an umbrella group of organizations focused on women's rights, represented more than 7 million members, and urged the club to open up to women immediately, so that this issue would not be relevant "when the tournament is staged next year."

As the 2003 Masters Tournament was looming, Augusta National's leadership responded vigorously to Burk's letter and the not-so-subtle threat they felt it contained. In an overnight counter, the chairman of the club, William "Hootie" Johnson, wrote that he found Burk's letter "offensive and coercive," and refused to have any further communication with her or the NCWO. As the apparently more powerful party, Johnson could fire back and also decide the rules of the game. In this case, he interpreted the rules to mean that he could ignore his critic.

The press pursued the story, however, and ignoring Burk was not an option.[xxxix] Recognizing this, Johnson published a three-page defense in which he argued that "The message delivered to us was clearly coercive. . . . We will not be bullied, threatened or intimidated. We do not intend to become a trophy in their display case," and, "Our membership alone decides our membership—not any outside group with its own agenda." This did not end it, and as the story continued to attract media attention, Johnson held a news conference at which he declared, "If I drop dead right now, our position will not change on this issue. It's not my issue alone. I promise you . . . our position will not change."

Johnson's varied and assorted responses supply a primer for some of the ways the group in power resists pressure from the outside. In his first communication, you should note the chairman did not deny the facts. He never said Augusta National had women members over the long course of its history, and so could not deny obviously discriminating against them. Surely at some point in the past seventy-plus years, at least one woman golfer deserved an invitation to the join the club. However, neither was he responsive to Burk's complaint. Instead, he asserted that her letter was offensive and that his organization would not be pushed around or intimidated. He gallantly stood up to the onslaught of this "outside group," which clearly did not appreciate the place of Augusta National in American sports lore. This golf club whose members included the richest and most powerful men in the country assumed the (underdog) position, with their beleaguered leader standing firm at the barricade and waving the Gadsden flag with its rattlesnake and DON'T TREAD ON ME motto. Hootie was not a man to be bullied. His (non)response is a nice example of a common way strong groups counterattack threatening outgroups, and the feminists of Burk's organization were clearly that. Rather than meeting the issue head-on, the majority diverted the disagreement to a tangentially related issue, so instead of dealing with sex discrimination, the chairman asserted his determination and courage to stand strong against bullies. This is an admirable sentiment, but it has little to do with gender equality. Even more, the response shifts the roles of the protagonists. The Augusta National Golf Club, whose membership numbers the country's elite, was portrayed—by Hootie—as being at the mercy of a coven of tyrannical feminists.

Still skirting the issue, Johnson then asserted that all the (male) members of the club were on board with its all-male policy, suggesting unity in the ranks. You might have noticed that this response still does not deny the basis of the outsiders' complaint. The claim of unanimity is important, however, because it suggests that the outsiders are not likely to induce the club's members to flock to its side in the dispute. In responding to a challenge from the outside, from an out-group, the stronger targeted organization often demeans the opposition, trumpets its solidarity, shifts the argument to more amenable grounds, and does not give an inch. Generally the strong will appeal to one or another of these tactics, but Johnson won the trifecta—he tried them all, and he largely succeeded. Augusta remains a bastion of rich white male golfers. Representation of black men is minimal, and of women, it is nonexistent.

A Penny for Your Thoughts . . .

The majority's refusal to respond directly to a minority group's accusations is a common tactic that often accomplishes its goal. Why do you think it succeeds? The sad truth is that the success of this kind of "answer by misdirection" depends on a listless, uninformed, or unconcerned audience. Is that a reasonable assessment of some of us? There's strong evidence that it is. More than twenty-five years ago, three researchers published a measure they called the "need for cognition" scale. It has become a widely used psychological test that is designed to identify differences among people in their "general tendency to engage in and enjoy effortful cognitive endeavors."

In other words, the researchers created this instrument to distinguish people who find it pleasant to think hard from those who find it hard to think. The scale was developed on college students. Imagine that—college students who do not like to think! Later research—literally hundreds of studies have been conducted with the scale—has involved other, more representative samples of the population, and the results across all groups are largely the same.

The research shows that people who score high on the need for cognition scale tend to seek out, and think about, information they need to make sense of their world, and they enjoy doing so.[xl] People with a diminished need for cognition are inclined to listen and go along with others' interpretations, especially if they view these "others" as experts or members of their in-group. They follow the lead of these other people when deciding how they should think and behave.

A sampling of some of the items of the scale gives a flavor of the instrument. If you're feeling particularly thoughtful, you might like to answer them. On the actual test, each item was followed by a scale like the one shown below the item set:

---

1. Thinking is not my idea of fun.

2. Learning new ways to think doesn't excite me very much.

3. I only think as hard as I have to.

4. I like tasks that require little thought once I've learned them.

1	2	3	4	5
Strongly Agree	Agree	Neutral	Disagree	Strongly Disagree

If you answered any of these questions in the strong affirmative, you probably should put this book down and take a nap. In the scale's introduction, the instructions say that there are no correct or incorrect answers to the items, but to a thinking person this seems like a misprint. The sad conclusion we can draw from this research is that many people, even those numbered among the nation's supposed intellectual elite, may be inclined to accept ideas or interpretations of issues simply because of who suggests them, rather than on the basis of the apparent validity of the information. People who are low on the need for cognition do not like to go to the trouble of thinking deeply about issues because they do not enjoy thinking. So how do they decide among the various alternatives that wait around every bend? They listen to what others say, and follow directions. They are suckers for incendiary propaganda and unscrupulous demagogues who are willing to ignore reality in their quest for greater influence or power, especially if these leaders can portray themselves as experts, trustworthy, and ingroup. Such spokespersons are especially powerful if they appear to have a direct line to the deity.

The Power's Edge

Let's consider some of the more common and perhaps egregious influence strategies and tactics used by the powerful. The list is far from complete, but it provides a flavor of the large advantages the strong enjoy in combating weaker groups' requests and demands. There is no doubt the playing field is uneven. The majority almost always has the edge, in part because it can use powerful influence strategies to which the weaker group usually is not privy, and because many of those who receive the majority's message are ingroup majority members themselves. If they are deficient in the need for cognition, they are prone to accept mainstream constructions of reality without much thought or argument.

The strategies the stronger group or its spokesperson employs to defuse a minority's attack will depend on the nature of the contender. The majority has an easier time of it if the complainant is not in-group, because it then can work to show its members that the critics are either irrelevant or threaten important group values. It can disparage and attack the out-group without concern, because the out-group does not play a role in the members' self-identity. In fact, drawing a distinction between us and them strengthens in-group identity.

Usually, the majority needs only to convince its members to ignore the out-group's attack. When the critics are out-group, the
folks in power can succeed in refuting them without undue consideration of the logic of their counterattack. This was Johnson's
first ploy. It did not work well, because the minority was not an
out-group to anyone other than his membership, it would not go
away, and it brought the issue to a larger venue than the membership of Augusta National. When Burk went public, she changed
the game. Let's follow the progress of the majority's self-defense
in this case study.

Majority Strategy 1: Emphasize the Minority's Out-group Status

Hootie's first retort, the most common line of defense for the majority when dealing with a pesky out-group, other than simply
ignoring the complainants, was to remind his members that their
critics were just that, an out-group. In his response to Martha
Burk, Mr. Johnson was proper, but his tone was aggressive. He
made it clear that he did not feel he was talking to an equal. He
did not need to go further, because on any number of sports call-
in shows, anonymous guest callers insisted Burk was a man-hater
and a lesbian who deserved to die. She received a number of let-
ters threatening her life (usually neatly printed in crayon). Whoever said golf was for sissies?

Those who opposed her position might not have understood the
deeper strategy of their aggressive responses, but in essence, attacks of this kind are designed to keep the critic from being seen as
part of the larger group, in this case, worthy Americans. The majority tries to discredit the out-group's credentials because by doing
so, it destroys the critic's credibility and moral authority, *at least for*

members of the in-group. Convincing in-group members that the minority is not a part of the group, that "they" do not belong with "us," effectively negates the minority's voice and legitimacy.

Leaders of the stronger (Augusta National) group have won the game if they can persuade the rank and file that their critics do not belong to the larger collective and, in fact, may be a threat. This out-grouping tactic has a powerful effect, because unless they threaten the in-group, out-group minorities usually are safely ignored—they do not exist, for all practical purposes. If a group does not exist, then nothing it says or holds dear needs be considered, much less accepted. The tactic of making a minority an out-group, however, does not work every time, because sometimes the weaker group cannot be smeared with the out-group paint.

Johnson tried this first line of defense with Burk and her NCWO, but it did not suffice. Although he convinced *his* group to stand firm—only two of approximately three hundred members resigned from the National—the issue had grown to involve more than just the club's membership. Now the contenders were playing on the international stage, and the Augusta club did not appear to be winning the match.

Majority Strategy 2: Claim the Minority's Demands Threaten Group Viability

The group membership question is only the first roadblock the larger group erects, but it is crucial, because if the minority cannot establish its in-group credentials, or is prevented from doing so by the actions of the majority, then for all practical purposes the influence process is stopped in its tracks. If the minority is not accepted as a legitimate (if strange) part of the in-group, it need not worry about crucial features of social influence, like how it presents its message, the unanimity of its voice, its persistence, consistency, whether the message somehow can be crafted so that it is seen as consistent with the general values of the majority, or whom the minority's request will serve or disadvantage.

If the minority fails the in-group test, its petition never leaves committee. It is critical, then, for the majority to push the minority into the out-group if it can. For Hootie Johnson, Burk and her group of 7 million women were the minority. From the standpoint of the members of his organization, this probably was true. In Burk's mind, the majority was the American people, and this is why she sought widespread coverage of the fight. For most observers, Burk's was the more sensible view. One of the reasons Hootie's arguments probably seem largely beside the point to most of us is that most of us do not belong to the Augusta National Golf Club.

As this drama played out, Johnson probably saw that the publicity he and his beloved organization were receiving was largely unfavorable, so he moved to the old "in-group viability threat" defense that often is used by the majority to neutralize the out-group. This defense requires the majority leadership to show the membership that the minority threatens its very existence. This approach is useful when the first line of defense is not. Its usage is common in business settings in which different factions come to different conclusions about how a process should proceed, how a campaign should be run, or how a recommendation or procedure should be implemented. In these circumstances it is difficult to define the opposition as out-group, even though they might hold positions diametrically opposed to one's own. After all, the members of the opposition work for the same firm, are keen on maintaining their livelihoods, seem willing to go to great lengths to ensure the viability of the company, and draw a paycheck signed by the same financial officer. Even when the majority includes the

CEO, ostracizing (or firing) the minority group is unusual. When he was CEO of General Electric, Jack Welch was renowned for his no-nonsense approach. He was quick to ditch managers whose productivity fell behind that of their peers. However, even Welch was not averse to disagreements with his staff, if their arguments were cogent (and panned out). In contexts such as these, there is not much room for using Strategy 1.

In using the second strategy, Hootie Johnson implied that the admission of women to the Augusta club would be a capitulation, accomplishing no more than giving Ms. Burk and her organization another scalp to hang on the wall. More important, he implied that the club would be irretrievably changed if this were to take place. Handing over the right of the club to enroll the members it wished to an outside feminist group would ruin Augusta National, and neither he nor the members would surrender club membership selection to a bunch of outsiders. That this was not what his critics were asking for was neither here nor there (see Strategy 1).

If the minority cannot be discredited as out-group, the majority may try to show that its proposals threaten the basic structure, perhaps even the continued existence, of the larger group. If the fundamental basis of the group is compromised by acceding to the minority, expect robust majority resistance, because we use the group to define ourselves, and changing it threatens our self-identity. Suppose you were a member of a fiscally conservative political party, whose battle cry was "No new taxes." The party holds other views as important—government is too big, entitlements have to be restrained or cut, and so on. You might be able to argue for maintaining some public programs, like Medicare, but you could not argue for raising taxes and still retain your party membership card. Your position would cut to the very heart of the organization. The membership could not accept it, and you would be redefined as being out-group, a threat to the viability of the grand old "no new taxes" party.

Majority Strategy 3: Raise the Threat of Minority Self-Interest

A related majority-resistance tactic is to question the vested interests of the minority. What do they have to gain by the majority's acquiescence to their demands? What will it cost us? Minority groups always are faced with this question, and their likelihood of success is much greater if they can show that the majority has as much to gain as they do if the requisite changes are made—that the minority is not arguing simply to gain a special advantage, although of course it is recognized that they, too, will gain if they attain their goals. The majority can resist influence by arguing that it will be unfairly disadvantaged if it accedes to the minority.

Affirmative action laws provide a useful example of this tactic in action. Generally, these laws are not particularly well received by the majority of white Americans. A poll conducted by Quinnipiac University in June 2009 showed that 55 percent of its sample believed that affirmative action should be abolished, and only 36 percent felt it should be retained. More than 70 percent of the respondents believed that the goal of diversity was not sufficient reason to give preference to minorities in either government or private sector jobs.[xli] One would think that the majority would rule in this case, but the minority sometimes can win even in cases such as these, when the imbalance of opinion is massive. The University of Michigan's successful defense of its affirmative action rules in its admissions procedure (chapter 5) against strong opposition involved showing that its use of race in admissions decisions advantaged both white and black students. If it had not been able to convince the court of this, the university would not have prevailed.

Majority Strategy 4: Analyze the Appeal and Counter

Even if the minority successfully navigates the shoals of the first three majority tests, it cannot assume a safe harbor, as the majority then engages in a close analysis of its message, which, as noted, includes a less-than-disinterested attention to the minority group's motives. Returning to Augusta, let's assume that Burk's minority had eluded Hootie's initial traps. If the minority had been in-group, this would be an easy assumption: The in-group minority cannot be cast out into the out-group darkness, nor can it be demeaned, as in-group members are not fair game for derogation. However, the logic of in-groups' appeals can be attacked. If its message is not strong and persuasive, its entreaties will be dismissed. For the out-group minority, the test is even more stringent, because everything that can be used against it will be.

Even assuming the minority develops an extremely persuasive communication does not guarantee instant success, because under these conditions, the majority's movement will not be seen on the focal issue, their central appeal, but on a related issue or issues. These indirect changes, as we've seen, sometimes are sufficiently large to induce a delayed change on the issue at the heart of the controversy. This does not seem to have occurred in the case of the Augusta club. The majority in this case was able to weather the tempest, maintaining its exclusivity and its membership, but whether it will be able to weather future storms, should they arise, is another question.

Influence Tactics

It is important to consider the counter-communication tactics the stronger group uses to hold off an insistent minority. You have seen these tactics in action many times, and they can be extremely powerful.

Majority influence tactics can be grouped into three main categories, which I have labeled ignore/condescend/punish, the big lie (with constant repetition), and the kitchen sink. They often are used in combination, but sometimes a single approach works just fine. The landscape of repudiated persuasion attempts is strewn with the debris of all three tactics, and I would be surprised if you did not recognize them immediately.

Ignore/Condescend/Punish

One of the best examples I have seen of the ignore/condescend/punish tactic occurred when I was a student in graduate school. A famous psychologist from another university was visiting my school and gave a wonderful lecture about his popular theory of persuasion, which was the culmination of nearly a decade's work. Almost everyone was impressed with the speaker's intelligence, wit, and insight, but some of us were bothered because he had not addressed a scathing attack on his labors that had been published only a few months previously. When we (probably discourteously) asked him about the well-argued and well-documented attack on his most important intellectual accomplishment, he professed ignorance, and then not too subtly lashed out at his tormenter—"I'm afraid I haven't seen that paper [ignore]. But then, I rarely read his work [condescend]—it's never impressed me much [punish]. Let me get back to you on that. . . ." Of course, he never did. Afterwards, we judged the probability that he had not read the critical work as close to zero.

At a somewhat grander level, think of Barack Obama's ignore/condescend/punish response to the birthers, the minority movement that continuously and heatedly raised questions regarding his place of birth. The birthers provoked this furor over Obama's birthplace because the U.S. Constitution requires the president be a natural-born citizen of the United States, and they insisted that Obama was not. Therefore, he was not eligible to serve, should be replaced forthwith, and presumably thrown into jail for impersonating a citizen. Mr. Obama's supporters asserted that that issue should be off the table for anyone capable of reading a birth certificate or an old newspaper's birth announcements—and use logic or common sense—but despite evidence to the contrary, the birthers continued to insist on Obama's foreign nativity and consequent ineligibility to lead the country.

A certification of live birth from the State of Hawaii and newspaper announcements of Obama's birth published in 1961, when it allegedly occurred, were not persuasive to the birthers even though two successive Republican governors of Hawaii seemed to find the evidence compelling. These documents were rigged, the birthers argued, they were all part of a giant conspiracy cooked up decades earlier, apparently before Obama could even spell the word *president,* much less think about running for the job. For many, these assertions lacked substance or logic, but they were held firmly by some, even by some who entertained the notion of taking Obama's place on the throne—and who could produce a U.S. certificate of live birth.

Obama's original response was to ignore the birthers. During his campaign, he desultorily published a short form of his birth certificate, and birth announcements from two Honolulu papers, and then ignored (or avoided, according to the birthers) the issue. Even after he won the general election, however, the birthers would not cease and desist. If anything, their claims became even more insistent, their accusations more strident. In office, Obama's response now became one of bemused condescension, much like parents might treat a favored child they have just caught trying to teach the family's pet cat to swim. At a National Prayer Breakfast in February 2010, for example, he said, "Surely you can question my policies without questioning my faith. Or, for that matter, my citizenship." By March 17, 2011, St. Patrick's Day, the furor had intensified further. Alluding to his (very) distant Irish heritage, America's first black president stated, "Now, speaking of ancestry, there has been some controversy about my own background. Two years into my presidency, some are still bent on peddling rumors about my origins. So today, I want to put all those rumors to rest. It is true my great-great-great-grandfather really was from Ireland. . . . I can't believe I have to keep pointing this out."

At that point, he still was condescending, gently mocking those who would not quit. He did not lash out at the birthers, for to do so would suggest that his position was in need of defending, and the furor was probably more damaging to the opposition party than to him. However, when he had enough of the controversy, he published the State of Hawaii's official "long form" of his birth, and hit hard, saying, "I know there is going to be a segment of people for which no matter what we put out this issue will not be put to rest. But I am speaking to the vast majority of the American people, as well as to the press. We do not have time for this kind of silliness. We've got better stuff to do." His initial ignore response had turned to condescension, and then to punishing.[22] Obama's prediction was right. A book published weeks

---

[22] It is interesting to take a moment to consider the birthers' communication tactics. They had little to no hope of succeeding, but following the rules, they were consistent with their message, and they persisted. Although this minority probably will lose this battle, at least they had adopted the approach that gave them the best chance. Not all minorities succeed, even when they do everything right. Sometimes the majority just has too much firepower.

after the more or less definitive proof of his birth in Hawaii, *Where's the Birth Certificate?: The Case that Barack Obama is Not Eligible to be President,* soon climbed to the *New York Times* best-seller list!

When the Majority Adopts Minority Influence Tactics

The majority sometimes adopts minority tactics, probably unwittingly, and this almost always turns out badly. This is especially true when the majority is newly established and is put on the defensive. The majority's ill-considered sprint to minority status is commonly seen in politics or in jury trials, especially when the defense has a weak case. Those who followed the trials of Kenneth Lay, the founder of Enron, and Jeffrey Skilling, its CEO, saw this mistaken tactic in action. Enron's corporate malfeasance was obvious. The greed of the corporation's leadership was breathtaking. They apparently had not learned the common Wall Street dictum, "Pigs get fat, hogs get slaughtered." Through illegal manipulation, Enron had sent the California economy into a tailspin, grafted billions of dollars from nearly everyone else with whom it came into contact, and the two men on trial were said to be the beneficiaries of much of it.

Obviously, with their multimillion-dollar ski lodges, two-hundred-foot yachts, and unbelievably sybaritic lifestyles, Lay and Skilling numbered among the wealthiest in the land. They had money, power, and influence. Yet, their lawyers adopted a minority-oriented defense that depended on the jury accepting these richest of Americans as in-group, as being just like you and me, in short as everyman. Lay's coterie of lawyers argued that Enron's years of chicanery occurred without Lay's knowledge. Their argument: "Imagine if you had been in their chairs. You could have been fooled just as easily. They're no different from you and me." True, maybe, but where did they think all that money was coming from?

As history would show, the jury didn't buy it. The appeal to a common social identity was never going to work. The minority-inspired social identity defense—"Look, Ken was just one of the boys"—was doomed from the start. Ken was not like you and me, unless you have a billion dollars in the bank, a bunch of houses, a fleet of expensive autos, and an unbelievable yacht. On the other hand, the defense did not have much else to work with, and justice prevailed.

The Kitchen Sink

The "kitchen sink" is another tactic often used to derail an opponent. We have seen its use in our earlier discussion of California's Proposition 8, which sought to ban same-sex marriage (chapter 8). In fighting this proposed measure, you will recall, those who favored maintaining the legal status of same-sex marriage had a single message that they needed to drive home, which was that gay people, as bona fide citizens of the country, deserved the same rights as everyone else. They could make this statement in any of a number of different ways, but the gist of their message needed to be the same in every case: We are part of the larger group and deserve to be treated as such.

Their opponents did not agree, but they rarely attacked that proposition head-on. Rather, they raised dozens of other issues, some of which were clearly untrue—the gay lifestyle would be taught in the schools as a desirable option, churches would lose their tax-exempt status, and others that seemed of dubious quality—same-sex marriage will weaken the very institution of marriage, and so on. Those supporting same-sex marriage were forced to stay on message or spend scarce resources combatting these wildly varying charges. It did not matter that their opponents' information could be disproved; merely responding to the many attacks the opponents of same-sex marriage forces threw at them would draw the minority off message. They did respond, were taken off message, and partly as a consequence, lost the battle.

Strictly speaking, the kitchen sink is not a technique reserved exclusively for the group in power. So long as an influence source can command an audience and has sufficient credibility to assure that it is not summarily dismissed, it can throw the kitchen sink at the adversary and get away with it. Usually, this tactic is used by the powerful to resist change, but even minority groups can take advantage of it if they satisfy the requirements of an attentive audience and some degree of credibility.

This technique works well because the group attempting to exert influence must keep on point when arguing its position, and this is especially true of the weaker of the contenders. It must not deviate, and must work to ensure that its message is not diluted by side issues. The competition is not required to cooperate.

In a weak versus strong contest, the strong often launches a variety of counters in defense of the status quo, and they are under no obligation to ensure that the issues raised in their defense are relevant or even true. Frequency counts. It is a sad fact that many of us are unwilling or unable to do the mental arithmetic to untangle complex (and sometimes even simple) issues. Remember the research on people's need for cognition? It does not paint a pretty picture of the cognitive acuity of our best and brightest. Often, we decide the better of two arguments by counting. "I've heard ten arguments against this proposal, and only two in favor, so the no's have it." This approach rewards frequency over argument quality. Logic is a common casualty when frequency is used to judge the credibility of a communication.

The Big Lie

The big lie is another technique that has been used by many, for many years. It works well for the majority, and even can be adapted for use by the minority, if the majority is complacent. The technique requires the influence agent to fabricate a story about the opposition and to push it *relentlessly*. In a nutshell this is how it works, according to Hitler's Reich Minister for Public Enlightenment and Propaganda, Joseph Goebbels:

> **If you tell a lie big enough and keep repeating it, people will eventually come to believe it. The lie can be maintained only for such time as the State can shield the people from the political, economic and/or military consequences of the lie. It thus becomes vitally important for the State to use all of its powers to repress dissent, for the truth is the mortal enemy of the lie, and thus by extension, the truth is the greatest enemy of the State.**

Think back to the 2004 presidential race involving John Kerry and George Bush. When Kerry decided to make a run for the presidency, his strategic plan was evident from the first day of his announced candidacy. He would base much of his appeal to voters on the fact of his service in the war in Vietnam. His demeanor was soldierly, and his audience during his announcement of his intention to run for the presidency was stacked with former soldiers with whom he had served. Throwing his hat in the ring, he announced to all that he was ready to serve.

The soldier-diplomat link that Kerry was trying hard to establish was challenged by a group who called themselves the Swift Boat Veterans for Truth.[23] They argued vociferously that Kerry's

---

[23] The group's name referred to the type of boat that Kerry commanded during the war in Vietnam.

heroic standing as a soldier was a myth, a bright and shining lie that the American people needed to understand and reject. Kerry and his campaign were caught flat-footed. How could anyone question Kerry's war hero status? He had been awarded a Bronze Star, a Silver Star, and three Purple Hearts, having been wounded three times in service of his country. Nothing doing, his detractors argued, none of his wounds were all that serious. What the Swift Boat Veterans chose to disregard is that an inch or two in either direction and his wounds might have become extremely inconvenient. The Silver Star is the nation's third highest combat medal; it commends distinctive gallantry in action against the enemy of the United States. His commanders at the time commented on his gallantry, which bordered on selfless recklessness. He seemed willing to sacrifice his life for the men in his command—yes, he sometimes took grave chances in doing so, but his judgment was always vindicated, as his men survived many close scrapes.

The so-called Swift Boat Veterans simply ignored the accounts of Kerry's commanding officers, who recommended his citations, and even of those of the men who had served with Kerry on the very mission he won the Silver Star. They branded him a showboat, reckless and cowardly, whose actions were always self-serving and always exaggerated. They were not happy that he had come out publicly against the war after his discharge, and called this action a betrayal of his fellow soldiers.

Weeks passed before Team Kerry responded to the Swift Boat Vets, who, incidentally, had ample funding from those actively opposed to the election of a Democratic president.[24] This delay was important, because it created the impression that there might be some truth to the story. Otherwise, what took them so long?

---

[24] Sam Fox, a right-wing billionaire, had financed the campaign. Bush later sought to appoint him ambassador to Belgium. The Senate blocked the appointment, but he was appointed during a Senate recess.

Many voters who had once assumed Kerry's war hero status had begun to rethink their position. At a minimum, some degree of doubt in Kerry's self-presentation as a statesman-warrior had developed around his candidacy. This was a problem, as part of his planned appeal was to show how his early military service, combined with his years in politics and his impressive Senatorial career qualified him to the nation's toughest job. The uncertainty created by the Swift Boat crew was a massive distraction, and in the end, it ruined Kerry's chances. Voters did not necessarily change their attitude about the candidate, but the attack on Kerry's courage did affect their interpretation and acceptance of everything he said.

What should Kerry have done? This is difficult to say, because to claim in response to his detractors, "Yes, I am a genuine war hero," seems so self-serving that it would not have flown. The public does not like braggarts, but others might have picked up the torch sooner than they did. The response to an attack that should not have surprised the Kerry camp was a clear indication that they did not understand the nature of the opposition. In all his previous campaigns, his opponent had smeared his opposition. In his race for governor of Texas, Mr. Bush (or rather, perhaps, his adviser, Karl Rove) mounted a whisper campaign using a push poll to slander his opponent, Governor Ann Richards, with innuendos of rampant lesbianism in her staff. In the South Carolina presidential primary, Mr. Bush's opponent, John McCain, was slandered with yet another whisper campaign alleging that McCain had fathered an illegitimate daughter, who also happened to be African American.

This was the sort of campaign Rove ran. He had a history of using lies and innuendo to smear and weaken his opponents. It was his normal way of running campaigns, so it was puzzling that Kerry's camp was caught off guard by the Bush attack. If anything, the Rove-Bush smear approach was business as usual. This sort of thing seemed to happen every time Mr. Bush ran for public office, and almost every time Rove ran a campaign. But the Kerry camp clearly appeared to have been stunned by the standard Rove tactic of attacking the opponent's strong suit, and the election was lost because of their campaign's lack of understanding of the rules of influence.

This analysis to this point begs the question of the appropriate response. What should Kerry have done? There are many things that a response to illogic or the big lie should be, but one of them is not a logical argument. It is impossible to fight illogic with logic. Kerry and his campaign tried to do so, but he would have been better served if his advisers had counseled him to mount a withering personal attack on his opponents, the Swift Boat Vets, Sam Fox (who funded the Vets), and even his opponent, Mr. Bush, whose own war record was open to serious question, and who would not disavow the scurrilous attacks beyond saying that he was not paying for them. A character assassination war would not have been pretty, and would not have raised the debate above the sewer level, but it would have worked better than the more admirable (if ultimately, losing) strategy Kerry chose.

We see similar tactics used today in many political contests, by members of both political parties. The big lie, if repeated enough, can work because it sometimes is easier to accept than to perform the mental effort to challenge it, especially by those with a low need for cognition, for whom thinking hard is unpleasant. And it is difficult to challenge a lie that is repeated time after time after time, especially if it is not countered rapidly, as John Kerry learned. This is why both major political parties now engage full-time "truth squads," whose job is to respond immediately to any information produced by their opponents that they deem fabricated or dishonest.

Let's Get Subtle: Innuendo Effects

Sadly, the big lie does not have to be that big. Harvard professor Dan Wegner showed in some exceptionally interesting research that even innuendos can bring an individual's reputation into question.[xlii] Wegner showed college students a set of newspaper headlines that referred to different people who were said to be running for public office in Seattle, Washington. According to the author,

> One headline appeared as a direct incriminating assertion (e.g., "BOB TALBERT LINKED WITH MAFIA"), another took the form of a question (e.g., "IS KAREN DOWNING ASSOCIATED WITH FRAUDULENT CHARITY?"), a third was phrased as a denial (e.g., "ANDREW WINTERS NOT CONNECTED TO BANK EMBEZZLEMENT"), and the fourth headline was a neutral assertion intended to serve as a control (e.g., "GEORGE ARMSTRONG ARRIVES IN CITY").

After reading the headlines, the students had to evaluate the various people named in them. Of course, the researchers were careful to associate the names they used with all four of the different outcomes mentioned in the headlines, and they balanced the order of the headlines across their sample of subjects. As might be expected, the person linked with the incriminating assertion (BOB TALBERT LINKED WITH MAFIA) was rated very unfavorably relative to the person in the control headline (GEORGE ARMSTRONG ARRIVES IN CITY). But the person associated with the innuendo (IS KAREN DOWNING ASSOCIATED WITH FRAUDULENT CHARITY?) was not any better off than the subject of the directly incriminating assertion. Karen was judged as being just as evil as Bob in this example, even though she was not accused of a crime—the headline merely raised the question of her involvement in a fraud. The denial headline produced judgments intermediate to those found in response to the control and the accusation headlines. At a general level, research on the innuendo effect seems to suggest that merely raising a question about a person's or a group's motives or the legitimacy of their appeal may effectively torpedo their effectiveness.

It gets worse. Wegner and his collaborators wondered if the credibility of the source would affect the strength of the innuendo effect, so they created a study similar to the one just described, but attributed the headlines either to a well-regarded newspaper (*The New York Times*) or one that most people do not see as a paragon of veracity or news ethics (*National Enquirer*). The credibility maneuver worked: People viewed the *Times* as significantly more credible than the *Enquirer*, and this made a difference, at least for those who received the incriminating assertion. The highly credible source, *The New York Times*, was more effective than the incredible one, the *Enquirer*, when incriminating assertions (BOB TALBERT LINKED WITH MAFIA) were made. However, the innuendo worked just as well as the accusation, and in the case of innuendos, the source did not matter. The headline IS KAREN DOWNING ASSOCIATED WITH FRAUDULENT CHARITY? had as big an effect on people's evaluations of Karen as the incriminating one (KAREN DOWNING LINKED WITH MAFIA), and it did not matter if it appeared in the *Times* or the *Enquirer*![25]

These results demonstrate that the source makes a difference when a direct accusation is made, but when we're talking innuendo, source seems irrelevant. Even worse yet, further research by

---

[25] Remember, the names and headlines were changed systematically, so sometimes Karen was incriminated, sometimes she went on vacation, and sometimes she denied wrongdoing, just as did Bob Talbert. These results were not specific to person or gender.

this same team showed that although denying the implications of a negative innuendo did not make matters worse, it did not make matters any better either. Denials do not reverse the innuendo effect.

Some Sobering Implications

This book is concerned with the ways the weak can enhance their likelihood of success with a strong opponent, but even when it follows all the rules laid out throughout the book, the minority never evens the odds. Like playing against the house in Las Vegas, the minority is always at a disadvantage. However, this does not mean that it never wins. Sometimes it does so by adopting the persuasive tactics used best by the majority. Sometimes it wins by the power of its persuasive arguments. Sometimes it lulls the majority into accepting a position it ordinarily would reject if its members were thinking hard. All these positive outcomes, at least from the minority's perspective, require active minority group members laboring to put their message on the table. The majority is under no such requirement. Often, it is sufficient for the stronger group simply to decline to attend to the weaker one's appeals. When the minority accepts this response and fails to push its agenda, the tactic is sufficient to defuse the minority's efforts and it allows the majority to go on as it always has.

Reviewing some of the strategies and tactics of persuasion the majority often uses should prove both enlightening and familiar. These tactics are encountered commonly, and they often are engaged in direct opposition to minority influence. To be most effective, the majority *sometimes* finds it necessary to understand the strengths and weaknesses of the minority when choosing the offensive or defensive tactic it will use. The minority, on the other hand, *always* must understand the strengths and weaknesses of the majority if it is to get its message across.

Although abbreviated, this review was meant to provide some idea of the uphill fight the minority must wage. And it demonstrates how the majority uses various means of deflecting the minority's entreaties to protect its privileged position. The minority's failing to understand the majority, and the majority's likely response to their appeals, usually results in the minority coming out on the losing end. It is important to realize that the majority has an impressive arsenal at its disposal, and this chapter has just scratched the surface of what it can do—but that's another story.

The New Rules of Influence

It does not require a majority to prevail, but
rather an irate, tireless minority keen to set
brush fires in people's minds.

—*Samuel Adams*

The history of most minority groups is a history of failure,
but failure is an avoidable outcome if you know the rules of
influence—and follow them exactly. In this final chapter, we'll go
over the rules. If you've jumped ahead and skipped everything
that came before, you might get some of the rules right, but you
probably will fall short of effective. The new rules of influence are
not like Dad's old scripts. They are dynamic and depend on a
good understanding of the context. The requirements are stiff
and must be followed, but they also require you to understand the
situation so that you can apply them intelligently. One size does
not fit all.

I have argued throughout this book that being an underdog
does not inevitably consign you to persuasive impotence. As we've
seen, the powerful do not always win the influence game, and the
weak do not always lose it. And even though the minority rarely
attains all it seeks, at least immediately, its actions can cause the

majority to bend, to make concessions on issues related directly or indirectly to the focus of contention. Sometimes, those making the concessions are not even aware of doing so. These accommodations are important because they pave the way for later adjustments on the critical issue, for delayed changes of attitudes and behaviors.

Looking back over ancient and recent history shows that unsuccessful minority groups have inevitably failed to adhere to the rules that have been exposed throughout this book, whereas minorities that prevailed adhered strictly to the rules. Minorities fail in many ways, but they succeed in exerting influence only when they follow the guidelines detailed throughout this book. Past minority successes were largely a matter of luck, as the rules of influence for those without the power to compel compliance have not been laid out explicitly before now. So how then did earlier minorities make good? They succeeded because they stumbled into doing precisely the right thing at the right time. Through luck or circumstance they followed the rules of influence that you now have in hand. Outsiders seeking to improve their chances of success must follow these rules, which have been uncovered over the past forty years of intense research. As promised in the first chapter, the rules are not complicated, but neither are they easy to apply. Failure to adhere strictly to them spells trouble, and violating the first rule, unquestionably the most important, almost always spells failure.

Rule 1. Be Accepted as In-group, as a Legitimate Part of the Larger (Majority) Group, as Part of "Us" rather than "Them"

The first and most important rule of influence requires that the members of weak or unpopular groups be accepted as legitimate members of the larger collective—the group they are attempting to influence. The minority, in other words, must become in-group, seen by the larger group as perhaps a bit quirky or unusual or misinformed, but "one of us" nonetheless—You may be an idiot, but you're our idiot. This does not necessarily imply that the minority must sacrifice its individual identity. Although "passing" or striving to be indistinguishable from the majority sometimes is necessary, there are many ways of becoming in-group and still maintaining individuality. A common and useful method of integrating with the larger group is by appealing to a larger, more inclusive identity, one that contains within itself both the majority and the minority factions. As we saw in chapter 3, the Tutsi of Rwanda did not do so, and suffered extermination of hundreds of thousands at the hands of the more powerful Hutu. They did not or could not incorporate themselves into the larger Rwandan body politic, and so became increasingly isolated, marginalized, and ultimately brutalized.

You might wonder in light of this genocidal action and of many others that readily come to mind—the near extermination of the Tamil Tigers at the hands of the powerful Sinhalese in Sri Lanka is another grisly example—whether the "shared identity" approach ever succeeds. Many believe it can, that it is a useful tactic in attempting to defuse mutually destructive intergroup war.

In his second State of the Union speech, Barack Obama showed a clear understanding and appreciation of the first rule, and the means of satisfying it, even in a country of growing and increasingly intense political divisions.[xliii] Obama gave his speech shortly after a disturbed young man attempted to assassinate a member of the U.S. House of Representatives, Congresswoman Gabrielle Giffords, in Tucson, Arizona. In this catastrophic attack, the assassin shot nineteen people, six fatally. Using this horrific event to call for an end to the viciousness that had come to characterize much of the political discourse in the country, including that occurring in the U.S. Congress, the president in his State of the Union address said,

> It's no secret that those of us here tonight have had our differences over the last two years. The debates have been contentious; we have fought fiercely for our beliefs. And that's a good thing. That's what a robust democracy demands. That's what helps set us apart as a nation.
>
> But there's a reason the tragedy in Tucson gave us pause. Amid all the noise and passion and rancor of our public debate, Tucson reminded us that no matter who we are or where we come from, each of us is a part of something greater—something more consequential than party or political preference.
>
> We are part of the American family. We believe that in a country where every race and faith and point of view can be found, we are still bound together as one people; that we share common hopes and a common creed; that the dreams of a little girl in Tucson are not so different than those of our own children, and that they all deserve the chance to be fulfilled.

Unmistakably calling for a recognition of the bonds that unite all citizens of the country, despite political differences, Obama emphasized an overarching identity, "we are part of the American family," to lessen the rancor that had become so characteristic of political interactions in the country. It is difficult to know whether his plea will succeed or fail. After all, merely pointing to the rule does not guarantee that anyone will follow it, but his attempt to evoke a common identity for the warring factions in American political life was wise and necessary. As an obvious minority group member for many years, Barack Obama learned and understands the first rule of minority influence.

The Rule in Action

The in-group minority often is the source of considerable innovation. Microsoft's shift from a massively successful programming and operating systems development and sales machine to a major player in the Internet came about as a result of a small in-group minority moving the establishment. The principal movers and shakers in the momentous decision of the company's hierarchy to change its successful business model, you will recall, were two young innovators who were not even remotely a part of the ruling junta. Sinofsky and Allard were at the beginning stages of their careers in a hugely successful business behemoth. Though Sinofsky was Bill Gates's technical assistant, neither he nor Allard had been around long enough to have keys to the executive washroom. However, they had a vision and a set of unusual skills and abilities that had atrophied among many in the company's hierarchy, the ruling class of Microsoft. To realize their vision, to achieve their goal, they had to show the powerful majority that their skills and abilities were essential to the company's continued dominance.

Sinofsky was considerably more in touch with the technologies driving this brave new world of communication (and sales), the Internet, than his boss. And he saw the immense financial benefits that would accrue to those who played a commanding role in the Web's evolution. He had something to offer the majority, and he was aware of the growing presence of Netscape Navigator, a Web browser that threatened to allow users to access their files across the network regardless of operating system. As Microsoft was primarily an operating systems company with a large market share, this possibility was a major threat to its continued world dominance. Sinofsky knew that by emphasizing the threat, he might gain a hearing. Allard was a programming whiz who possessed skills and abilities that his bosses probably never dreamed of, and certainly did not possess themselves—and he could see and articulate how the proper system could benefit any company that controlled it. He, too, had something to offer the larger group of nonbelievers. After some fits and starts, Microsoft's Internet Explorer was born, and was to play a commanding role as a Web browser that still controls the market. For most people, the names Erwise or Viola WWW do not ring a bell. These were among the earliest Web browsers, the trailblazers. Their names are unfamiliar to most because they were eaten by Microsoft, whose entry into the World Wide Web was made possible because a small and powerless minority in the company was in tune with the latest developments in the field, saw the changes in the digital world that were soon to take place, and succeeded in persuading Microsoft's power brokers that the company must evolve or face insolvency.

In most companies, ideas advanced by young mavericks pushing for a revolutionary change in a wildly successful business would be rejected outright. However, these spokesmen for a minority position had lots of things going for them, the most important of which was everyone's recognition of their legitimacy as members in good standing in the company, and a deep admiration for their technical abilities and the passion with which they made their case. Sinofsky and Allard were recognized as an in-group minority, a legitimate part of the whole. By combining this common group identity with their rare technical abilities, Netscape's threat, and the promise that the majority might reap great benefits by acceding to their (surprising) ideas, they were able to affect the beliefs and actions of the company's leadership, even though technically their position was a minority view when they originally pitched it.[26]

---

[26] Their minority status did not continue for long. Sinofsky is now a Senior VP at Microsoft, and Allard is the company's Corporate VP. They obviously fit into the hierarchy, even though they did not belong at the time of their assault on Gates or Microsoft.

Minor Exceptions to the Rule

The first rule is primary. Unless it is satisfied, in most circumstances the chances of the dissident group having any impact on the majority are negligible. Under some rare and unusual conditions, however, even the first rule can be circumvented, but these situations are exceptional. The outsider possessing a rare and special skill may influence the majority group's behaviors, and even beliefs, in contexts in which that special talent is required and recognized as essential. Your heart surgeon probably is not a member of your in-group, but it is likely that you will listen carefully to everything she says, even going so far as to change your diet and exercise regimen—if the stakes are high enough.

In situations in which the majority has not established a position, and in whose outcome it is not particularly invested, even out-group minorities can be influential. In those contexts, in fact, minorities might enjoy a slight persuasive advantage by virtue of their relative rarity. Minority group members draw attention because they are different, as do most rare or unusual people or objects, and this attention can be turned to advantage under highly prescribed conditions. If the minority's message is strong, the attention it attracts because of its unusual status can help its cause. An interesting example of the "unusual draws attention" formula is found in E*Trade Financial's ads that feature a talking baby playing the stock market and offhandedly giving investment advice. It's a fair bet that most of us have never seen or heard a two-year-old giving stock tips, and this might explain the success of the ad campaign. In circumstances involving the rare or unusual, we attend. The minority is rare and unusual, by definition, and so we might attend to and think about its message. Assuming the message is strong and logical, it might carry. If it is weak or illogical or incredible, the attention it draws will kill its chances, because attending closely to weak messages exposes their flaws. In general, it is unwise to bet the house on the out-group minority being widely and consistently persuasive. Under the constrained conditions I have described, the out-group can affect the majority, but these circumstances are not common.

When the issue matters to the majority, outsiders cannot prevail unless they are accepted by the larger group as a legitimate part of the collective. The first rule rules in all but the rarest circumstances. On issues that matter, you must be viewed as belonging to the group on some level if you are to exert influence. It does not matter that you hold beliefs or possess features that are distinct from the great mass of your fellow group members, if you are to prevail, you must be accepted as a legitimate part of the whole. If you are not, your chances of influencing the majority are practically nonexistent. Members of the Catholic Church's Curia, the officials that form the governing body of the Church, may respect the Dalai Lama and consider him a holy and admirable man, but it is not likely that they would accept his version of the virgin birth of Christ. He is an outsider in this conversation, and his views carry little weight. When talking about the sanctity of human life and the need to love and help our fellow human beings, his views will carry weight, because in this instance he is part of the larger group of men commonly viewed as devotees of charity for all people.

The Presentation Rules

Becoming accepted as "one of us" by the ruling group's membership is necessary, but it is not sufficient to guarantee persuasive success. How in-group dissidents present their appeal is critical. Rules 2 through 5, the Holy Trinity plus one, guide this process. These rules are combined here because they all are focused on how the minority must present its message. All these rules need to be satisfied by the minority in its appeal. It doesn't help if one or two of the rules are met, and the others are not. That is a recipe for failure. To succeed, the minority must develop its message and style of presentation so that each of these requirements is met. This is not easy to do, but no one ever said it would be. The rules that must guide the minority's presentation and presentation style follow.

Making the Case

Rule 2. Be Persistent: Don't Retreat and Don't Compromise

Rule 3. Be Consistent: Stay on Message

Rule 4. Be Unanimous: Everyone Must Be On Board

Rule 5. Be Flexible: Adjust Your Message to Circumstances

The reasons for these rules are easy to understand. A minority group's initial persuasive foray is likely to be met by the majority with benign neglect. If the weaker group fails to persist, nothing will happen. Lack of persistence on a contentious issue also may signal weakness or uncertainty. Either way, this is the death knell of persuasion. Conceding a point, compromising, or shifting a position may be read by the majority as a willingness to backpedal or give in on other positions, and the majority will try to take advantage of any lack of consistency. Remember, the majority is intent on maintaining the status quo. It is content to leave things as they are. An inconsistency in the minority's argument seriously deflates its moral standing, and encourages the majority to seek out other weaknesses in its arguments. Similarly, an inconsistency among the minority's members suggests to the majority that the position is not uniformly accepted within the contending group, and this leaves considerable room for resistance.

When the majority sees the minority gaining adherents, it often tries to buy it off by offering it some crumbs. Co-opting is a great strategy, and it works if the minority is willing to compromise. When the minority accepts the crumbs, its cause is lost, as acquiescence usually spells the end of persistence and fractures the unanimity of the group. The departure from persistence, consistency, and unanimity effectively blunts the thrust and the moral standing of the minority's position. If the majority's buy-off tactic does not work, brute force often does, but it is difficult to maintain force for long, and its use almost always has negative repercussions for the majority in the long term.

A modern example of a minority movement that refused to be bought off and maintained persistent pressure on the majority can be found in the events surrounding the Egyptian people's overthrow of President Hosni Mubarak in 2011. This revolution began with mass protests on January 24, 2011, and ended in his resignation only a few weeks later on February 11. Many have termed this a peaceful or bloodless revolution, but it would be hard to sell this description to the families of the men and women who died in the streets attempting to secure a new direction for the country (estimated at more than three hundred by the UN), or the hundreds more who were injured or "disappeared" while exercising rights that most of us take for granted. This revolution was not bloodless, nor was it easy. The speed with which it occurred might mislead the casual observer to assume otherwise, that it was nothing more than a pleasant stroll down the broad avenues of Cairo, but the reality was quite different.

When it started, no one knew what would become of the protestors on the streets. Past protests had been met with violent responses that left many civilians incarcerated, wounded, killed, or terminally "disappeared." Would Mubarak send in the tanks, much as the Chinese leaders did when unrest flowed into Tiananmen Square in 1989? How would the army respond? Would anyone come out alive in a confrontation with the government's tanks and armed brigades? No one knew the answer to these questions on January 24, but they went to the streets nonetheless, and started a chain reaction that engulfed the Middle East in a frenzy of regime change, the so-called Arab Spring of 2011.

Despite the questions of life or death, the people of Egypt responded to the call for change, broadcast through every available medium, and this unorganized mass, certainly a large and determined minority, prevailed. It prevailed due in part to its size, but its persistence and refusal to be bought off by the compromises that dribbled out of President Mubarak's office day by day and hour by hour really turned the tide. To maintain its position of privilege, the leadership tried desperately to co-opt the protestors in a vain attempt to defuse this seeming force of nature. First it offered some minor concessions: the president appointed a vice president. He was considering lifting the martial law that had been in effect for a mere thirty years. Prices would be adjusted, maybe. Corruption might be studied. In a major departure from form, the newly appointed Vice President Suleiman would meet with some of the more influential groups in the protest. None of this worked, as the protestors maintained their demand for wholesale changes in the governance of the country.

When a ranking member of the Muslim Brotherhood met with the new vice president, he described the encounter as follows: "We cannot call it talks or negotiations. The Muslim Brotherhood went with a key condition that cannot be abandoned . . . that he [Mubarak] needs to step down in order to usher in a democratic phase." It is clear that the goals of Egypt's leaders and the minority revolutionary movement were incompatible. In this game of chicken, one side or the other had to give way, and Mubarak was the first to blink.[xliv]

The protestors' refusal to bite into the forbidden fruits of concession, and their persistence in the face of great danger and even greater odds of failure were responsible for their victory. U.S. Secretary of State Hillary Clinton got it right in a speech at George Washington University, which she delivered shortly after Mubarak abdicated, when she observed, "Egypt isn't inspiring people because they communicated using Twitter. It is inspiring because people came together and persisted in demanding a better future." Persistence is an essential prerequisite of minority influence. If it is not a feature of the minority's approach, the minority will fail.[xlv]

It Won't Be Easy

The minority must expect resistance on all issues of contention with the majority, because the minority almost inevitably promotes positions that the majority views as being at odds with its vested interest. If this were not so, there would be no need for the minority to invoke the rules of influence. Every group would have a fair and equal chance of making its points and winning the day, but this level playing field is more likely found in fertile imagination than real life. If, as has been shown, the first response of the majority to the minority's appeal is rejection, then it is obvious that a nonpersistent minority does not have much chance of accomplishing anything. A less-than-determined minority that slinks away to lick its wounds after a few feeble forays into the majority's ring will lose the match. The status quo, which always favors the majority, will overwhelm all pressures for change. A minority willing to compromise or that continually changes or adjusts its demands will fail. A minority whose members do not present a united front will fail. With all this failure in the air, it should be easy to see that the minority's chances are not great. If it is to prevail, the weaker group must be persistent, it must not compromise, and all its members must be on board. The opponents of the minority take great comfort in a single turncoat, and this is probably why such "black sheep" are so universally despised by the group whose trust they betray.

Size Matters

Research suggests that large minorities are more likely to succeed than small ones. With large minorities, only a few converts can transform minority to majority. Strong minorities also have the benefit of credibility. It is more difficult to discount the position of 49 percent of a larger group than 3 percent of the group. However, size isn't everything, and even strong in-group minorities that fail the persistence test do not prevail.

Early in his presidency, for example, President Richard Nixon ventured eastward to confer with many of Europe's leaders and to deliver an address to the North Atlantic Council. Visiting England, Vatican City, France, and Germany, Nixon was impressed with the pomp and circumstance that attended European political and religious leaders. He was particularly impressed with the livery of the palace guards in many of the capitals he visited. On his return to the then friendly confines of Washington, D.C., he decided to redesign the White House police force's uniforms along regal European lines to be more in keeping with the grandeur of his recently acquired (White) house. To many, this turned out to be one of the most memorable accomplishments of his trip, as Mr. Nixon himself designed a uniform that raised torrents of laughter from even the most devoted Republicans. Wags of the time variously described the uniform as "belonging in Radio City Music Hall" or a musical comedy. The outfit was "festooned with gold braid" and "nipped at the waist with black leather gunbelts." The uniform featured "black vinyl hats trimmed in gold [that] suggested, by turns, a Ruritanian palace guard, a Belgian customs inspector, and Prince Danilo in *The Merry Widow*."

The point is not to make fun of President Nixon's imperial pretentions, or his marginal abilities as a clothing designer, but rather to point to the fact that after being met with less-than-stifled guffaws, the uniforms quietly disappeared—some say to a marching band somewhere in the Midwest. The president in this instance belonged to a truly tiny minority who liked the uniforms. Almost no one else in the country did, except perhaps the members of his innermost circle of advisers and loved ones, whose true attitudes have never been publicly disclosed. Many of these devotees risked prison to carry out the wishes of the president—remember Watergate?—but apparently even they could not stifle their laughter when the guards arrived in their new threads. The powerful in-group minority in this case did not persist, and as would be expected, did not prevail, despite numbering among its members (perhaps its only member) the most powerful man in the world at the time.

Contrast Mr. Nixon's much appreciated lack of persistence on the White House police guard uniform issue with the tenacity of Richard Chambers, a logging equipment salesman and avid outdoorsman. An Oregonian, Chambers had a habit of collecting litter on his hikes and climbing trips. In 1968, beer and soft drink companies had distributed more than 170 million bottles and nearly 300 million cans in Oregon—and many of these apparently were deposited along the trails Chambers loved to hike. He decided to do something about it. He wrote to a friend in the Oregon legislature and proposed to ban all nonreturnable cans and bottles. To promote the law's odds of passage, he ultimately proposed to require a five-cent deposit fee on returnables. The law was crafted carefully, but was defeated in the legislature.

The governor, Tom McCall, was in favor of Chambers's bottle bill, but the men had fallen out over another environmental issue. McCall subsequently offered his own bill, which required a deposit on cans and bottles that contained beer, water, and carbonated sodas. Despite stiff opposition from the beverage industry, the law passed this time and has served as a model for many other states. The Oregon bottle bill has subsequently been expanded and strengthened, and has made an important contribution to the ecology of the state. In 1974, just two years after the law went into effect, bottle and can litter had been reduced by nearly 85 percent.[xlvi]

Although the Oregon bottle bill was to have much further reaching consequences than Nixon's White House police uniform issue, at the time the bill probably was not seen as crucial to the fate of the Western world. It was passed, however, and has made an important difference to the quality of the environment, to conservation, and to the general welfare. In this case, the change was effected by a minority, originally one man, Richard Chambers, and later, Tom McCall, who took on the establishment and through persistence and strong arguments was able to succeed. McCall had an advantage of being governor, but he, too, faced immense odds. His in-group status was important—Chambers did not enjoy this advantage—but it was not enough. Without persistence and consistency of argument, the law would not have become a reality and the positive changes it has caused would not have been realized. Persistence in the face of sometimes strong opposition is necessary if the minority is to prevail, and this is true regardless of the issue: It was necessary for Nixon, who failed owing to a lack of persistence, and it was necessary for Chambers and McCall, who ultimately succeeded because of it. Had these men retreated from the field after their first reversal, their contribution would have been forfeit.

Credibility of an Information Source

The persistence and single-mindedness of Chambers and McCall worked wonders because their message was strong, but also because they had gained considerable credibility over the course of their interactions with the public. Credibility has been studied for the past fifty years in psychological laboratories. The research shows that it is largely determined by two features, expertise and trustworthiness. Expertise is concerned with the source's credentials, with the question of whether its information is valid or true, and trustworthiness has to do with the source's likelihood of gaining from your following its advice.

In this case, both men had established their expertise—much of McCall's work as Oregon's governor been devoted to ecological issues, and Chambers was well known as an authentic outdoorsman who spent most of his spare time hiking in the wilds of that beautiful state. What's more, neither man stood to make a dime from the bottle bill's passage. After an initial setback, the bill passed and the rest is history. The credibility these men had established had much to do with people's perceptions of their expertise and trustworthiness. They could have been viewed as eco-zealots, and might have been dismissed as rigid and incapable of understanding the larger issues surrounding their efforts. Certainly the bottling industry tried to portray them in that way. Their opponents argued that supermarkets would be buried under tons of empty bottles and cans, and that this would place an intolerable burden on them. The proponents of the bottle bill, however, would not back down. Rather than being perceived as rigid zealots, they were viewed as flexible and rational, as they offered proven solutions to the "buried under a ton of empty cans" argument. Flexibility involved solving the problems raised by their opposition, while tenaciously maintaining their position.

The minority seeking to move the majority to its way of thinking must satisfy both credibility criteria. If it falls below either the expertise or the trust bar, it has blown its chance. To bolster perceptions of its expertise, the minority's appeals must be persistent and consistent. It must walk a taut tightrope in carrying out this presentation strategy, because minorities that *rigidly* pursue their goals lead the majority to mistrust the information they provide. And what is rigidity? It is best described as extreme persistence and consistency without considering changing conditions. The minority must be consistent in the thrust of its position, but it also must be attuned to the environment in which its demands are made. If it is not, the majority's general attribution is that the minority is not trustworthy, because a failure to adjust demands to changing conditions leads people to mistrust the information they are given. A source's consistent immobility in the face of changing circumstances usually results in the source being viewed as so self-interested that it cannot be trusted. This seriously weakens its case, reducing its chances of persuading anyone.

Research conducted in Switzerland has confirmed this observation. In this study, the subjects listened to a speech that argued strongly for major changes in the Swiss Army. In Switzerland, all men must serve in the army. It also is important to know that at times in recent history, the army had been used by the government to quash what many Swiss people thought were legitimate strikes and demonstrations.[xlvii]

With this background, let's consider the study. It took a standard form. The researchers tested their subjects' attitudes toward the army, and also their feelings about conscientious objection. The subjects were apprentices—they were not wealthy people who would be expected to reject the speech outright. The initial measures showed that the apprentices were not particularly supportive of the army, and they were favorably disposed toward those who refused to serve on the basis of conscience.

Then the apprentices listened to one of two almost identical speeches. All heard a speech that bluntly contended that the army was an instrument of repression, an organization that quashed opposition views and stifled freedom in the service of the wealthy upper classes. Much of the talk was drawn from the writings of extreme left-wing groups, so the language of the persuasive speech was extreme. The speaker argued that revolutionary action from the inside was needed to weaken the army's stranglehold on the country's workers, and went on to say that conscientious objection was *not* a particularly useful or politically informed action, terming it "an excessively personal method."

Later in the message, the two speeches diverged to allow a test of the effectiveness of rigidity or consistency. The subjects assigned to the "rigid" speech group heard the speaker say, "In the struggle against [the army] . . . we think that means such as conscientious objection are false, personal . . . and quasi-reactionary." This sentence signaled not only that the speaker favored internal struggle, but that he rejected a response that he knew most of his audience favored as legitimate and reasonable—conscientious objection to military service.

Subjects assigned to the consistent but *flexible* message condition heard, "I would like to come back to our position on conscientious objection, which I expressed badly just now. We think that conscientious objection which is collective and organized is a good and valuable way of fighting the army. I simply wanted to say that we also think it important to contend against the army from the inside."

The central objective of both arguments was to fight the army from the inside, and this argument was consistent across the two speeches. However, in the rigid speech, the possibility of the apprentices moving to a middle ground was all but eliminated. It was all or none. You are with us or against us. In the consistent but flexible condition, subjects still heard an anti-army message, but it was consistent without being rigid. And it turned out that it was much more persuasive than the inflexible presentation.

The distinction between rigidity and consistency is not easy to realize in practice. The path the minority must tread is more like a tightrope than a wide boulevard, but it is essential that the distinction be understood and respected. One path leads to a successful change, the other to out-and-out failure. Vernon Allen and David Wilder, two leading social psychological theorists, said it very well when they observed,

> Even the in-group minority must recognize the dangers of majority rejection and be ready to combat this disadvantage with persistence and consistency. However . . . consistency and persistence must be tied to reality. If the reality changes, then the minority's persuasive appeal has to change as well. The minority cannot be rigid in its approach . . . [it] must alter its behavior to account for changing social situations.[xlviii]

Rule 6. Make the Subjective Objective

How often have you heard or said, "We'll just have to agree to disagree"? We resort to this expedient when we are at an impasse, when no further amount of persuasive argumentation will move either of the contending parties to the other side of the fence. If you think about it, this sentiment "works" only when one or both parties see the issue as involving subjective judgments, not objective reality. It makes no sense to "agree to disagree" about the capital of Ohio. There is a correct answer to this question. It is an objective fact. The source of the seemingly intractable chaos that exists in the interactions between Israelis and Palestinians is the subjective nature of the evidence that both sides use to support their arguments. I am aware that this statement will make me an enemy in both camps, a rare tour de force in the annals of persuasion, but how else is the inability to come to a rational solution to be explained? Each group believes that their arguments are grounded in the bedrock of objective truth. Both contenders have God on their side, and it is difficult to argue with God. That being the case, neither side feels the need to give an inch. How can we explain any of this other than to understand that the issues and interpretations under consideration are functionally subjective? This does not mean that there are no hard (objective) facts that can be brought to the table in this debate, but even when they are, their relative weight accorded by the warring factions differs enormously, as do their interpretations, and who's to say that your weighting scheme or interpretation is any better than mine? Subjective judgments can be effective, but success is considerably less likely when the issue rests on preferences rather than objective, verifiable facts.

We encounter these conflicts between objective facts and subjective opinions constantly. Deciding on the neighborhood that has the best elementary school for little Jennie should be an easy job. Hard data regarding students' standardized test scores are available, so the choice seems obvious, except it isn't. Even standard scores must be interpreted. Did the children from the contending schools start out the same, are the kids at the better-scoring school too concerned with social climbing, does the school tolerate behavior you find unacceptable, teach unacceptable dogmas like evolution or creationism (take your pick), and so on. All these considerations affect judgments and decisions, and all of them are subjective. The job of the persuader is to frame the issue in such a way that the objective evidence is unmistakable and undeniable, and more important, forms the basis of the argument. Moving the issue under debate from subjectivity to objectivity, from preference to fact, greatly enhances the outsider's chances. The minority *can* succeed when the issue is viewed by the larger group as involving subjective judgments, but its odds of success are greatly diminished.

It works this way because of the different functions that subjective and objective judgments are meant to serve. If we are dealing with a subjective preference, we generally are most interested in learning the likelihood that others *like ourselves* share the preference. If you are crazy about cars and have formed a strong attachment to this year's Jaguar sports machine, you will want to know what other car nuts think. The opinions of people who are not involved with automobiles are not nearly so interesting to you. You seek similar others. Expanding on this idea suggests that if you are in a majority group, the opinions and preferences of fellow majority group members on subjective issues will be preferred to those of the minority, even if the minority is in-group.

When making objective judgments, the focus is on finding the truth. Who utters it is secondary, so it follows that fellow majority group members do not have an advantage in objective judgment contexts. In fact, there is evidence that when attempting to form objective judgments we are more interested in information provided by those who are different from us. Plenty of explanations have been advanced for this preference, but its implication is that when objective judgments are under consideration, members of the majority will be more attuned to in-group minority voices than fellow in-group majority members. What this all means in practice is that if you are in a battle with the majority of your group, and have satisfied all the earlier rules of influence, it will be to your great advantage to move the argument onto objective grounds. Your chances of persuasive success are much greater if the discussion is viewed by the combatants as involving objective facts rather than subjective preferences.

Rule 7. Do Not Expect Direct Influence: Be Attuned to Indirect Influence

The majority is never keen to give up its advantages. When displaced and moved into the minority, the former majority group members often find their circumstances greatly diminished, so as a rule they are unlikely to welcome a minority's attempts to change the status quo. This reluctance to give up a privileged status is understandable. Why should we be expected to change the rules of the game that have allowed us to enjoy the top dog position?

Although the majority often declines to comply with the minority's demands, even legitimate ones, it has proved willing to give ground on issues that are related, though not identical, to the minority's position. So for example, staunch Roman Catholics may be strongly opposed to abortion, as this is their Church's irreversible position. A parishioner's call for a reconsideration of this position is likely to be firmly rejected. However, as a result of the parishioner's (rejected but well-argued) appeal, some majority group adherents may become somewhat more accepting of contraception, which also is contrary to the Church's official position, but may be less extremely held by the larger group. In this case, the minority has not moved the mountain, but the mountain has shifted a bit in the minority's direction.

If the change in the majority group members' attitude toward contraception is pronounced, this change will put pressure on related attitudes (among them, beliefs regarding abortion) to follow. With extremely strong attitudes, this process by which the indirect change drags the direct attitude in its direction is less likely, but with attitudes that are less central, indirect change can have a powerful effect on later, direct changes.

The opposite process in which the indirectly changed attitude reverts to its original position is more common. Unless the indirect change is great, the likelihood of the changed indirect attitude to spring back to its original value is high. However, if the indirect attitude is strongly modified as a result of the minority influence process, and the minority is aware of this change and builds on it, then it can parlay the indirect movement to pressure the belief that was the target of the persuasive attack in the first place.

Under normal circumstances, the majority almost never immediately accepts the minority's position. If it does change in the direction of the minority, it does so by the complex indirect-then-direct change process described here. Under the best of circumstances, the majority will concede a point that is related (but not identical) to the minority's demands. This need not be a conscious ingratiating tactic. Often, the majority group members are not even aware of their concession. They need not be if the minority senses the concession, is encouraged by it, and continues its agitation for change. Building on the indirectly changed circumstances, it has a great chance of prevailing.

The take-home message from this description of a somewhat roundabout process is that it is unrealistic for minority group members to assume that their appeals for change will be immediately welcomed by the majority and their petitions granted wholesale, without a fight. Regardless of the apparent legitimacy and logic of the appeal, the majority's instant acceptance of the minority's earnest and sometimes justified requests is a pipe dream. It will not happen.

WILLIAM D. CRANO

Consider the recurrent and heated debate over the plight of gay and bisexual soldiers in the U.S. military. Homosexuality has been grounds for dismissal from the U.S. Army from the time of America's Revolutionary War. Starting in the 1970s, the growing gay rights movement turned up the heat, continually pressuring the leaders of the country to remove this ban on service. They were not successful until 1993. At that time, owing to President Clinton's frequently voiced campaign promise to overturn the ban on gay soldiers, conservative forces in the Congress sought preemptively to pass a federal law outlawing gays in the military. The law would formalize the practice that had been in place by presidential directive since 1950.

Clinton, as usual, outmaneuvered his opponents. Owing to his political and persuasive skills, the Don't Ask, Don't Tell compromise was reached. Soldiers were not to be asked about their sexual orientations by their superior officers (don't ask), but they were not to divulge their sexuality (don't tell). The directive stayed in force till 2010, when Congress repealed the law, and now gay servicepersons may serve in the armed forces. This example serves as a useful reminder that one crucial determining factor in minority success is perseverance. Without it the initial and almost always predictable negative majority rejection will hold, and progress will not be made.

In addition to perseverance, the minority should be attuned to any concessions made by the majority. This sometimes can be difficult, as the concession might not always be immediately obvious, either to the minority *or* the majority. It is not required that majority group members realize that they have made a concession that in theory should placate the minority. In some cases the process appears spontaneous, an automatic response made to preserve the integrity or cohesiveness of the group. It is not necessarily a mindful or considered tactic. However, the minority attuned to the sometimes subtle concessions made by the majority can succeed in moving the majority on the central focus of its complaint— but it helps to recognize the majority's complicit reaction and proceed from there. Returning to the abortion-contraception example, if the minority recognizes the majority's softening on the issue of contraception, it can continue to press this advantage in further debates. Obviously, if the softening position is not recognized, minority group members would not feel they had much to gain by focusing on this topic, and the opportunity could be lost. However, if the change were recognized, the minority could use it as an entry into the larger debate of the ethics of conception and childbirth. This is not to say that even a mindful minority will succeed in this instance. Sometimes minorities fail even when they follow the script. But it is certain that they will fail if they do not recognize their advantage when it presents itself.

Postscript

The seven rules of influence developed in this book seem relatively easy to understand. They are. And they may seem easy to follow. They aren't. Although understanding the rules is not difficult, following them in the highly charged contexts in which weaker groups contend with stronger ones can be exceptionally difficult, but the record of successful and failed minorities clearly shows that honoring the rules can result in success, and failing to honor them almost always spells failure. Disregard any of these rules and the game is over for the minority. There are exceptions to the rules—they have been laid out earlier in this chapter—but it is important to understand that these exceptions occur in unusual and unlikely circumstances. The minority that bets on the long shot may succeed, if the stars align perfectly, but it is much more likely to fail unless it shortens its odds by following the rules to the letter.

If the underdog follows the rules of influence; if it works to be accepted into the larger group; if it remains consistent, persistent, united, and flexible; if it is patient and changes the debate from subjective preference to objective fact; if it is alert to even minor concessions; and if it follows these concessions and adjusts its methods accordingly, it can succeed, and in many cases, will succeed. Armed with this information, you can move stronger opponents to your side of the table. You will not always succeed, because the majority always has the advantage. But if you follow the rules of influence, you will massively enhance your likelihood of success.

Acknowledgments

In developing this book, I drew information and inspiration from a host of researchers whose work forms the basis of my arguments. My first debt of gratitude goes to them, many of whom are not acknowledged elsewhere in this book. Their insights and hard work enabled me to develop the ideas I advance throughout this work. Intellectually, I am especially indebted to two giants of the field of social psychology, Serge Moscovici and Henri Tajfel, whose brilliance changed the face of scholarship in my discipline, and whose combined visions and intuitions have allowed me to develop the *rules of influence*. On a more personal level, I must acknowledge my friend for decades, Larry Messé, whose friendship and incredible intelligence had much to do with my own development as a social psychologist, and who is indirectly responsible for all of this. All who knew Larry miss his brilliance, but mourn even more his kindness, wit, and basic humanity.

My agent, Eric Lupfer, has been a source of encouragement and good advice, and has contributed to this book from beginning to end. Without his good advice, I might have been able to avoid many hours of work, as there would have been no book to work on. Matt Martz, my editor at St. Martin's Press, also has proved a strong and positive influence. It became clear to me in all our interactions that he took the lessons of this book to heart. What more could an author wish for? The people at St. Martin's Press have been great, and are responsible for the look and feel of this book.

Finally, I am happy to acknowledge the two people who are most directly responsible for this book seeing the light of day, my son, Brian, and my wife, Suellen. Brian and I spent many interesting hours talking about the ways the weak can influence the strong, and his consistent badgering to engage the long and arduous process of writing this book ultimately convinced me. Having done other books, I knew the toll that a project of this magnitude can take, and so resisted for a time, but his consistent needle was not to be denied. Finally, I must express once again my love and gratitude to Suellen, to whom I have dedicated this book. Many authors thank their partners for putting up with them while the writing was under way, and I do so as well. More than that, I thank mine for her truly excellent critique of everything I wrote. While I might have disagreed at times with her ideas, they were always worth arguing over. Finally, and perhaps most important, I thank her for putting up with me for the past thirty years. Without that basic training, I would never have learned how the weak have the remotest chance of influencing the strong.

Endnotes

INTRODUCTION: THE MINORITY RULES . . . OR DOES IT?

[i] Oakland's flirtation with legal marijuana production for medicinal purposes has yet to play out, but the state and federal authorities do not seem inclined to cooperate with the Oakland plan. An interesting piece of reportage of the ins and outs of this issue was written by J. Bennett, (2010). "Oakland's Growth Industry: Legalized Marijuana Farms," in *Newsweek*. You can retrieve it on the Web at http://www.newsweek.com/2010/07/21/oakland-legalizes-marijuana-farming.html?from=rss. The state and federal reluctance to see large profit-making marijuana farms spring up was reported in the *Los Angeles Times* by John Hoeffel. It can be found at http://www.latimes.com/news/local/la-me-medical-marijuana-20110702,0,1515449.story.

[ii] Modern psychological study of ostracism has been spearheaded by Kit Williams. For a sample of his work see: Williams, K. D. (2001). *Ostracism: The Power of Silence*. New York: Guilford., and Williams, K. D. (2007). "Ostracism: The Social Kiss of Death." *Social and Personality Psychology Compass, 1*, 236–247.

[iii] The original study on the phenomenon of "basking in reflected glory" can be found in Cialdini, R. B., and colleagues (1976). "Basking in Reflected Glory: Three (Football) Field Studies." *Journal of Personality and Social Psychology, 34*(3), 366–375.

[iv] Arthur Schlesinger's autobiography and journals (edited by his son) are mandatory reading for anyone interested in the half century beginning in the 1950s. Two useful references are: Schlesinger, A., and Schlesinger, S. (Eds.). (2007). *Journals, 1952–2000 / Arthur M. Schlesinger, Jr.* New York: Penguin, and Schlesinger, A. M. (2000). *A Life in the Twentieth Century: Innocent Beginnings, 1917–1950*. Boston, MA: Houghton Mifflin.

[v] The original, and still one of the best books on groupthink was written by Irving Janis. Here's the reference: Janis, I. L. (1972). *Victims of Groupthink: A Psychological Study of Foreign-Policy Decisions and Fiascoes*. Boston, MA: Houghton Mifflin. In addition, a review of twenty years of work

on groupthink is available in Turner, M., and Pratkanis, A. (1998). "Twenty-five Years of Groupthink Research: Lessons from the Evaluation of a Theory." *Organizational Behavior and Human Decision Processes, 73*, 105–115.

vi Some authors have discussed the negative features of the devil's advocate, and I agree with them if the advocate is allowed to spout any objection he or she wishes without regard to plausibility or the possibility of testing its validity. If the role is used properly, however, I think even doubters of the role might be converted. For an interesting discussion of the scary features of devil's advocacy, see Kelly, T., and Littman, J. (2005). *The Ten Faces of Innovation: IDEO's Strategies for Defeating the Devil's Advocate and Driving Creativity Throughout your Organization.* New York: Doubleday.

vii A scientific study on the eradication of polio can be found in Strebel, P. M., and colleagues (1992). "Epidemiology of Poliomyelitis in the United States One Decade After the Last Reported Case of Indigenous Wild Virus-Associated Disease." *Clinical Infectious Diseases, 14*, 568–579.

CHAPTER 1: WHO AND WHAT IS A MINORITY?

viii Stories about Jack Welch abound in the business community, maybe because Welch seems to like to write about himself. There's lots to say, and some of the best is found in Lane, B. (2008). *Jacked Up: The Inside Story of How Jack Welch Talked GE into Becoming the World's Greatest Company.* New York: McGraw-Hill, and Welch, J., and Byrne, J. A. (2001). *Jack Straight from the Gut.* New York: Warner Business Books.

ix The details of this study can be found in Seyranian, V., and colleagues (2008). "Dimensions of Majority and Minority Groups." *Group Processes and Intergroup Relations, 11*, 21–37.

x An exceptional analysis of the psychological dynamics that might have given rise to the Abu Ghraib prisoner torture can be found in an impressive book by an author who has long been fascinated with the mundane features of exceptionally evil behavior. If you're interested, you would do well to read Phil Zimbardo's (2008) *The Lucifer Effect: Understanding How Good People Turn Evil.* New York: Random House.

xi p. 47. Details of this study can be found in Atuel, H., and colleagues (2007). "Media Representations of Majority and Minority Groups." *European Journal of Social Psychology, 37*, 561–572.

CHAPTER 2: HOW OUR GROUPS DEFINE WHO WE ARE

xii Michael Hogg, a superb experimental social psychologist, has written extensively about extremism and self-uncertainty. For a flavor of his important work, which has relevance in almost any context in which uncertainty of the self is evident, see the following: Hogg, M. A. (2006). "Self-conceptual Uncertainty and the Lure of Belonging." In R. Brown and D. Capozza (Eds.), *Social Identities: Motivational, Emotional and Cultural Influences* (pp. 33–49). Hove England: Psychology Press/Taylor & Francis (UK). Hogg, M. A. (2007). "Uncertainty-Identity Theory." In M. P. Zanna (Ed.), *Advances in Experimental Social Psychology, Vol 39* (pp. 69–126). San Diego, CA: Elsevier Academic Press. Hogg, M. A., Meehan, C., and Farquharson, J. (2010). "The Solace of Radicalism: Self-uncertainty and Group Identification in the Face of Threat." *Journal of Experimental Social Psychology, 46*, 1061–1066.

xiii For a really charming book on one of mankind's great minds, see Chesterton, G. K. (1956). *Saint Thomas Aquinas: The Dumb Ox.* New York: Doubleday.

xiv Details of this expectancy study can be found in Lamb, C., and Crano, W. D. (in press). "Evidence of a Self-fulfilling Prophecy in Parents' Estimates of Their Children's Marijuana Use."

xv Henri Tajfel was one of the giants of twentieth-century social psychology. A brief biography can be found in an appreciation written by Steven Reicher. http://www.easp.eu/activities/own/awards/tajfel.htm. A sampling of work is published in the following: Tajfel, H. (1978). *Differentiation between Social Groups: Studies in the Social Psychology of Intergroup Relations.* Oxford, England: Academic Press. Tajfel, H. (1978). *The Social Psychology of Minorities.* London: Minority Rights Group. Tajfel, H. (1982). "Social Psychology of Intergroup Relations." *Annual Review of Psychology, 33*, 1–39. Tajfel, H., and Turner, J. (2001). "An Integrative Theory of Intergroup Conflict." In M. A. Hogg and D. Abrams (Eds.), *Intergroup Relations: Essential Readings* (pp. 94–109). New York: Psychology Press. Tajfel, H., and Turner, J. C. (1986). "The Social Identity Theory of Inter-Group Behavior." In S. Worchel & L. W. Austin (Eds.), *Psychology of Intergroup Relations* (p. 57). Chicago: Nelson-Hall.

Expanding on Tajfel's life story is a fascinating book by Peter Suedfeld, which details the autobiographical accounts of a group of eminent Jewish social scientists who, as youth, were forced to survive the holocaust. See Suedfeld, P. (Ed.). (2002). *Light from Ashes: Social Science Careers of Young Holocaust Refugees and Survivors.* Ann Arbor, MI: University of Michigan Press.

CHAPTER 3: YOU IN OR OUT?

xvi Two excellent analyses of the Rwandan genocide are to be found in Berry, J. A., and Berry, C. P. (1999). *Genocide in Rwanda: A Collective Memory.*

Washington, D.C.: Howard University Press, and Gourevitch, P. (1998). *We Wish to Inform You that Tomorrow We Will Be Killed with Our Families: Stories from Rwanda.* New York: Farrar, Straus & Giroux.

xvii   Henri Tajfel provides a wonderful discussion of in-groups and out-groups in a paper titled *Social Identity and Intergroup Behavior.* This important theoretical contribution can be found online at http://ssi.sagepub.com/content/13/2/65.full.pdf.

xviii A good introduction to the scientific writing on in-groups and out-groups, and the need to be part of "us" rather than "them" can be found in the four research papers referenced here: Brewer, M. B., and Gardner, W. (1996). "Who Is This 'We'? Levels of Collective Identity and Self Representations." *Journal of Personality and Social Psychology, 71,* 83–93. Housley, M. K., Claypool, H. M., Garcia-Marques, T., and Mackie, D. M. (2010). " 'We' Are Familiar but 'It' Is Not: Ingroup Pronouns Trigger Feelings of Familiarity." *Journal of Experimental Social Psychology, 46,* 114–119. Perdue, C. W., Dovidio, J. F., Gurtman, M. B., & Tyler, R. B. (1990). "Us and Them: Social Categorization and the Process of Intergroup Bias." *Journal of Personality and Social Psychology, 59,* 475–486. Thomas, E. F., McGarty, C., & Mavor, K. I. (2009). "Aligning Identities, Emotions, and Beliefs to Create Commitment to Sustainable Social and Political Action." *Personality and Social Psychology Review, 13,* 194–218.

xix   Telling insights into Steven Sinofsky's thinking can be gained by reading his book on strategic management. This book, written many years after he and J Allard helped turn Microsoft's business model on its ear shows a refinement in Sinofsky's thinking, but the bedrock ideas that were there in the early days of Microsoft's entry into the wild world of the World Wide Web are still apparent. So, if you're interested in how an exceptional thinker thinks, you might want to check out Sinofsky, S., and Iansiti, M. (2010). *One Strategy: Organization, Planning, and Decision Making.* Hoboken, NJ: John Wiley.

xx   Marilynn Brewer has written extensively and creatively about the complexity of relations between in- and out-groups, and suggests that in-group loyalty does not necessarily signal out-group hatred. This fits with my own impression, which is that out-groups often are simply ignored as nonexistent—unless they pose a threat to the identity group. Two of Brewer's important papers are especially useful in illuminating this line of thinking: Brewer, M. B. (1999). "The Psychology of Prejudice: Ingroup Love or Outgroup Hate?" *Journal of Social Issues, 55,* 429–444. Brewer, M. B. (2007). "The Importance of Being We: Human Nature and Intergroup Relations." *American Psychologist, 62,* 728–738.

CHAPTER 4: RESIZING GOLIATH

xxi John Quincy Adams was one of America's most interesting political figures. He was a prolific and incisive social critic, and his keen eye tells us much about the life and politics of the Colonial period. Two useful sources of his thinking can be found in Allen, D. G., Friedlaender, M., and Taylor, R. J. (Eds.). (1981). *Diary of John Quincy Adams*. Cambridge, MA: Belknap Press of the Harvard University Press, and online at http://www.masshist.org/jqadiaries/.

xxii Two of Asch's most important studies are summarized in the following: Asch, S. (1956). "Studies of Independence and Conformity: I. A Minority of One Against a Unanimous Majority." *Psychological Monographs, 70*(9), and Asch, S. (1951). "Effects of Group Pressure upon the Modification and Distortion of Judgment." In H. Guetzkow (Ed.), *Groups, Leadership, and Men*. Pittsburgh, PA: Carnegie Press. A more complete guide to Asch's thought is available in his still-influential textbook: Asch, S. (1952). *Social Psychology*. New York: Prentice Hall.

xxiii For a detailed description and discussion of this study, see Koeske, G. F., and Crano, W. D. (1968). "The Effect of Congruous and Incongruous Source-Statement Combinations upon the Judged Credibility of a Communication." *Journal of Experimental Social Psychology, 4*(4), 384–399.

CHAPTER 5: THE HOLY TRINITY (PLUS ONE) OF MINORITY INFLUENCE

xxiv If you are interested in political campaigns and in influence in general, you have to read this book. The reference is Carville, J., and Begala, P. (2002). *Buck Up, Suck Up . . . and Come Back When You Foul Up: 12 Winning Secrets from the War Room*. New York: Simon & Schuster.

xxv Research on the door-in-the-face effect has produced results that on close consideration show people sometimes behave in quite illogical ways, unless we see reciprocation as a necessity of social interaction. If you consider the phenomenon in this light, then the originally strange results of the door-in-the-face research make perfect sense. For a research example of the phenomenon in a different cultural setting, see Lecat, B., Hilton, D. J., and Crano, W. D. (2009). "Group Status and Reciprocity Norms: Can the Door-in-the-face Effect Be Obtained in an Out-group Context?" *Group Dynamics: Theory, Research, and Practice, 13*, 178–189.

xxvi The research by Jud Mills and Jerry Jellison plays an important role in my discussion of a source's believability, and the contextual factors that influence this important feature of persuasion and social influence. The research is very well designed, and the results are crystal clear. And, the report is only four pages long. You should read it: Mills, J., & Jellison, J. M. (1967). "Effect on Opinion Change of How Desirable the Communication Is to the Audience the Communicator Addressed." *Journal of Personality and Social Psychology, 6,* 98–101.

CHAPTER 6: MAKING THE SUBJECTIVE OBJECTIVE

xxvii An inside the White House picture of the Cuban missile confrontation is found in Kennedy, R. F. (1969). *Thirteen Days: A Memoir of the Cuban Missile Crisis.* New York: W.W. Norton. Of course, with documents of this type, bias in the presentation of the issue must be considered. Even so, this is an exciting read.

xxviii The interview with al-Janabi is published in *The Guardian*. You can read this, and view a short video showing Colin Powell using al-Janabi's "intelligence," along with discussion of his work. This is a sad commentary on the United States' use of faulty intelligence data to entangle the country in a war that many would have voted to avoid if the truth had been told. See http://www.guardian.co.uk/world/2011/feb/15/defector-admits-wmd-lies-iraq-war.

xxix If you want more explicit details about this study, see Gorenflo, D. W. and Crano, W. D. (1989). "Judgmental Subjectivity/Objectivity and Locus of Choice in Social Comparison." *Journal of Personality and Social Psychology, 57,* 605–614.

xxx This study, which establishes the importance of the objective or subjective nature of the persuasion focus, can be found in Crano, W. D., and Hannula-Bral, K. A. (1994). "Context/Categorization Model of Social Influence: Minority and Majority Influence in the Formation of a Novel Response Norm." *Journal of Experimental Social Psychology, 30,* 247–276.

CHAPTER 7: THINGS ARE NOT ALWAYS AS THEY SEEM

xxxi The details of this important study can be found in: Pérez, J. A., and Mugny, G. (1987). "Paradoxical Effects of Categorization in Minority Influence: When Being an Outgroup is an Advantage." *European Journal of Social Psychology, 17*(2), 157–169. This study was in my opinion the beginning of our understanding of the indirect influence effects found when the in-group minority attempts to move the majority.

xxxii The studies reported on these pages are the bases of the model of persuasion I have developed, and that I have detailed in this book. It would be worth your time and effort to read Alvaro, E. M., and Crano, W. D. (1997). "Indirect Minority Influence: Evidence for Leniency in Source Evaluation and Counterargumentation." *Journal of Personality and Social Psychology, 72,* 949–964. This research presents some unusual results that fit perfectly with the theory that we had developed, and that is described here.

xxxiii The leniency contract is complicated, but its predictions have held up every time we've tested it. If you want more details on this predictive model, see Crano, W. D. (2001). "Social Influence, Social Identity, and Ingroup Leniency." In C. K. W. De Dreu and N. K. De Vries (Eds.), *Group Consensus and Minority Influence: Implications for Innovation* (pp. 122–143). Malden: Blackwell Publishing, and Crano, W. D., and Seyranian, V. (2007). "Majority and Minority Influence." *Social and Personality Psychology Compass, 1*, 572–589. A wide-ranging discussion of the leniency contract and other models designed to predict the influence of minorities on the majority can be found in Martin, R., and Hewstone, M. (2010). "Majority vs. Minority Influence, Message Processing, and Attitude Change: The Source-context-elaboration Model. In M.P. Zanna (Ed.), *Advances in Experimental Social Psychology,* Vol. 40, pp. 237-326.

xxxiv The delayed direct change prediction of the leniency model was tested explicitly in Crano, W. D., and Chen, X. (1998). "The Leniency Contract and Persistence of Majority and Minority Influence." *Journal of Personality and Social Psychology, 74*, 1437–1450. The results of the study strongly confirmed our expectations.

CHAPTER 8: GETTING IT ALL WRONG

xxxv The remarkable saga of Ignaz Semmelweis has been chronicled many times. His life seems to hold a unique fascination for epidemiologists and members of the medical profession. A good biography is found in Carter, K. C., and Carter, B. R. (2009). *Childbed Fever: A Scientific Biography of Ignaz Semmelweis.* New Brunswick, NJ: Transaction Publishers. Ignaz's own book also is worth reading for historical purposes: Semmelweis, I. (1818–1865). *The Etiology, Concept, and Prophylaxis of Childbed Fever.* Madison, WI: University of Wisconsin Press. Finally, you might like to read a modern statistical analysis of Semmelweis's data, compiled nearly 150 years after he died. Semmelweis greatly respected data, and unlike many of his rivals at the time, was guided by objective evidence. This work is by Bromeling, L. D. (undated). "Studies in the History of Probability and Statistics: Semmelweis and Childbed Fever. A Statistical Analysis 147 Years Later." Find it at http://www.mdanderson.org/education-and-research/departments-programs-and-labs/departments-and-divisions/division-of-quantitative-sciences/research/biostats-utmdabtr00504.pdf.

xxxvi The principal contributors to the proposition to ban same-sex marriage were the Mormon Church and the Catholic Church's Knights of

Columbus. See deTurenne, V. (August 20, 2008). "Knights of Columbus Tip the Balance with Big Anti-Gay Marriage Donation." http://
latimesblogs.latimes.com/lanow/2008/08/prop-8-post.html, *L.A.Times.*
McKinley, J., and Johnson, K. (November 14, 2008). "Mormons Tipped
Scale in Ban on Gay Marriage." http://www.nytimes.com/2008/11/15/us
/politics/15marriage.html?_r=3&pagewanted=1&hp&oref=slogin, *New
York Times.* Pyrah, J. (September 15, 2008). "LDS Contribute Millions to
Fight Gay Marriage." http://www.heraldextra.com/news/local/article
_84a8a9bf-6851-56a1-8c36-f170e8cd9f13.html, *Daily Herald.*

xxxvii This incisive observation is taken from J. Rauch (Oct 26, 2008). "Prop.
8s Ads' Invisible Gays: Campaigns for and against Prop 8 avoid showing gays." http://www.latimes.com/news/opinion/la-oe-rauch26-2008
oct26,0,3675742.story. *Los Angeles Times.*

xxxviii For background on the Rev. Rick Warren's stand on gay people, read Be-
liefnet. (December 17, 2008). "Rick Warren's Controversial Comments
on Gay Marriage." http://blog.beliefnet.com/stevenwaldman/2008/12
/rick-warrens-controversial-com.html.

CHAPTER 9: THE EMPIRE STRIKES BACK

xxxix pp. 239–249. Some background on the Augusta flap can be found in an
article at http://www.golftoday.co.uk/news/yeartodate/news02/augusta5
.html, and Wolfrum, W. F. (nd). "Martha Burk's Fight against Augusta
National's All-Male Policy Gaining Momentum, She Says." http://
www.worldgolf.com/features/martha-burk-fight-against-augusta-na-
tional-all-male-policy-6700.htm.

xl Work on the need-for-cognition scale is detailed in the following articles:
Cacioppo, J. T., and Petty, R. E. (1982). "The Need for Cognition." *Jour-
nal of Personality and Social Psychology, 42,* 116–131. Cacioppo, J. T.,
Petty, R. E., Feinstein, J. A., and Jarvis, W. B. G. (1996). "Dispositional
Differences in Cognitive Motivation: The Life and Times of Individuals
Varying in Need for Cognition." *Psychological Bulletin, 119,* 197–253,
and Cacioppo, J. T., Petty, R. E., and Kao, C. F. (1984). "The Efficient
Assessment of Need for Cognition." *Journal of Personality Assessment,
48,* 306–307.

xli Details of this poll ("June 3, 2009 - U.S. Voters Disagree 3-1 With Soto-
mayor On Key Case, Quinnipiac University National Poll Finds; Most
Say Abolish Affirmative Action") can be found at http://www.quinni
piac.edu/x1295.xml?ReleaseID=1307.

xlii The important study on innuendo effects should be required reading for
anyone interested in persuasion and the subtleties of influence tactics,
and can be found in Wegner, D. M., Wenzlaff, R., Kerker, R. M., and

Beattie, A. E. (1981). "Incrimination through Innuendo: Can Media Questions Become Public Answers?" *Journal of Personality and Social Psychology, 40,* 822–832.

CHAPTER 10: THE NEW RULES OF INFLUENCE

[xliii] The full text of President Obama's second State of the Union Address can be found at http://www.npr.org/2011/01/26/133224933/transcript-obamas -state-of-union-address.

[xliv] A fascinating interview with a leader of the Muslim Brotherhood on the conditions they had established in the Egyptian people's fight for freedom can be found at http://www.independent.co.uk/news/world/africa /egyptian-government-offers-concessions-as-street-protests-continue -2206333.html.

[xlv] Hillary Clinton's observation on the role of social media in the Egyptians' overthrow of Mubarak is worth thinking about. You can see it on http://www.necn.com/pages/landing_weather?blockID=410977& tagID=55 735.

[xlvi] For an analysis of the Oregon bottle bill, see J. Mitchell (October 1, 1992). "Happy Birthday Bottle Bill." *The Oregonian*: pp. F01.

[xlvii] Details of this study can be found in Mugny, G. (1975). "Negotiations, Image of the Other and the Process of Minority Influence." *European Journal of Social Psychology, 5,* 209–228.

[xlviii] This quote was taken from Allen, V. L., and Wilder, D. A. (1978). "Perceived Persuasiveness as a Function of Response Style: Multi-issue Consistency Over Time." *European Journal of Social Psychology, 8,* 289–296. It contains a wealth of information and insights into the process of minority influence—and it was published more than thirty years ago.